CROSSROADS
A JIT SUCCESS STORY

**The Coopers & Lybrand
Performance Solutions Series**

**Linking Theory and Practice
to Develop Unique Solutions
for Contemporary Performance Issues**

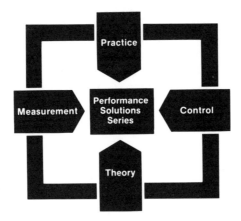

Other Titles in This Series
*Beyond The Bottom Line
Measuring World Class Performance*

Carol J. McNair, William Mosconi, Thomas Norris

CROSSROADS
A JIT SUCCESS STORY

*Robert Stasey
and
Carol J. McNair*

Dow Jones–Irwin
Homewood, Illinois 60430

© RICHARD D. IRWIN, INC., 1990

Dow Jones-Irwin is a trademark of Dow Jones & Company, Inc.

All rights reserved. No part of this publication may be reproduced, stored in a retrieval system, or transmitted, in any form or by any means, electronic, mechanical, photocopying, recording, or otherwise, without the prior written permission of the copyright holder.

This publication is designed to provide accurate and authoritative information in regard to the subject matter covered. It is sold with the understanding that the publisher is not engaged in rendering legal, accounting, or other professional service. If legal advice or other expert assistance is required, the services of a competent professional person should be sought.

From a Declaration of Principles jointly adopted by a Committee of the American Bar Association and a Committee of Publishers.

Sponsoring editor: Jim Childs
Project editor: Jean Roberts
Production manager: Diane Palmer
Production services: Editing, Design & Production, Inc.
Typeface: 11/13 Century Schoolbook
Printer: The Maple-Vail Book Manufacturing Group

Library of Congress Cataloging-in-Publication Data

Stasey, Robert.
    Crossroads : a JIT success story / Robert Stasey, Carol J. McNair.
      p.   cm. — (The Coopers & Lybrand performance solutions series)
    ISBN 1-55623-284-5
    1. Just-in-time systems. I. McNair, Carol Jean. II. Title.
III. Series.
TS157.S77   1990
658.5′6—dc20   89–23250
                                                                                CIP

Printed in the United States of America

1 2 3 4 5 6 7 8 9 0 MP 6 5 4 3 2 1 0 9

*To the family and friends that supported me as I
struggled, and cheered when I was done,
and to Mike especially, for opening doors and horizons.
C. J. McNair*

*To the family, friends, and Coopers &
Lybrand partners who supported my efforts.
Special thanks to Eugene M. Freedman,
Leonard I. Olin, and H. Michael Gleason
for their encouragement.
Robert Stasey*

PREFACE

Just-in-Time [JIT] manufacturing is making a bold entrance into traditional American manufacturing plants. Few companies, though, are reaping its benefits because of a failure to understand the process and its underlying philosophy. Our objective is to describe the challenges that managers implementing JIT will face in the hope that they will more quickly reap the benefits that JIT manufacturing can provide.

Our approach is unusual in presenting what is normally considered to be technical material. Its focus is on the process of implementation and the people behind it. Based on a real JIT/TQC project and its results, our objective is to capture the flow of decisions and events, taking poetic license when the reader would benefit.

This book is more than a story. It describes the technical features of JIT/TQC, discusses its merits, key features, and the rationale behind the methods. Our intent is to make learning vital and challenging, and technology enjoyable and productive. It is education by example, rather than by rote and detail.

It is important for the reader to understand the techniques used in this book. Technical discussion has been woven into the story. While many techniques might have been used to move from one to the other, we chose a simple one. Major transitions between story and background or between differing time periods are marked by a row of asterisks. When you encounter them, get ready to shift gears. While great care has gone into making these transitions smooth and logical, it remains for you, the reader, to judge whether our efforts have been successful.

Banyon is a fictional name, as are those of all the characters. This is the major "license" we have taken with the characters and facts. The sequence, and nature of the events, are based on an actual JIT implementation; we have added facts based on our mutual experience, and added drama to keep your interest. Hence, any resemblance to real people, companies, or situations is purely coincidental.

This has been a challenging project for us. Bob reached into his past, often to find facts that didn't fit. Patiently, he would retell the story until it made sense and events fell into place. C. J. fought a writer's battles, pushing herself when her resolve seemed to fail. Without Bob, the book couldn't have been written. Without C. J., it wouldn't have appeared in this form. We take pride in what is truly a joint effort.

No project is ever completed without the help of others, and this one is no exception. First, Walter Stasey gave unselfishly of his time in editing the first draft of the book and in providing useful comments. Gordon Shillinglaw, Professor of Accounting at Columbia University, gave both advice and encouragement when the authors needed it most. Jim Childs, Senior Editor at Dow Jones-Irwin, patiently pushed the book along, with cheerful but stern resolve. Finally, we wish to thank H. Michael Gleason, Managing Partner of Coopers & Lybrand Management Consulting Services, New York, for his continuing commitment and support of the project and the authors.

Robert Stasey
Carol J. McNair

TABLE OF CONTENTS

PROLOGUE   1

1   DISCOVERING JUST-IN-TIME   9

Just-in-Time: What It Is and Isn't   *Keeping Product Moving*   *Tying JIT to the Past*   *JIT Improvements Include the Back Office*   *JIT Is Different*   *Interdependence Is Reality*   *Identifying Nonvalue-Added Activities*   *Doing the Right Job*   *Getting to JIT*   *Back at Banyon*   *Just-in-Time: Getting Started*

2   CRAFTING A PLAN   25

Putting a Plan Together   *Step Two: Organize for Success*   *Step Three: Education and Awareness*   *Step Four: Housekeeping—Preventive Maintenance*   *Step Five: Quality Improvement*   *Step Six: Uniform Plant Load*   *Step Seven: Redesigning the Process Flow*   *Step Eight: Setup Reduction*   *Step Nine: Setting Up a Pull System*   *Step Ten: Setting Up Supplier Networks*   *A Final Step: Locking In the Solution*   *First Steps at Banyon*

3   A FOCUS ON QUALITY   44

Learning about Quality   *Defining and Finding Quality Improvements*   *The History of Quality*   *Quality in the Age of Efficiency*   *Total Quality Control*   *The Basics of TQC*   *Creating a Simple Process*   *Eliminate Waste*   *Making Problems Visible*   *Create a Climate for Improvement*   *Putting Structure Around the Quality Effort*   *A Team for Quality*   *Selecting a Candidate for Study*   *A Visit with a Surprise Ending*

| 4 | A SERIES OF FAILURES | 61 |

Two Strikes . . . The First Attack on Setups   The Monday Morning Blues   A Fresh Start   Getting Involved   Closing the Loop: Checkpoints and Measures   Statistical Process Control   Doing It Right: An Ongoing Commitment

| 5 | THE DOLLARS AND SENSE OF QUALITY | 76 |

The Beginnings of Trust   Defining the Cost of Quality   The Cost of Preventing Errors   Detection: Inspecting Quality In   Costing the Mistakes   Quality Costs Outside the Plant Door   Banyon's Cost of Quality   Recapping the Quality Management Process   Breaking the Production Mentality   A Framework for Action   Identifying Problem Areas   Making Quality a Design Issue   Banyon's TQC Results: Final Notes

| INTERMISSION | 92 |

| 6 | JIT: THE HARD FACTS | 95 |

A Technical View of JIT   Uniform Plant Load: Marching to a Beat   Kanban: Simple but Effective   Vendors and Measurements   Technical? It's Logical   Choosing a Pilot   Eleven Steps to Success   Communication: The Essential Element   Choosing the Team   A Light on the Horizon   Using Consultants: Sometimes Yes, Sometimes No

| 7 | INITIATING THE CYCLE OF SUCCESS | 112 |

Teaching the Basics of JIT   Cause and Effect: Ishikawa Fishbone Diagrams   Defects: Diamonds in the Rough   Pleasant Surprises and Good Beginnings   Putting JIT to Work   A Rapid Response   JIT: More Than Technique   The Multiple Dimensions of Control

| 8 | SURPRISES AND SUCCESSES | 130 |

Understanding JIT   A Multidisciplinary Team   The President's Line Diagnostic Report   Value Added: Disheartening Results   Inventories: Compensating for Mistakes   A Solution: The Conceptual Design   Kanban in Action   Synchronized Movements and Plant Design   Matching Schedules to New Capabilities   Dealing with Success   Learning the Meaning of Group Technology   Success and New Beginnings

9	THE HUMAN SIDE OF JIT	150

Participation: The Basic Element of JIT Management   Mastering Change   JIT Implementation: Evolution Not Revolution   *Creating the Learning Organization*   Success: Setups, JIT, and Balance   *Expanding JIT to Other Lines   Success: It's Even Better with Effort*   The Dangers of JIT: Management by Stress   *Hidden Dangers   Crisis in the Management Ranks*   Banyon's JIT Implementation: A Summary

INTERMISSION		169
10	PUSHING INDIVIDUAL INCENTIVES OUT THE DOOR	174

The Shortcomings of Individual Incentives   Solutions Abound . . . Which One to Choose?   Exploring the Scanlon Plan   Setting the Stage for Change   An Emerging Incentive Plan   *Time, Time, and More Time   Problems and More Problems*

11	GAINSHARING: A COMMITMENT TO EQUITY	194

The Elements of Change   Criteria for Successful Gainsharing   Equity Is Not Easy to Achieve   *Fair Division of Dollars   Building Consensus   Issues and Answers   Problems with No Easy Answers   Lunchtime Conversations*

12	NEGOTIATING WITH CORPORATE	208

Managing through Pressure   Narrow Minds and Ultimatums   A Glimmer of Hope   Corporate Compromises   A Change of Command   A Negotiated Plan

INTERMISSION		225
13	A SECOND CHALLENGE: MEASURING SUCCESS	232

A Broken Control Loop   Visible Measures of Success   *New Measures for New Objectives   Matching Measures to Performance*   Doesn't Time Mean Money?   *Space? Where the Buffalo Roam . . .   Quality: Key to Ongoing Success   WIP: Liability, Not Asset*   Clear Results

14	ACCOUNTING COMES OUT OF THE CLOSET	248

Controllable Costs   *The Logic Behind Excluding Depreciation*   What's Broken?   A Changing View of

xii   Table of Contents

Labor   Reporting to Corporate   *JIT Accounting Meets Corporate*   *Providing Information to Management*   *Tricking the MRP System*   *Moving through Labor Inventory Accounting*   Final Points

EPILOGUE   270

15   POSTSCRIPTS   273

What to Do When Volumes Fall Off   Design for Manufacturability   Closing the Loop: Suppliers and JIT   *The Essence of a Supplier Network*

INDEX   281

Silhouettes in motion, a synchronized flow of material through cells, like water coursing through sand. Where once mountains of inventory hindered flow, Kanban trays stand alone. The journey to Just-in-Time manufacturing, while never complete, is underway.

PROLOGUE

Clouds and sunshine took turns, moving in a synchronized dance across the sky. A balanced movement with no winner or loser. Only partners, painting the landscape in changing colors.

Ben thought the day quite fitting. He was about to give the last talk of his Banyon career. Yet, it was also the first day of a new life. Sunshine and shadows, past and present.

Julie remained quiet at his side. She was inflective today. During the hour long trip from Banyon she had barely said a word. Ben did not push her to talk. She would participate when the time was right for her. To ask her to do otherwise would be to take unfair control.

Within moments they reached the red brick building that was their final destination. Ben began to reach for the door handle, then paused to allow Julie to open it instead. With a slight incline of his head and a smile, Ben went through the open door. Julie followed, at once the leader and the led. It was a day of transition, of the old colliding with the new.

* * * * *

"Three years ago the plant looked like a warehouse. Inventory was everywhere, growing daily, pushing people and machines out of the way with storage racks. Today we're winning the 'Battle of the Bulge,' thanks to the discipline of Just-in-Time manufacturing."

Ben was in his element, energizing the audience the way he had energized Julie and others at Banyon. Julie was

Ben's lieutenant during their battle to implement Just-in-Time (JIT) manufacturing at Banyon's midwestern plant. More than a machine, JIT had proved to be a management technique, a way of life. It had changed the way they manufactured products and permanently altered their goals, their management styles, and their lives.

"The plant we'll discuss is located in the midwest," Ben continued. "It recently hosted a visit by the Association for Manufacturing Excellence, who designated it a "world class manufacturing" site. They saw the plant in action, making parts and assembling high-quality product. They saw success."

"I don't know of any other plant that has made such dramatic changes in product quality, JIT manufacturing technique, gain-sharing, and performance measurement, let alone in just four years. As its plant manager, I am proud of these accomplishments, and I am honored to share the experience with you."

* * * * *

Ah, yes, the plant. Banyon is a job-shop manufacturer, producing counters, count controls, and programmable controls for the business machine, machine tool, and metal fabrication industries. Sales are about $30 million per year. It occupies 140000 square feet, and employs about 400 men and women. It is vertically integrated and capable of all steps in the production process, starting with the molding of plastic counter housings through final assembly and testing. This capability extends to more than 70 separate processes, from screw machines to plastic molding to production of printed circuit boards. Banyon is a high variety producer of a broad range of products using complex process flows. A perfect candidate for JIT, right?

In describing the plant to his audience, Ben tried to describe the chaos at Banyon before its conversion to JIT. "It is difficult for me to visualize how we got product out the door in those days, or, more precisely, how we got the right product out the door while maintaining quality. Fire fighting was everyone's job."

* * * * *

Julie was a great expediter. In fact, she took great pride in her ability to find orders and expedite them through the production maze. "Expediting. I was a high-priced clerk," Julie mused, "getting product out to meet order deadlines." Expediting had been Julie's main job from the time Alex Martin left Banyon until Ben arrived. It was what she knew best, and it was the best way Julie knew to keep top management off her back.

Julie excelled at Banyon. She could charm line supervisors into running her jobs by playing the frazzled but understanding manager who had to placate a customer. This is what greeted Ben when he took over as plant manager: turmoil, a job shop with 6,000 catalog items, 12,000 parts, and 80,000 routings. Did anyone know what was going on? Could anyone? But they could fight fires and win Probe Awards of Excellence in the process.

* * * * *

"I don't know how many of you run plants, but I can tell you that when I took over Banyon's operations my friends thought I was crazy. I was a financial manager and a good one. Why did I swap my education and a soft job for a dirty factory? Truthfully, it was the kind of challenge I wanted. At the time I was 6 feet, 6 inches tall and weighed 220 pounds." Ben smiled as he delivered his favorite one-liner. "Today I'm 5 feet 6 inches and barely keep the scale above 145. It was one heck of a challenge."

Julie listened, wishing that this wasn't the last time she'd be listening to Ben as her boss. Tomorrow he'd simply be a friend.

"There was a cartoon in the paper recently that pictured a king going to war. A salesman selling weapons arrived and sought an audience with him. He told his aide, 'I don't have time to talk to salesmen; I have a battle to fight.' Of course, the salesman's Gatling gun would have helped him win the battle. I was that king in 1978 when I heard about Just-in-Time. I said, 'That stuff is crazy. The claims of 50, 60, 70 percent reductions in setup time and comparable reductions in inventory aren't believable; not only that, how could JIT possibly apply to a job shop? But I'm going to show you how it does apply." As Ben continued with the story, Julie reminisced.

* * * * *

Shortly after Ben had taken over at Banyon, he and Julie went to a local association meeting to see a presentation on Just-in-Time manufacturing by John Boyer of Regent Electric. It was well done, but it raised more questions than it answered, leaving Ben and Julie more than a little skeptical.

"Can you believe it?" Julie exclaimed. "How can he stand there with a straight face and say he got those results in such a short time? Does he think we were born yesterday? And he says he's glad his company was pushed into 'Just-in-Time.' I don't believe it, or that it works the way he says it does."

"Julie, I agree with you, but I can't dismiss everything John Boyer says," Ben replied. "I just read an article on JIT in a trade magazine, and it made the same claims. While I'm in the market for some solutions to our manufacturing problems, I'm not in the habit of chasing fads. The claims don't seem realistic. Careful use of exaggeration, though, is the hallmark of good salesmen. What John Boyer is selling, though, is a mystery to me."

Ben was looking for answers to problems he had encountered at Banyon, and that was why he and Julie had come to the presentation. As the new plant manager, he faced severe challenges. He had to get the plant moving, get profits up and costs down fast. Top management had pushed his predecessor, Alex Martin, out of the job, and Julie was not ready for the responsibility. So Ben was sent in. He was a bit green, but he had more years of management experience than either Julie or Alex. And he liked changes and encouraging people to take on new challenges.

"I know you've always kept the plant going and done a good job of it," Ben continued. "But, Julie, we need a better answer than working harder to clean up the mess. If companies are experiencing huge improvements in quality and lowering their costs by using Just-in-Time, then we have to consider it. JIT appears to focus on improving throughput time and process flow controls. Maybe it can make our jobs easier."

Julie listened calmly to Ben's response, amused and skeptical at the same time. "I thought I was the one who got carried away. You know, the soft touch for a good sales pitch. Ben, I know you've got a tough job to do. And if JIT can help, I'm willing to try it. But, I'm not sure that it isn't just fluff. What can it do for us that Materials Resource Planning (MRP) isn't doing already?"

"Julie, we don't need to make any changes immediately. I just started, and everything I do is new. Maybe we can think about this as we go along. That way, when I'm settled and we know that we really need it, we can work on the project the right way. You know, do the research, put together a plan, and get top management to give us a hand. Right now, I agree, let's get things under control."

Little did Ben and Julie know that later in the week the ideas they had heard at the Just-in-Time conference would dramatically affect their lives, much like a lifeline thrown to a drowning man.

* * * * *

"Ben, why did Probe send someone here to present this award? The last 10 awards just showed up in the mailroom," Julie gasped. Trying to keep up with Ben when he was walking through the plant was like doing roadwork with Mike Tyson. Julie struggled along, ankles wobbling as high heels slipped on the flat cement floor. Slip and recover. Wobble and gasp. Lacking a bit in elegance, she managed to keep up.

They rounded the last corner and entered the employee cafeteria. The Probe representative, Al Brown, Vice President of Materials, was there with Banyon's Vice President of Sales. Ben and Al exchanged greetings and moved to the platform that had been erected so that the employees could witness the achievement award. Introductions behind them, Ben and Julie sat down to listen to the praises Al was about to heap on Banyon as a supplier.

Al took off his tie and discarded his prepared remarks.

In a folksy manner he said, "You are outstanding quality producers in America today, but you're not good enough. Do you know what the defect level is for your product? It's 3.3 percent. Do you know what it is for your Japanese competitor? It's zero, 100 percent quality, an absolute necessity for us to survive in the future." To say that he had everyone's attention was an understatement. While his remaining remarks were full of praise for Banyon's performance, there was no doubt that Al had something else to say to Ben and Julie before he departed.

After the presentation, the workers went back to their stations, and Ben and Julie took Al on a plant tour. At the end of the tour, they stopped at Ben's office. Al said to them, "Ben, congratulations on the 11th award. Only 1 percent of our 2,500 suppliers earn the award each year. And your company is one of only two to win 11. By the way, we're going to have some seminars on statistical process control (SPC) and Just-in-Time manufacturing. I suggest that you attend."

"With what you'll learn added to what you already do, we'll expect a 20 percent price reduction on next month's shipments. We're going to a preferred vendor system, and if you don't qualify—that means reducing your defect rate to zero and lowering your costs at the same time—then, well, you won't make the list."

Al let the other shoe drop, and the worst of all nightmares came true. Since Ben and Julie were speechless, he continued. "The point of going to a preferred vendor arrangement, Ben, is to stop doing in-house inspection. Inspection adds cost, not value, and it's a cost we can't afford if we're going to stay competitive. We expect your components to work. And if they don't, you shut down our line and you're no longer our supplier. It's as simple as that."

"Probe isn't asking for your profits, Ben. We value you as a vendor. But we're asking you to share with us a part of the savings you'll realize by using these new techniques. We're entering a new world, and Probe intends to be part of it. Do you?"

Ultimatum delivered, Al left. Ben and Julie left for lunch with little appetite. A drink was in order.

Ben's mood was angry and bitter. Julie? Well, she was glad that Ben was plant manager. She had wanted it with all her heart, but now she was glad to serve as an underling; her job wasn't on the line.

They chatted over lunch, going over both Probe's ultimatum and the concepts they had heard at the JIT seminar the day before. Their world had suddenly changed, and Ben, at least, was not about to let the challenge go unmet. If Probe, and later GRI, intended to jettison them, they were in for a surprise.

Several hours later they returned to the plant where they spent the rest of the afternoon developing a game plan. Ben wanted Julie to get to work on learning how to implement the new manufacturing techniques. He had a plant to run, and spending countless hours in the library hunched over books or scurrying between seminars was out of the question. That would be Julie's job. She would gather information and brief Ben once she knew what it all meant. The careful, well-planned implementation Ben had wanted went up in smoke. The process of change wasn't going to be pretty because they needed results now.

CHAPTER 1

DISCOVERING JUST-IN-TIME

Ben and Julie were ready to try Just-in-Time if that was what was required to keep Probe as a customer. But the usual problems encountered with any new plan surfaced immediately. Where should they start? Banyon was a job shop, and one thing never clear in a job shop is what can be changed without upsetting the ability to meet customer demand.

The fact that money was unavailable for process redesign or for new machinery meant that Ben and Julie faced tremendous obstacles in implementing JIT. Banyon was a subsidiary of a company whose major emphasis was on profits. When Ben called Herman Randolph, the division head, to ask for help, Randolph had simply said, "Not with Banyon's money you don't. You can do anything you want within those four walls, but you meet your profit goals or you're out!" It was a rude awakening.

No money, a job shop, extreme time pressure, and Probe wants a 20 percent price cut next month—not an environment from which new ideas naturally spring. Yet, perhaps it is. Crisis motivates people to change, and Ben and Julie faced an extreme crisis; they had to succeed. And JIT was just a new way to route material on the plant floor, wasn't it? What could be so hard? It wasn't long before they learned that they were in for bigger challenges than anticipated as they faced changes that reached inside their own lives.

JUST-IN-TIME: WHAT IT IS AND ISN'T

"Julie!" Ben never yelled, but he was close. "What in the devil is Just-in-Time? You've been talking to me for two hours now, and all I'm getting is fluff. OK. So you've only attended one seminar. But can't you give me a clear, concise answer? I need something I can see and feel, not maxims like 'the process of continuous improvement.' I can't run this factory with proverbs. Take today and tomorrow if you have to, but come back with facts."

Wow, someone got up on the wrong side of the bed. His mood was understandable, though. Ben was under pressure from top management to increase profits. And he was expected to do this with existing resources. The ultimatum from Probe increased the pressure. If what Ben needed was details on JIT, then Julie would get them. She took out the business card of one of the speakers she had heard at the seminar, called him, and set up an appointment for early afternoon. Meeting set, Julie reread the brochures on JIT she kept in her desk drawer.

The discussion began in a straightforward manner. Good thing, too, as Julie was not technical; and she needed facts, not a sales pitch.

* * * * *

Just-in-Time (JIT) has excited the manufacturing world in the past few years. To hear people talk about it, JIT is the golden ring when it comes to seeking manufacturing efficiency. While that mystique may be justified to some extent, many companies go into JIT with erroneous perceptions of what it is.

JIT is not:
- An inventory program.
- An effort that involves suppliers only.
- A cultural phenomenon.
- A materials project.
- A program that displaces MRP.
- A panacea for poor management.

JIT is an enterprise-wide operating philosophy that has the elimination of waste as its basic objective. As noted by Dr. Chou, a renowned JIT expert, "Waste is considered anything other than the minimum amount of equipment, materials, parts, space, and workers' time absolutely essential to add value to product." The key phrase is "adding value." JIT strives to identify activities that do not add value and eliminate them.[1]

* * * * *

"Adding value, wasn't that what the Probe vice president said? Isn't that what they're doing?" Julie mused. "Probe must be using JIT. And, if that's right, they're trying to get their vendor system under control just like the books recommend. We're on the receiving end of JIT, and it isn't a lot of fun. Yet, maybe it can work here."

Julie read on, skipping lunch, in the hope of finding the elusive link that would help her "see and feel" JIT, a way to convey it to Ben.

KEEPING PRODUCT MOVING

The essential feature of JIT manufacturing is the concept of waste, of defect prevention, of quality at the source. Today, quality is no longer defined by acceptable levels of scrap, nor is it to be inspected by sorting good from bad at the end of the manufacturing process. To a proponent of JIT manufacturing, then, waste is defined as any unneeded, nonvalue-adding activity at any stage in the production cycle.

This concern with waste is based on the use of time, time being the one element all aspects of the manufacturing process, including back office activities, have in common. Every

---

[1]This section is excerpted, with permission, from the Coopers & Lybrand document "Straight Talk on Just-in-Time," based on a presentation by William A. Wheeler III, made to the South African Production and Inventory Control Society in June 1986.

activity uses time. People are paid for renting their time to the organization. And inventory is a store of time, time to completion. No completion, no revenues, and no money to pay for more time.

* * * * *

Julie was confused by the time concept. While it seemed like common sense, she knew that the final report card was the bottom line. All this talk about time seemed irrelevant.

"Hmmm. This concern with time. I remember John Boyer describing inventory as a time bomb. I understand why it's important to be efficient, but this 'total throughput time' is a puzzle. And measuring the entire company this way, even my work, is hard to grasp."

Julie was trying to understand the key role that time played in JIT manufacturing. It is called "Just-in-Time," but Julie thought that meant the delivery of inventory to the plant floor at the precise time it was needed and that's all. Wasn't this just a refined inventory technique? She turned her attention back to her reading.

* * * * *

The total time a product spends in the manufacturing process can be broken down into several components:

$$\text{Total time} = \text{Move time} + \text{Queue time} + \text{Process time} + \text{Inspect time} + \text{Setup time}$$

Of this entire list, only process time adds value; the rest add cost.

* * * * *

"JIT breaks what we do in the plant into 'time buckets' instead of tasks or routings. Inspection is a task in our current system, but 'move'? We don't measure 'move', at least not as far as I know. And this concept of adding value, does it mean that only process time adds value? Don't we need to do the rest of these things to get good product out the door?" Julie read on, feeling like she was getting lost in a maze of jargon and abstract theory. Yesterday's foothill loomed like today's Everest.

Tying JIT to the Past

JIT is often described as an inventory technique. This couldn't be farther from the truth. What JIT means is solving problems, eliminating the root cause of variation in the production process that makes inventory a necessity. Inventory in a typical plant is like insurance, insurance that a problem in one area won't affect work performed in another. When problems creating the need for insurance are solved, then inventories disappear from the plant floor.

In the early years of the 20th century, a group of engineer-scientists led by Frederick Taylor set out to improve the efficiency of man and machine on the plant floor using a stopwatch to time movements of workers during the manufacturing process. Stories abound of workers sandbagging the engineer with the stopwatch. Given the natural aversion of people to being controlled, the stories are most likely true.

What the scientific management group ignored in their efforts to bring efficiency to the plant floor was inventory. Inventory was seen as a store of value; it was a defined asset on the balance sheet. Their focus was on men and machines, wasted if idle or inefficient. Inventory did not lose value sitting on the plant floor, but idle workers and machines represented orders not filled and profits lost.

JIT recognizes that idle inventory costs as much as idle labor, perhaps more. The accounting system, it is true, never metered the cost of inventory-based idle time directly. And unreported numbers are ignored. Attention is targeted at numbers management can see. While everyone knew that inventory was an expensive solution to the problem of coordinating complex processes occurring in the factory, it wasn't a factor entering directly into performance evaluations, and, hence, it was acceptable.

To JIT, inventory is the enemy. JIT concepts don't provide the means to manage inventory better or to track it through the manufacturing process. JIT seeks to eliminate inventory wherever possible by streamlining process flows and getting rid of islands of inventory between machines. It is a new form of management, not a new software program or technology.

* * * * *

Julie paused. She had been reading for an hour. She had a handful of notes and a queasy feeling in her stomach. "What am I missing? This part sounds like a history lesson. OK. So we can't forget the past or we make the same mistakes again. That I understand. But where are the facts, the plans for putting JIT in place? What does it look like, and what changes to the plant are needed? And, do the changes stop in the plant?"

JIT Improvements Include the Back Office

While failing to track inventory use efficiency can be traced to the concept of inventory as an asset, increased efficiency can also trigger redesign and improvement of back office functions: a more efficient flow of paper. Think of an office as a manufacturing process, one in which paper flows through various departments and manufacturing stations to result in a product: customer payment for merchandise delivered. Eliminating a pause in the flow is the same whether on the plant floor or in the back office. Are nonvalue-adding activities performed because the nature of the flow is not understood? Does paperwork emerge from the end of its cycle in the same way product emerges from the plant?

The focus of JIT is on management of process flow to eliminate nonvalue-adding activities. This is the concept that this book will bring to life by describing a true implementation with the trials, pitfalls, successes, and failures of the real world. It is a management concept as applicable to a bank as to a manufacturing firm. It is based on analyzing the "cause for pause." A pause is waste—time gone never to be replaced. It is time that keeps a customer waiting, resulting in lost sales and damaged reputations.

JIT Is Different

"This is starting to sound like marketing! Analyze the cause for pause. How do I do that? We have over 70 different processes. This sounds less promising by the minute!"

What Julie was beginning to grasp, however tentatively, is that Just-in-Time manufacturing is more than an inventory control technique. JIT is a new way to think about the manufacturing process; it attacks the assumptions that underlie American manufacturing. Being efficient in a JIT sense means more than getting product out the door quickly. It means getting it out right and only in the quantity needed. JIT is discipline.

Anyone who has seen JIT work becomes a convert. A lot of waste exists in American manufacturing and *service* organizations today. This "fat" came from having enough market power to set prices and create demand. This market power is disappearing, and so are many companies that used to be giants of American manufacturing. But JIT is not a quick fix to be picked off the shelf and put to work on the plant floor. The benefits that JIT can provide are documented, as suggested in Table 1–1, but these results don't come from just setting up manufacturing cells, but from changing how the manufacturing process is viewed.

JIT sets up a "pull" system in contrast to the prevailing "push" system. By pulling rather than pushing orders through the plant and the office, it sets up a series of internal "customers" that trigger movements of products and paper. If there is no customer demand, there is no activity. If production did occur, it would quite likely be waste. Idle machines and people, the nightmare of managers, still reflect unused capacity, but no longer unacknowledged waste. It means that orders are needed, or that production problems need to be solved.

* * * * *

Julie needed to think, so she decided to go for a walk. While the plant might not be Central Park, it would get her feet back on the ground. "I think I'll stop to chat with Mike

TABLE 1-1
Opportunities (Percent Improvement)

Reductions	Automotive Supplier	Printer	Fashion Goods	Mechanical Equipment	Electric Components	Range
Manufacturing lead time	89	86	92	83	85	83–92
Inventory:						
Raw	35	70	70	73	50	35–73
WIP	89	82	85	70	85	70–89
Finished goods	61	71	70	0	100	0–100
Changeover time	75	75	91	75	94	75–94
Labor:						
Direct	19	50	29	5	0	0–50
Indirect	60	50	22	21	38	21–60
Exempt	?*	?*		?*	?*	?–22
Space	53	n/a	39	?*	80 (est.)	39–80
Cost of quality	50	63	61	33	26	26–63
Purchased material (net)	?*	7	11	6	n/a	6–11
Additional capacity	n/a	36	42	n/a	0	0–42

*Unknown.

Source: Coopers & Lybrand.

Gannon. He always cheers me up, and I need a lift right now." She set off for the tool crib where Mike could usually be found.

"Mike, you've got to help me! I'm up to my eyebrows in problems. Ben thinks I can help him get out of the fix with Probe by using something called 'Just-in-Time' manufacturing. Cripes, I think I'm going down for the count!" Julie was smiling, but just barely.

"Hello, sunshine!" Mike said. "So, the new boss has you on 'Mission Impossible.' I was talking to a buddy over at Regent where they put this technique in place. He says it isn't so bad, except they moved all the inventory off the floor. No place left to nap or play cards! What's the world coming to?"

"Mike Gannon, you never stop moving all day long. But don't let Ben hear you; he doesn't know you like I do, and he might take you seriously," Julie chided. "Now, cheer me up; I need it!"

Mike tried his best. He joked with Julie and told her the latest gossip on the plant floor. In the end, Julie left feeling little better than when she had arrived. "Back to the slave pit, Mike. If you get a chance, ask the warden to send in bread and water. Or arsenic, if I don't get an answer for Ben."

INTERDEPENDENCE IS REALITY

Mike described the biggest visual change that JIT brings to the factory floor, the disappearance of work-in-process inventory. A plant converting to JIT takes on the look of an empty warehouse. Emptiness does not signal a lack of value-adding activity, but the elimination of waste.

Inventory buffers on factory floors separate activities performed in different areas. If a problem erupts in one area, it doesn't shut down the rest of the plant. Everyone is buffered, and production continues. But the source of the problem might be in the first assembly stage, and everyone afterwards diligently and conscientiously adds cost to bad parts.

In the design and movement of materials and paper, JIT

recognizes clearly that the entire process is linked, from receipt of raw materials through manufacturing to delivery of finished product, and to receiving payment from the customer. While the buffering or independence of each function may encourage a manager to believe that the assets available are producing at their optimum, there is no real control of the process. How can improvements be made if there is little true understanding of where problem spots are, or what needs fixing? The managers at Banyon had already encountered this problem.

Removing buffers can shut down an entire factory because of a problem in one area. The process flow design of JIT ensures that this will happen; nothing is pulled from preceding stages, and work stops. But is running defective product and fixing it later, which results in scrap and risks poor quality goods sneaking through inspection to the customer, a better way to operate? That this view prevails in American business management is reflected in the widely held belief that improving quality increases cost. In JIT this accepted tenet is rejected. If a quality problem shuts down a line, there is little doubt that it will become readily apparent. The problem is then isolated and fixed with a minimal amount of rework and scrap.

* * * * *

Julie was back at her desk, confused. She continued reading the article that had caused her to pause. The author was finally getting to facts she could understand and embrace.

Identifying Nonvalue-Added Activities

There are a few simple tests that can be used to identify areas where nonvalue-adding activities occur:

- Does an activity, for example, inspection, transportation, receiving, purchasing, and expediting, add cost without changing the physical or chemical characteristics of the item?

- Do parts or paperwork stop or pause at any point during their journey through the manufacturing site?
- Is an operation performed to compensate for something that was not done properly the first time?

If the answer is yes, a nonvalue-adding activity is taking place. Each such nonvalue-adding activity is a candidate for reduction or elimination. This frees time for critical activities left undone because everyone is too busy fighting fires. JIT doesn't mean getting rid of people, it means getting rid of nonvalue-adding activities.

* * * * *

"I wonder if I'm supposed to figure out how many times we pause for each of these categories? If this is serious, we have a long way to go before we're done. At the presentation John Boyer said you never get done. I can see why!" Julie jotted down a list of questions and made several notes about likely areas to begin her analysis. It was progress, however meager.

Doing the Right Job

JIT eliminates situations in which good people do the wrong job right. It sets up a cycle of improvement in which the individual achieves satisfaction by adding value to the product and contributing to the success of the firm. Everyone has a say in the final outcome. JIT is people-oriented. It depends on people to succeed, not machines. And it reflects the following two tenets:

1. Identify and eliminate the "cause for pause."
2. If you can't use it now, don't make it now!

Getting to this level of understanding of the processes and activities performed in an organization is a team effort. Organizations implement JIT, not individuals.

* * * * *

"Boy, this stuff is great, but how do I start? The list of questions gave me some ideas, but I need one clear candidate to start the experiment. Ben wants a plan for action, and I don't know where to start. Identify the cause for pause. I could be at this the rest of my life. If every time the product pauses is waste, then we're doing a lot more wasting than value-adding." Julie was both dismayed and intrigued by the puzzle of JIT. It bore a disturbing resemblance to a "Rubik's cube."

"It seems impossible. But maybe when I talk to the plant manager at Regent Electric, who did this and succeeded, I'll get a handle on how to implement JIT. Maybe that will help. I truly hope so, or it's not going to be fun when I get back."

GETTING TO JIT

Julie arrived at Regent, and after waiting a few moments, was ushered into John Boyer's office. While he finished a call, Julie looked around.

The walls were filled with charts and graphs of all kinds, on-time shipments, plant load, first pass quality levels, levels of work-in-process inventory, changeover time, and on and on. An endless sea of charts and graphs, all suggesting that JIT was working at Regent. Inventories were radically down, on-time deliveries were approaching 100 percent, and changeover time was heading toward zero. It was impressive, and, obviously, testimony to a manager who placed emphasis on operating results over accounting data.

John Boyer finished his call, and Julie turned her attention to him. This was a crucial afternoon, and she had to pay careful attention to what John had to say.

"Julie Higgins, isn't it?" John Boyer started. "Sorry for the delay, Julie, but I try to keep on top of things. That was a foreman letting me know there's a problem in a component we just received. The line is down, and he's on track to fixing it. If need be, we'll get another shipment today at the vendor's expense, of course. If he can't meet our specs, he has a problem."

The Probe attitude again. Julie wondered if these guys would like to be on the receiving end of the ultimatum. This was answered quickly.

"You know, we have to be tough on our suppliers," John continued. "We're a JIT supplier to Anderson & Anderson, the computer company, and if we let poor quality out the door, we lose at the other end. That's the story in JIT. In the end, it requires a commitment to quality throughout the vendor chain. The big guys start it, and they push it back on their suppliers. You meet the demands, or look for business elsewhere. Most companies are dragged, shoved, or pushed into JIT by a major customer."

"And they kick and scream and yell and look for an out. Well, because we were pushed, we're now a JIT producer. And we've never been so profitable or successful in our history. Success breeds confidence. We're not only producing for Anderson & Anderson, but also for the Japanese. It's a result I'm proud of."

"John, you got me very interested in JIT when I attended your seminar several days ago," Julie responded. "But I really don't understand what it is and where to start. I thought that you might be able to help me. You see, the story you just described fits Banyon exactly. One of our major customers just delivered an ultimatum to improve quality and cut cost, or else. They're demanding an immediate response, and we don't know where to begin."

Julie went on to describe Banyon's manufacturing facility, the types of products it made, and the high level of variety in both machines and products that typified the plant floor. John Boyer listened and made a few notes. When Julie paused, he responded quickly.

"Julie, first you have to understand the plant the way it is today. If you can find areas where quality is not up to snuff, and which cause rework and product failure downstream whether in house or at the customer, you'll have a place to start. But you can't short-circuit the learning process. Converting to JIT is more than rearranging a few machines or putting more emphasis on in-line quality. Your people have to change their view of the manufacturing process, it's objectives, their roles, who's in charge, and where the plant is going."

"Don't underestimate the changes that you and the people at your plant will have to make. If you don't understand JIT for the major change it is, you'll fail. Oh, your company may improve, because JIT takes root even in poor soil, but you won't be able to keep the improvements rolling. You'll fight and claw for each step, and the strain on you and your people will be immense. If you're going to do it, do it right. We didn't, and we made our lives a lot harder. In the end, we finally realized what JIT was, and we made the final transition. If not, I'd be back fighting fires rather than talking to you."

The rest of the afternoon passed quickly. John Boyer took Julie on a plant tour, where she talked at length with line personnel, supervisors, and managers about JIT and its impact on Regent and on their jobs. As her visit ended, John handed her a well-worn flyer about JIT. "It's yours, and I hope you understand what it means. It was our bible, simple though it may seem."

BACK AT BANYON

Julie returned to the office late. While the trip to Regent had been enjoyable, it had raised more questions than it had answered. And she still didn't know how or where to start, how to frame the JIT concepts so Ben could, in his own words, "see it and feel it."

Julie sighed as she entered the office. It was dark and quiet, and although a good time to work, it was also a lonely time, when the obstacles littering the path ahead loomed menacingly. Closing her office door cut the darkness down to size; but it didn't matter. Within a few moments she was hard at work crafting her proposal to Ben, and the hours passed quickly.

The next morning Ben arrived to find Julie leafing through several flyers on Just-in-Time seminars being offered in the area. While she didn't look as though she had slept at the office, it was obvious that she hadn't slept much.

Stopping in front of her desk, Ben wondered why she

was working so hard. "Julie, did you go home last night? If you didn't, go home now."

"I went home, but I couldn't sleep. So I came in early. I don't have any clear answers for you, but I think we should go to a few classes to get a clearer idea of what JIT means. The trip to Regent was informative, but I think we need more information before we try to implement JIT." With this, Julie looked up at Ben, concern and uneasiness showing on her face.

Ben was quick to respond and put Julie at ease. "If you think that's best, I agree. I'd like to think that we know better than to try something we don't understand. You set up the seminars, and I'll clear my calendar. We've got the summer, I figure, to gain an understanding of JIT, but by September we'd better be ready to implement it."

* * * * *

Julie and Ben went to several seminars, some at Probe, others at local universities and consulting firms. Slowly they came to an understanding of JIT, at least partially. What they grasped, we'll see later, was its technical aspects, not its total message. That knowledge came from trial and error, lessons learned on the firing line.

Just-in-Time: Getting Started

This book details the true story of JIT implementation at Banyon. While the company name used here is, of necessity, fictional, the story is not. Throughout, our objective will be to address the real problems facing managers and companies that try to put JIT into place. The truth is neither as pretty nor as neat as "how-to" manuals might suggest. And the path followed by your company may well differ from the one described here.

This is not a cookbook; it is reality. Hopefully, through the unfolding of events at Banyon, the benefits, sacrifices, and changes that Just-in-Time brings will be easier to understand. The goal is to help you and your company make the transition to excellence and to find your own path to success.

* * * * *

Julie walked slowly to her car. It had been a long day, but it would be only one of many long days. How could a concept as simple as "continuous improvement" require such hard work? Because it meant never being satisfied, always pushing to be better. Like a world-class athlete, Banyon had to go into training working long and hard to become the best. Competition does not suggest tranquility, it means pushing, always pushing, to stay one step ahead.

CHAPTER 2

CRAFTING A PLAN

Summer passed all too quickly for Ben and Julie. They completed the last of the seminars and were ready to begin the JIT start-up in early September.

Julie spent most of the Labor Day weekend reading *Creating the Corporate Future* by Russell Ackoff. She had discovered it on one of her trips to the library, but hadn't found the time to read it until now. It wasn't easy to read, but it fascinated her nonetheless.

"I wish I really understood these concepts. Somehow I know that JIT is like the interactive systems he describes, but no matter how many times I read some of these sections, I just don't understand what he means. Well, I'll use what I do understand. The book won't go away."

Julie's favorite quotations came from Ambrose Bierce, a master of pithy statements. "I think I'll use this one on planning to start my report to Ben, a bit of humor before drudgery."

> **plan**, *v.t.* To bother about the best method of accomplishing an accidental result.
>
> Ambrose Bierce[1]

"Cute. Now, what does Ackoff say about developing a plan? He lists the steps somewhere." Julie flipped through the book, finally locating the following sequence:

---

[1]Ambrose Bierce, *The Devil's Dictionary* (Cleveland: The World Publishing Co., 1911).

> To succeed, the implementation plan must include:
> 1. The nature of the task to be carried out.
> 2. The relevant goal or objective.
> 3. Who is responsible for carrying it out.
> 4. The steps to be taken.
> 5. Who is responsible for each step.
> 6. The timing of each step.
> 7. The money allocated to each step, if any.
> 8. The critical assumptions on which the schedule is based.
> 9. The expected performance and when it is expected.
> 10. The assumptions on which this expectation is based."[2]

"This makes sense. If I dig through the articles I've got on JIT, I can start to match this list to what we're supposed to do to implement it. The diagram on the 'JIT Cycle of Success' had a lot of steps in it. That's a good place to start." Julie hunted for a while, finally finding the diagram John Boyer had given her a few months before. " He said that this was their 'bible', and maybe this is why. It lists the steps in implementation, but can we fill in the rest of the details Ackoff says we need?"

The diagram Julie pulled out is Figure 2–1. She began to work slowly through the diagram and what it meant for Banyon.

PUTTING A PLAN TOGETHER

"Planning comes first. That's comforting," Julie thought as she began. "I wonder what planning means in a JIT setting? It can't be much different from what Ackoff says needs to be

---

[2]Russell Ackoff, *Creating the Corporate Future* (New York: John Wiley & Sons, 1981), p. 234.

FIGURE 2–1
Cycle of Success

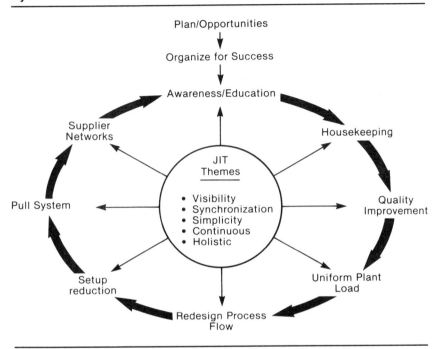

Source: Coopers & Lybrand.

done in general, so I'll assume it means setting up a flowchart and developing ways to track results against the plan."

* * * * *

To get the most out of JIT, there must be a good plan. It took a while for Banyon's plan to emerge, regardless of the advice and reading materials they received. And the plan had to be revised once Ben and Julie saw what confronted them.

While planning is an obvious first step, far too many companies jump into a JIT implementation without adequate preparation. As with Banyon, each is responding to a crisis, grabbing at JIT as a life jacket. "Cherry-picking" the areas for improvement leads to a few partial successes, but once policy or accounting issues arise, the JIT effort gets derailed or confined to a single area or function.

There is an inherent danger in JIT implementation, a tendency to create "islands of JIT" without ever integrating it into the whole system. Companies that fall into this trap never gain the true benefits of JIT and often reap only temporary improvements on the plant floor. Recognizing this danger is an important part of the planning process.

* * * * *

"We probably need to lay out a list of candidates for JIT cells, areas where we can get the work flow organized. That will require some input from Dick Williamson in engineering as well as Ben and some other key players. I'll leave that part blank for now. If we pick the best areas, then we ought to get results, and maybe we'll get some support from corporate." Julie began jotting down potential areas for improvement.

"A good area is one in which both the people and the process are willing to change and capable of changing. And it can't be a critical area, because we can't shut down the plant while we figure it out. Maybe the circuit board area would be good, but I think I'll wait to talk to Ben and Dick first. What's next?"

Step Two: Organize for Success

Julie remembered reading about this in the brochure. There was a need for a team. Thumbing through the brochure, she came across two points she had underlined in her first reading of the material:

> To implement any major innovation, such as JIT, there must be an underlying organizational structure—a group of people that are dedicated to seeing the process through. It's their job, and they have the power and the expertise to put the new system in place. . . . One of the most common reasons for failure of JIT is the lack of top management support. Why? Because the change process consumes time and money. It can be done on a shoestring, but this loads the deck against

success. Whether a "champion" is chosen to lead the cause, or a team used right from the start, is not as important as the fact that an organization changes its structure—that it places a priority on the JIT project. And, this priority includes support at the top.

"Do they really mean we have to have top management support, I wonder? If they do, we're doomed, because we just can't get it. Well, I'll simply redefine top to mean Ben for now; he runs the plant and signs off on everything that happens. But that won't change the facts; we don't have the financial resources we need for this project."

Julie was beginning to grow, seeing the plant and management's role in it in a different light. She was also beginning to think more like Ben, looking for ways to get action without waiting for the last shred of doubt to disappear. In the past she would have abandoned the project because Banyon didn't fit the perfect plan. Yet time after time Ben kept saying, "Let's get it done. If we try harder, we can overcome these problems. Action is what counts." So when Julie confronted shortcomings in Banyon's resources, she acknowledged them but looked for ways to get around them, to get where she had to go despite the obstacles.

"Well, we've got the team and the incentives, even if they are informal. Assuming that, what's next?" Julie moved on, beginning to understand what implementing JIT really means.

Step Three: Education and Awareness

Education is the next step in the JIT cycle. It is, in fact, a major cost in JIT implementation. Everyone is being asked to change, to adopt a new approach to manufacturing. They need to see the benefits of the change, how it is going to affect their jobs, and where to start. This knowledge comes through education in the cooperative, sharing vein of group discussion, not by lecture.

Change is often perceived as a threat to a person's security in the company. This can lead to resistance and sabotage, all in the name of saving one's job. The irony is that a failure to change can result in the loss of jobs as customers turn to suppliers that can meet the demands of the new manufacturing environment. Threats, though, of this kind do not aid the change process. They set up an "us versus them" mentality that may be impossible to overcome.

* * * * *

The impact of change on people kept reappearing in the articles and books Julie read. She tried to envision how Ben would handle the change process at Banyon. When he had first come to the plant everyone, including Julie, had found him distant. They gave him a green eyeshade in the early months because he acted more like an accountant than a plant manager. Recently, though, Julie saw that Ben had a good sense for people. Whether it would extend to the level of understanding that the books talked about, though, was an unanswered question. He wasn't managing through group interaction. He took comments and listened, but the decision was always his, no matter what.

Julie underlined the next passage. She decided to put it word for word in her memo to Ben.

> Through group interaction, individual involvement, and a true understanding of what JIT means, the change process can succeed. Contrary to much existing folklore, individuals do want to do a good job, to help their company succeed. But, a cog in the machine, one that is ignored unless it causes problems, does not see beyond the immediate job and its demands. Everyone should be involved in trying, and probably failing at first, to improve operations. In the long run employee involvement is the essential element in assuring continuous improvement.

"This sounds like Ackoff's 'participation' concept. And isn't continuous improvement the same as never being satisfied? Ackoff talks about this in terms of systems theory and a lot of other concepts. Let's see. Where is that quotation again?" Julie was back to digging through the books. "I've got to get organized. I spend most of my time looking for things."

The quotation Julie was looking for was the following: "If each part of a system, considered separately, is made to operate as efficiently as possible, the system as a whole will not operate as effectively as possible."[3]

"Now that's as clear as mud," Julie grunted. "I wonder why I thought it would be important? It seems to say that if everything is not linked, running the entire plant full speed still won't guarantee success. This may be part of what awareness means in a JIT setting, but it just doesn't seem to make sense. Shouldn't every activity and every process be optimized? That's what I learned in school."

"The JIT books talk about line balancing and synchronizing the flow. That I can understand. But systems? I'll have to think about this for a while. It seems like we're connecting pieces of a puzzle when we put JIT in place, and supposedly, this will make us run better. But it might also mean that every time a problem crops up, all production stops. Ben's not going to like that. So much for awareness. I think the main point is that we need to set up training once we decide what JIT is. Now, what does this little diagram hold in store for me next?"

Step Four: Housekeeping—Preventive Maintenance

"Housekeeping! Housekeeping?" Julie exclaimed. That's not a way to incorporate change! That can't be a key step on the path to manufacturing perfection!"

Or can it? At home messy drawers and unpacked boxes can lead to frustrating treasure hunts, or more precisely, wasted hours sifting through junk to find something misplaced. Many factories are like messy drawers, piles of inventory are everywhere. Tools are left wherever they were last used or tossed into corners. Finding a specific order or part can be a challenge when the factory floor is in chaos.

---

[3]Ibid., p. 18.

"This doesn't mean dusting the machines. Thank God, because that certainly isn't a value-adding activity in my book. Things just get dirty again!" Humor aside, Julie jotted down a few thoughts from the brochure.

> The message is not "Cleanliness is next to Godliness." The real issue is one of responsibility. Responsibility and pride of ownership, of a work area, a piece of equipment, or a product. . . . Having everything in the right place can definitely improve productivity. . . . Yet the pride carries far beyond any immediate benefit that an organized workplace and a visible process flow can provide. It translates to success, both on the plant floor and in the marketplace. Success creates a pride of achievement, a pride that many worry is gone in American business.

Responsibility, that term was also used in the implementation outline in Ackoff's book. Julie found that encouraging, because she believed that people should be held accountable for their actions as well as the tools they were given to do their jobs. "But I'm a prime example of the messy drawer syndrome. Look at this pile of paper! I wonder if any system can get me to be neater. Ha! I've always been a pack rat and probably always will. Well, I've written it down, even if I'm not sure I take it seriously. Sounds like Aunt Grace, 'A place for everything and everything in its place'."

* * * * *

Housekeeping means more than simply keeping the workplace neat. It also means putting an emphasis on prevention instead of correction. Total preventive maintenance (TPM) is the term used to convey this concept. It means proper maintenance of machines before they break down and stop production. In a clean work area a visual check can be made of line and machine status, and problems, such as oil leaks, can be fixed because they can be seen.

TPM transfers day-to-day ownership of the machine to the worker. The person operating the machine is given the right to stop it if unusual noises or problems arise. Pride comes with ownership, and success with pride. At Andrews Controls, Inc., TPM led to early detection of a critical problem in several coil-winding machines, preventing a total plant shutdown. It's a concept that works for everyone involved.

Eliminating the cause for pause, therefore, means more than organizing a workstation; it means analyzing the process itself to see where an hour of effort today can save a day of downtime tomorrow.

Step Five: Quality Improvement

This is the beginning for most JIT implementations. Why? For two reasons: (1) JIT assumes that quality is under control, and (2) facing the seeming impossibility of improving quality while reducing costs, managers look here for results. Ben and Julie didn't have time. They had to improve quality; it was the principal requirement.

Ben faced a 100 percent test of all finished products in order to meet Probe's quality standards. He knew this would cost much more than the current system of sample testing being used by quality assurance (QA). It was obvious to Ben that this was a major problem. As he saw it, he faced the impossible, a 100 percent test of finished units *and* at the same time a lower price to Probe.

JIT manufacturing eliminates variance from the process. It is based on stopping the line to fix problems when and where they occur. If process quality capabilities are a problem, then quality has to be addressed first.

Reality seldom matches JIT implementations presented in the press and at conferences. While all facets must eventually be covered, each manager lives in a real world with real pressures. This means that the path that seems easiest to a JIT consultant may not work in every setting. Improving quality gives results, results that others can see and believe. If an implementation is started without top management's support, the focus has to be on getting the results necessary to get top management aboard.

Achieving the goal of zero defects takes time and effort. JIT manufacturing changes the definition and focus of a plant's quality programs; the emphasis is on continuously reducing process variances. Eliminating variance is the basis of statistical process control (SPC) procedures. Variances are neither expected nor built into standards, but isolated and studied in the hopes of removing them. By doing this, JIT manufacturing removes many of the existing reasons for variance absorbing inventory buffers.

In JIT manufacturing, it is important to remember that the operator, not a quality control technician, monitors and improves quality performance. This means that the operator has the authority to shut down the line if a problem is detected. Giving line workers this right may violate the chain of command in an organization. In reality, it shortens the feedback loop, reducing the time lost between the time a problem occurs and is corrected. In the final analysis, then, quality does not begin on the plant floor. It is built into a product at design because it is a key characteristic of competitive excellence.

* * * * *

"Quality is step five? No way! Ben and I have talked about this. If we have to stop the process every time we hit a defect, we'll never get anything out the door. It must mean that quality efforts are part of JIT, and that quality is pretty good before you start this process. If that's not what it means, it certainly is what it needs to be. Quality may be out of sequence according to the diagram, but it belongs up front in our case. I'll have to remember to put quality first when I draw up the flowchart."

Julie was right. Everyone at Banyon was beginning to learn what it meant to be a world-class manufacturer,[4] but there was still a long way to go. The quality improvement effort had started, but in a world of continuous improvement, it was obviously not over.

---

[4]Richard J. Schonberger, *World Class Manufacturing* (New York: Free Press, 1986).

Step Six: Uniform Plant Load

The next stage in the JIT cycle is developing a uniform plant load. Julie wasn't quite sure how this could be used at Banyon where they still operated like a job shop, but now the object was to understand the steps in a "normal" implementation. She and Ben would have to think through some of these issues together. Since her immediate goal was to be able to explain it to Ben, she wrote down the essentials.

* * * * *

Uniform plant load, or linear production, simply means that output is divided into even "buckets," one bucket for each production day or shift. The goal is not maximizing output, but producing only what is needed, no more, no less.

"Sounds good," Julie thought, "but what about personal incentive programs, for example, piece-rate pay structures? If you limit the total amount any individual can produce, how do you reward superior performance? Or even detect it? And if a plant already has a piece-rate bonus system, how can uniform plant load be achieved?"

* * * * *

Banyon had this problem and solved it, not by managerial mandate, but by joint effort between management and work force. It took a long time to reach an acceptable solution, but a plan was finally crafted and implemented.

Uniform plant load is not the final assembly schedule. It is a production rate for all components and assemblies synchronized with final demand rate. It is the establishment of an attainable cycle time which is constrained by the capacity of bottlenecks within the process. While this may seem an unusual method of planning production, plants have always been constrained. Recognizing the impact of bottlenecks in production planning can translate to reduced lead times and improved customer service.

Many line workers know that a particular machine or process is slow, but as long as the machine works, there are no complaints. The bottleneck is, therefore, acceptable. And while management might be frustrated by the inability to get more product out the door, identifying the problem area is not a simple matter without detailed process flow analyses. Consultants have made a lot of money helping companies find their bottlenecks. But a simple process and a dash of common sense can accomplish the same thing.

* * * * *

"Maybe this is what Ackoff was talking about, bottleneck capacity. No matter how fast you run the other machines, you can only produce as much as the slowest machine or process will allow. Makes sense. I wonder why I never saw this in any book at school. I have a feeling a lot of my old professors could learn from what we're doing. Maybe I should invite a couple of them over, but not until we have things under control." Julie's eyes were beginning to ache, so she set the papers aside and went out for a walk.

She thought about many things, not the least of which was that she should have put on a raincoat or taken an umbrella. It was drizzling, but Julie didn't turn back. The rain felt good, and she wasn't going to a beauty pageant. "Mom would yell if she saw me. I get so caught up in books that I lose what little common sense I have. Oh well! It'll make me walk faster."

Julie wondered where they should start in the implementation process. Planning had begun, but she couldn't see Ben following the lock-step path the diagram suggested. "Ben likes results and action. Some of the steps are hard to define, and that means the results could be fuzzy. John Boyer warned us about leapfrogging over basics in the implementation, but we just don't have the luxury of doing each step in order. Maybe we can do a couple of things at once, like line balancing, candidate selection, and education. The flowchart may help there."

Julie walked on. She had a set path for her walks so she could let her mind wander without being bothered with direction. It didn't come as a surprise, then, when she was back home before she realized it. "I could sit down and work again, but I doubt much more will go into my head. We don't start back for a couple more days, so I might as well relax while I have the chance."

The next morning Julie was back at the books. She picked up the brochure and began where she had left off. "Ah, we're finally getting to the cells. When I first heard about JIT, I thought cells first, but here they are way down the list in step seven. I wonder how many people get this step out of sync?"

Step Seven: Redesigning the Process Flow

Another common characteristic of JIT production is its basic U-shaped cell configuration. Moving machines out of functional departments, such as machining, into cells designed to complete a specific stage in the assembly path may seem to be a radical departure from existing practice. Actually, Alexander Hamilton Church talked about ranges of machines in 1929, and Henry Ford used this concept to set up the first assembly line.

* * * * *

"Thinking of Banyon as an assembly line is hard because there are so many products and so many routings. Ford had it easy, any color was fine as long as it was black. But then isn't that what the Japanese do? We can have one of their cars in a couple of colors and with or without an options package. A range of machines, though, is hard to visualize. I wonder what the key objective is?" Julie found her answer in the next paragraph.

* * * * *

In setting up a manufacturing cell, the objective is to eliminate any operations that don't add value, and then to group dissimilar, dedicated equipment together to assemble a particular subcomponent or product. Product families are groups of products that follow a common assembly path. They are the bases of "focused factory" manufacturing.

A standardized assembly path, common components, and flexibility are key elements of the cell concept. In implementing JIT, one objective is to push variety toward the end of the manufacturing process. If products consist of 70 to 80 percent standard parts and assemblies, adding bells and whistles at the end of the process is a low cost way to provide variety. One large company realized significant inventory savings simply by selling telephones separate from their covers. If new colors come into vogue, the company is not faced with a lot of obsolete inventory, just a few covers. Common sense got a nudge from JIT procedures.

* * * * *

"So it does mean standardization. I keep thinking that we supply dozens of different products, but really, they often look the same. Maybe we put a few more features on one counter than on another, but I bet we could do something to make this variety less costly. Do we even need all the models we have? I wonder if we ever asked our customers?"

Julie's thoughts mean that JIT is beginning to settle in. She is connecting the manufacturing process from design to the final customer and asking questions that quite likely have never been asked before. Is she simply smarter than most? No, Julie is quite normal. She is just beginning to put the pieces together; the hardest part was getting started.

Step Eight: Setup Reduction

"Setup reduction? I wonder why this is important?"

Inventory models, such as economic order quantity (EOQ), balance the holding costs of inventory against the setup costs associated with each batch of product. Setup time and cost play a major role in promoting long runs of product built to inventory, not to demand. Through careful analysis of the setup process, this time and cost can be reduced to zero, reducing run sizes and decreasing inventory levels.

Think of setup time as consisting of activities *external* to the process, that is, the machine continues to produce while preparations are made for the production of another product, and those that are *internal* to the process, that is, the machine stops while it is adjusted to produce another product. If both are performed when the machine is down, time is wasted. Performing external setup while another job is running, and reducing internal setup time, can reduce run size requirements significantly. In fact, as setup time moves toward zero, the optimal lot size approaches one!

JIT seeks to eliminate the cause for pause. Setup time is definitely a nonvalue-adding pause beyond some minimal level. Engineering studies are not the only way to identify setup time reductions. People who run the machines know them best and are likely to come up with the formula for success.

* * * * *

"Well, my answer seems to be that setup is a cause for pause. Funny, but I always thought of it as a constant, a fact of life. We've been using the EOQ model to plan optimum run sizes, and we've never questioned the time lost. If setups are easy and fast to do, then more real work can get out. I'll bet this would come as no surprise to Dick Williamson. He's been harping on the setup crew for some time to do more preparatory work before they shut down a machine. I might have to start following him around!"

Julie turned to the next page. "I'm finally getting to the end. Good! Oh-oh. A 'pull system'? What on earth does this mean? I don't recall reading about this before. I must have faded out when I was supposed to be absorbing it."

Step Nine: Setting Up a Pull System

The term *pull system* means that Kanban tools are being used to control the production process. Kanban, a Japanese term for a card used in inventory control, is most often associated in the United States with a rack or space for staging production. In an overlapped pull system, an empty space preceding a workstation acts as a signal to pull production along. If a rack or some other batch device is used, for example, to move parts from one cell to another, then the company is using a "linked" pull system. In either case, only an empty space or a rack can be filled. Demand triggers supply.

A pull system manages the flow of parts on the plant floor. It is a short-term approach that does not replace the long-term focus of MRP, but supplants it with synchronized production and simple process controls. A computer company uses an overlapped pull system that makes any problem instantly visible. For example, during a recent plant tour one line was down. The point where the problem occurred was easy to spot, all Kanban spaces prior to the attachment of the plastic dust cover were full, and subsequent spaces were empty. Until the defective covers were repaired or replaced, the line would stay down, a graphic example of the pull system in operation.

*****

This caused Julie to think. "This means inventory has to go. If we tried to put it all in baskets, we'd need a lot of them. Mike wasn't kidding when he said that JIT meant no more mounds to hide behind. I guess that less inventory is better, but it's scary to think about losing our buffers. What if we can't meet the final demand? What happens if we get an unexpected order?" Julie had many questions and few answers.

Like most managers, Julie had difficulty visualizing a linked flow of materials through a factory without buffers or safety nets. She was concerned that setting up a pull system might spell disaster. Customers often changed their minds, and the mix run in the plant could change two or three times a month. It just didn't seem possible that everything could be synchronized so well that all the long-standing problems of manufacturing would disappear.

Step Ten: Setting Up Supplier Networks

This book began with Probe pushing Banyon into JIT as Probe established a vendor network that would provide the stability necessary to support the JIT pull system. JIT is one form of vertical integration that establishes informal partnerships between suppliers and customers. If a vendor's failure shuts down a plant, the vendor will not survive. Conversely, many suppliers balk when facing JIT schedules.

Many companies are tackling these issues by establishing preferred vendor programs that consolidate orders and raise volumes provided by suppliers. Long-term contracts can simplify these agreements. The vendor always ships on schedule, and the customer always accepts the order. These guarantees go a long way toward removing uncertainties for vendor and customer.

For many companies, JIT adoption is triggered by a major customer's desire to set up a supplier network. And if the supplier can't respond by getting its suppliers to join the team, a brutal game of "monkey in the middle" develops.

* * * * *

"That finishes the formal diagram, but John Boyer has penciled in another step, 'locking in the solution.' If I remember right, he said that many JIT efforts fail in the long run because the measurements used to manage and evaluate the plant aren't changed. I'd better remember what he said about this, because it seemed pretty important to him."

A Final Step: Locking In the Solution

The final gauge of success of any implementation effort is whether the "entrepreneur" can leave. If the system is dependent on the presence and encouragement of one or two individuals, it will only survive as long as they are involved. Should they leave or tire, the entire implementation could end. Once solutions are achieved, new structures and measures have to be put in place to perpetuate the improvements.

If JIT implementation is completed without changing the performance evaluation and accounting systems, it will be a short-run phenomenon. People respond to the measurements used to evaluate them, and failing to change these measurements can result in an unraveling of JIT efforts.

FIRST STEPS AT BANYON

Julie had a detailed list of implementation steps ready for Ben when he returned from the long weekend. They used

Julie's notes to help choose the members of the implementation brain trust. Ben was convinced that a good team was the key to a successful JIT start-up.

"Julie, whom should we include on this team? I know we need Dick Williamson from Manufacturing Engineering and Paul from Quality Assurance. Who else?"

"I'd like to see both Ron Fennel, the product manager, and Mike Gannon included. Mike knows the people and the processes in the factory as well as anyone, and Ron has a good head on his shoulders." Ben agreed and asked her to set up a meeting for the next day.

"Tell them to set aside the whole morning," Ben said. "I want to come out of the meeting with an implementation flowchart. We need to pick areas to start the change process, and that means getting together with people who know the plant."

* * * * *

The next morning everyone met in the conference room. Ben brought sweet rolls and Julie arranged for coffee. As Ben looked around the room he could barely contain a chuckle. Ron and Paul were sitting on one side of the conference table, Dick and Mike on the other. "The thinkers versus the doers," Ben thought. The way people clustered in groups always interested Ben. "Likes attract!" Ben smiled to himself as he took off his jacket and waited for everyone to get coffee.

"I think each of you is aware of the problems we face. Probe is demanding higher quality and lower costs, and top management is unwilling to let up on profit targets or provide additional resources. We're caught between a rock and a hard place. Julie and I have spent a lot of time looking for an answer, and we think we have one. It's called Just-in-Time manufacturing. If we adopt it, we'll be changing the way we manufacture product."

Ben launched into a discussion of JIT using the "Cycle of Success" diagram. The managers in the room broke in at times asking about Ben's objectives, what certain concepts meant, and looking for examples.

Three hours later the meeting broke up. Everyone was

given a copy of several key articles on JIT and asked to spend some time thinking about the best place to start at Banyon. Another meeting was scheduled for Friday morning.

* * * * *

"Julie, do you think they understood what I was trying to say?" Ben wondered. "Some of the questions were right on target, but Paul just didn't seem to be with it. I hope I'm wrong, but I think he's going to be trouble."

"I don't know, Ben. You did a good job of summing up JIT, and they should learn a lot from those articles. I think we'll find out Friday one way or the other. What should we do between now and then?"

"Let's start the flowchart. I thought we'd get it done in this meeting, but it took a lot longer to explain the concepts than I anticipated."

"I still think you made a lot of progress, though."

"In what way, Julie? I talked, they asked questions, but I'm certain only part of the message was received."

"Part's better than none. So, boss, what do you have in mind? I'm not a graphic designer, so any 'flowchart' is going to flow only in intent, not reality."

"Then I'll draw, you think."

Ben cleared away the papers on his desk, then pulled a clean sheet of paper out. Pencils sharpened, they set to the task at hand.

CHAPTER 3

A FOCUS ON QUALITY

Most books about just-in-time confirm that quality improvements emerge from process improvements, as if JIT gives birth to enhanced quality. JIT assumes that basic levels of quality already exist, and that reducing lot sizes will make any remaining quality problems visible. If the production process is to be stopped every time a quality problem arises, there had better be an acceptable level of quality from the start. Otherwise, there will be a lot of "causes for pause."

Learning about Quality

Ben and Julie spent the rest of the afternoon going over the basics of JIT/TQC and setting up an implementation flowchart. While the basic steps were clear from the "Cycle of Success" diagram (See Figure 2–1), picking a candidate for the pilot study proved to be a challenge.

"Ben," Julie began, "how are we going to pick the best place to start? We can limit ourselves to areas that make Probe product, but you know that GRI's mandate was just as stern. The plant is complex; I hardly know what routings products take. Yet we're supposed to look at all of these processes and pick the one that will have the greatest impact on our quality performance. I'd like to see one of the JIT gurus figure out where to start at Banyon."

"It's hard, Julie, but we don't have a choice. We have to do it or find a customer for the orders we'll lose if we don't. Major customers can't be ignored. Let's think about it from a different perspective. JIT is built on the concept of teams, of going to the people who do the job to get answers. Maybe our new team will be able to help. I'm willing to put my money on our abilities, Julie. This is a good company with good people."

The rest of the afternoon they went over the basics of quality management, looking for the best way to frame the problem for the implementation team. Ben anticipated a few problems getting started because Paul, the Quality Assurance manager, was a firm proponent of "inspecting quality in." That was the way it had always been done, and if Paul had his way, that was the way it would always be done.

The implementation was embroiled in people problems from the start, problems without easy answers. Ben's "people sense" was his only guide. A team approach to implementing process improvements, the very basis of JIT, meant that people would drive the process and could derail it at any step. It was a nagging thought in the back of Ben's mind all the time.

DEFINING AND FINDING QUALITY IMPROVEMENTS

Quality improvement is an ongoing process, not a one-time program. Before a company can start, it must know what quality means to its customers. Is it—as Phil Crosby, a noted quality expert, suggests—best described as "conformity with requirements"? Or is it "fitness for use," Juran's description? Does putting statistical process control in place ensure that quality will improve?

Defining quality is the first step in improving quality. Webster defines quality as "that which makes or helps to make anything such as it is . . . a distinguishing property or level of excellence." Quality is meeting the customer's requirements; it starts with design and continues to post-delivery service. It means doing the right job consistently and knowing what the right job is.

Banyon had one advantage going into the change process. They knew what their customers wanted, at least as far as Probe and GRI were concerned. Meeting their requirements seemed to be impossible, but the mandate was certainly clear.

* * * * *

"Julie, can you get some information together on what 'Total Quality Control' means before tomorrow's meeting?" Ben and Julie were back at Banyon; it was after 6 P.M., and the day was far from over.

"I'll try, Ben. I have a book that examines quality from a couple of different angles. What do you need, and why? Do you think Paul will be that hard to convince? Quality is his job; we're simply giving him more direction on how to define it." Julie's looks betrayed her thoughts, and Ben was quick to respond to both.

"Think about this from his point of view for a moment, Julie. He's been working in quality assurance at Banyon most of his life. What he knows about quality he learned on the plant floor, not in a classroom. So, he has a limited view of what we're doing; but he's no dummy. He'll want to know what this means for his area in both the short and long run. We'll need to convince him that statistical process control won't hurt him or his ability to get his job done. So, will it be hard? We'll see. I just want to be ready, that's all."

Ben walked Julie back to her office. "You know, I keep assuming that you don't mind working late, Julie. You have to let me know if you need time off. I'm relying on you a lot, but you do have a personal life. Are you OK?"

"I'll let you know when I'm not, I promise." With that, Julie turned to the stack on her desk, and Ben walked back to his office. The quiet settled around them, isolated in space but joined in purpose. Facing greater obstacles than they knew, they toiled on late into the night, looking for answers.

THE HISTORY OF QUALITY

Building a competitive advantage based on superior quality is not a new idea. Ensuring that it is present, though, is a process that changes as the manufacturing and *service* environments change. In the early days of commerce, most goods were made by trained craftsmen who spent years developing their arts through daily practice. The technology of quality was in their heads and hands, and pride and concern for one's reputation provided the necessary incentives to ensure high levels of quality.

> as technology evolved, as commerce changed, as distances grew, and as complexities arose, there was a need for the work of many craftsmen to converge somehow. . . . Various inventions had to be created—forms of control, forms of quality planning, and the rest. Because of this phenomenon . . . we are looking (today) for new policies, goals, and plans, which will enable us to retain the benefits of our technological society but without enduring the breaks in those protective (quality) dikes.[1]

* * * * *

"Juran says the concept of quality has changed over time." Julie was hard at work on a quality memo. It was interesting to think that a concept that seemed to be straightforward was actually complex and dynamic. "If the concept of quality changes with how work is done, then the use of JIT/TQC may change what consumers expect. It's changed Probe unless they're schizophrenic, giving out quality awards with one hand while saying 'you've got to improve your quality' with the other." Julie read on.

Quality in the Age of Efficiency

In the early 1900s, Taylor changed the concept of quality to correspond with the demands of the emerging manufacturing environment in the United States. Believing firmly in the need to exploit the division of labor in order to get maximum

---

[1] J. Juran, "Upper Management and Quality." in *Quality, Productivity and Management*, ed. M. Starr (New York: Elsevier Science Publishing Co., 1987), pp. 278–79.

performance out of the manufacturing process, he built his system on the separation of planning and working. Planners made decisions, and workers executed them. Workers no longer bore responsibility for quality assurance; that was up to quality control inspectors.

Taylor's methods were alien to a culture where craftsmen and individual skills were vital elements in the manufacturing process. Giving control back to the worker and stopping the manufacturing process to fix problems as they occur is alien today.

The United States is at a crossroad today in its ability to manufacture good product to meet customer demand. The solutions suggested overthrow many of the tenets of scientific management in the short run; whether they do so in the long run remains to be seen.

* * * * *

Julie looked from her desk to the window. Thinking about what she was going to say at the afternoon meeting, she kept returning to the question, "Why?" Why did American manufacturing move away from a belief in the value of the individual worker? Why did anyone think that separating processes into their smallest parts could be a long run solution to any problem?

"Taylor keeps popping up. A person could blame him for all of our manufacturing problems. Well, he may have had the solution they needed in the early 1900s, but it's not working today. So much for history. How do I describe the concept of Total Quality Control (TQC) to Paul?"

TOTAL QUALITY CONTROL

Total Quality Control is one of the new concepts Julie and Ben had to explore. It sounded simple enough; apply the concept of quality control to every activity in the organization. There was only one way to do something, the right way. This meant that every individual in the firm, whether in engineering, marketing, manufacturing, finance, or personnel, had to focus on providing quality products and services to the customer. It is institutionalizing a process of continuous improvement.

The Basics of TQC

Julie picked up the last article from her quality pile. So far the articles had not helped much. Murphy's law prevailed; the last article proved to be the only one useful in structuring her memo. The article discussed the basics of TQC, starting with four principles:

1. Create a simple process.
2. Eliminate waste.
3. Make problems visible.
4. Create a climate for improvement.

The article claimed that implementing JIT/TQC was as simple as these four principles. JIT/TQC was described not as a computer software package to redesign process flow, but as the assumptions needed to frame the process flow that emerges from design.

* * * * *

"Oh, oh. This looks like the kind of jargon that raises Ben's blood pressure," chuckled Julie. "But if it starts out this way and runs on for another seven pages, it's got to say something useful." Julie read on, taking notes and thinking as the hours slipped by.

Creating a Simple Process

Creating a simple process begins with product design. In fact, fully 75 percent of a product's cost and most of the constraints in the production process are set in its design. If a product's specifications are at the outside limits of the machinery which makes it, then the difficulties encountered to turn out acceptable product will overwhelm all other considerations.

What is a simple process? A good example is McDonald's

quality control check. If you've ever been inside one of their kitchens, you've probably seen small plastic cards inserted in stacks of hamburgers. This is a simple quality control device. It signals the time by which the hamburgers must be served, a simple way to ensure quality.

Simplicity means removing all unnecessary steps, reducing the complexity of the operation performed, and designing the product to minimize the number of adjustments that need to be made. Today, most computer printer covers snap on instead of being fastened by screws. A one step assembly, simple in nature, has replaced a more complicated operation.

* * * * *

"We start with the old adage, 'Keep it simple, stupid!' Better not put that in the report. I won't get gold stars for irreverence when Ben is trying to gain support."

Julie, always irreverent, knew when to keep her comments to herself, at least most of the time. "On to waste. I wonder if this is going to be redefined too?"

Eliminate Waste

Waste is any process or activity that does not add value to the product. Scrap is visible waste on the plant floor. But this is not the only place waste occurs. Idle inventory is waste. Expediting orders is waste. If every pause a product makes is waste, and every buffer in the flow of product is waste, it is easy to find room for improvement. Waste is everywhere. And tolerance for waste in the competitive marketplace is evaporating.

Identifying waste requires a clear understanding of process flow. Engineers are trained to analyze process flow, but not in the context of the overall organization. Accountants know how to cost a process, but not how to analyze a process to isolate areas for improvement. Managers are trained to motivate people to achieve goals, but they don't know which goals will optimize long-run performance. Eliminating waste is a team effort.

* * * * *

"Go, team, go! I suppose we could start a cheerleading squad, but I think that's what Ben and I are. Well, if we need a team to get started, Ben is definitely on the right track by including Paul and others at the beginning." Julie turned back to the article.

Making Problems Visible

The complex reporting processes used by the management of most factories do not provide timely signals of problems. In fact, by the time a centrally generated report gets to the plant floor, the problems have usually been resolved. Real time systems can help reduce the lag between events and feedback to management, but common sense may provide the best signaling mechanism of all.

A simple, visible process flow means that a manager can see how well production is going by looking at it. Many JIT plants have installed windows so that supervisors can scan the line to spot problems. This sets up a basis for strong operational controls on real activities, not the downstream financial impact of those activities. Managers manage people and tasks, not numbers. Creating a visible process supports the return of the manager to the plant floor and provides an efficient and understandable way to monitor performance.

* * * * *

"It would be great to see how we'e doing just by walking through the plant," Julie mused. "Ben and I are out there all the time, but all I see is stacks of inventory interspersed with people. I know they're doing something, but what is always a mystery."

Create a Climate for Improvement

The Japanese change the culture of an organization so that it will respond to the demands of JIT/TQC. While physical modifications can be made to start the culture change, consistent reinforcement of the right performance and immediate recognition and resolution of problems is required.

Culture change is a slow phenomenon. It creates new relationships and expectations. In the final analysis, it is the beliefs held by people in the organization that must change. This will not happen overnight. That is why implementation is different for every company. People and their beliefs are different in each plant. Therefore, there are few universal truths when it comes to describing group behavior.

Consistent action on the part of management, a willingness to stick with the new system when something goes wrong, and trusting the team's solutions even when certain they won't work, are all necessary to create a climate for improvement. At Banyon, Ben had to change his own views as well as his style of management before the JIT effort would truly succeed.

* * * * *

"This is a lifetime's work!" Ben tossed the list of steps aside before looking up. He locked eyes with Julie, waiting for a response.

"But, Ben, . . ."

"But Ben what? You've given me four 'simple' principles. Now help me understand them."

"I wish I could. They are simple, and yet I don't know where to start applying them. Don't you?"

"Maybe. If I recall, Probe made a point of emphasizing that these changes have to take place in an 'experimental' setting . . . one site where statistical process control fits. If we're going to meet our improvement targets, I think we'd better focus on the site, principles or not."

Julie did not respond, at least not right away. Ben seemed to be confident about starting the project, while she continued to feel that she didn't understand what it would take to make the new process work. She enjoyed the research and learning how to motivate people to change, but she still wasn't sure they knew what it was they were trying to adopt. The focus on quality at least got them moving. She hoped it was in the right direction.

"Just look at Ben," Julie thought. "Here I am hesitating and looking for more facts, and Ben, as always, is controlled and confident. Once he makes up his mind, he doesn't look back; he moves forward with zeal. Banyon is an old-fashioned machine shop with a stodgy labor force that doesn't want to try anything new. Does he really think he can transform it into a new manufacturing environment?"

"I just don't know, Ben," Julie stammered. "I read and reread my notes, but there just isn't much there. If you know where to start, I'll gladly support your efforts, but I'm uncertain of where to start and unsure of what we're trying to do. Get results, that I do know. But TQC? There's no help in the four basic principles. Not help for today, for getting started!"

Now it was Ben's turn to think. Where was her self-confidence? Sure, this was going to be hard. Wasn't that part of the fun? If it were easy, everyone would be doing it. Well, if part of the process meant getting Julie excited about JIT, he would do it. The boss always had to act as if he knew where he was going and what he was doing. OK. So he wasn't sure. No problem. He was a quick study, and they were going to succeed.

"Let's look at the game plan we got at the seminar, Julie. Maybe that will help."

The outline is presented in Table 3–1. The first step is to select a candidate for study. While it sounds simple, choosing an implementation site requires a detailed understanding of

TABLE 3–1
Statistical Process Control (A Planned Approach)

Select a candidate for study
Define the process
Procure resources for the study
Determine the adequacy of the measurement system
Provide a control system
Select a method of analysis
Gather and analyze data
Track down and remove special causes
Estimate process capability
Establish a quality control plan for the process

Source: Coopers & Lybrand.

the existing process. Ben and Julie were on the right track in bringing the issues to the people who ran the machines.

PUTTING STRUCTURE AROUND THE QUALITY EFFORT

Three steps provide the basis for implementing a quality improvement program. First, there must be a clear understanding of what quality is for the product in question. Earlier, terms like *fitness for use* were suggested as a starting point. *Fitness* is a term defined by the customer's needs. Therefore, the first step in understanding quality is to learn the customer's needs and expectations.

The next step is translating these expectations into product specifications. Providing all the desired specifications may be impossible because they require different, conflicting standards. If this is the case, a quality strategy is needed. If only 75 percent of the desired specifications can be met, the choice of which to meet is critical. Quality is not a concept for the factory floor alone; it is a critical competitive characteristic of a product.

When these decisions have been made, the next step is to develop systems to ensure that the desired level of quality is achieved. In Banyon's case, customers didn't wait to be asked what features they wanted in the product; they delivered ultimatums.

Banyon faced implementation, the hardest part in any organizational change. It had to institute a process of continuous improvement that would serve as the backbone for the JIT system.

A Team for Quality

"What do you think, Ben? Can you put together a talk that will work?" Julie was looking over Ben's shoulder as he read her memo on TQC concepts. The second meeting of the implementation team would begin in 20 minutes. It would be a critical meeting; the flow chart that Ben and Julie had developed would be discussed, and a candidate for the pilot TQC effort chosen.

"Your background information helps a lot, Julie. I think what I'm going to do, though, is to start with the action list that you got at the Probe seminar. These are practical guys. They need to see a clear sequence of tasks, not a strategy. I need strategy; it helps me keep things in perspective. Anyway, it's about time to get this project underway." Ben and Julie walked down the hall to the conference room.

Selecting a Candidate for Study

The meeting started promptly at 9 A.M. Ben was always prompt, a fascinating characteristic to Julie, who was always 5 minutes late, whatever the event. For the last hour they had gone over her notes on quality as Ben put together a presentation. Julie was to play backup quarterback in case the discussion moved into areas in which Ben was less sure. Until then, she would just listen.

"I think each of you know that we were given an ultimatum by Probe to improve our quality or lose their business," Ben began. "I've had Julie looking into a technique called Total Quality Control, because this is Probe's recommendation. I thought today you could help us get started. We need your input to make this thing work. So, settle back and I'll walk you through what we've learned so far."

Ben launched into the implementation plan that he and Julie had developed. He kept waiting for the others to interrupt, but they didn't. Julie looked around, sensing a definite shift in mood since the first session. "I wonder what's going on here? Well, Mike is my best source. After this meeting is over I'll wander out to the plant and talk to him."

* * * * *

The first step in implementing total quality control is the selection of a good candidate for analysis. Good candidates are processes that will deliver a lot of "bang for the buck," where the maximum number of products will benefit from improvement, and where the individuals involved in producing product can be counted on to support management's efforts. The first operation chosen for improvement is a "greenfield" site. It provides the impetus for continued change, setting the tone for how changes will be received. A high probability of success is essential, because early failures can derail the entire JIT/TQC effort.

* * * * *

"Does this make sense to all of you? Feel free to cut in at any time." Ben paused. Looking to Paul for an answer, he was not about to start up again without one.

"Ah, well, Ben, I just don't like it. What are you saying? That inspectors will stand at every machine, or that you won't need inspection any more? If you are going to do this, I want to know how it's going to affect me and my people. Sounds like a bunch of schoolboy theory to me. You can't expect perfection or get it. And inspecting stuff in batches is just plain more efficient."

Ben did not respond immediately. He had guessed that Paul wouldn't jump on the bandwagon, but why was he so negative? Just like Paul to say no and mean it, up front. Talking to him was like talking to a brick wall. Well, if he wouldn't join the effort he would be sidelined, permanently.

"Paul, please listen to the idea before you reject it. We don't have a lot of options. I have to keep this plant running and make a profit. I can't do that if we lose our biggest customers, can I?"

* * * * *

Ben's discussion with Paul revealed the major problem with TQC; it threatens the security of the people being asked to put it in place. It is the equivalent of saying, "==Help me design you out of a job==." In approaching JIT/TQC, it is crucial that personal dynamics and motivational factors always be at the forefront. Few individuals are anxious to take an active hand in their own demise.

The hard facts are that a good program of quality control, such as statistical process control, minimizes the need for downstream inspection and workers who perform those tasks. Giving machine operators control over and responsibility for quality takes these tasks away from quality assurance. It is a necessary move, in that competitive survival relies increasingly on doing things right the first time. It is a change, however, with winners and losers. Early recognition of this issue can provide the time needed to develop alternative jobs for workers displaced.

* * * * *

"We all understand the problem, Ben." Paul took the role of group spokesman. "And we do have a quality problem, but it's not in this plant. It's in the 5041 microprocessors we buy from Dantel. Those parts cost 25 dollars each, and we lose almost 10 percent, 1 out of every 10, to one type of failure or another. If you want to fix this place, start there!"

Ben couldn't believe his ears. Was Paul saying that Dantel, one of their major suppliers, was the cause of their quality problems? Paul should know; quality was his job. "Do the rest of you agree with Paul?" Ben looked around the room, trying to see the answer in the faces of his managers.

Dick Williamson finally spoke up. "Paul came to me just yesterday with enough details to convince me that the problems lie outside the plant. I believe that JIT/TQC is the wave of the future, but I can't see how we can do a good job with bad raw materials. So if we're here to suggest a place to start fixing our problems, this seems to be as good a place as any."

"If all of you agree, then that's where we'll start. Paul, I'd like you to go out to their plant with me. Until we confront them face to face, we can't move forward. The rest of you start looking in your areas for other problems like this, or ones where we seem to be making mistakes. Let's get back together a week from now, same time, same place."

The meeting ended, and Ben and Julie went back to work. Julie set up a meeting with Dantel for the following week while Ben worked on his monthly report to corporate.

A VISIT WITH A SURPRISE ENDING . . .

Tuesday of the following week found Ben and Paul in Ft. Worth meeting with Dantel's management. Dantel rolled out the red carpet, even had the senior marketing manager meet them at the airport. Ben had briefly mentioned that there were problems with their latest shipments, and Dantel's management had assured him that they would do whatever was necessary to correct the situation.

The ride to the plant was pleasant. Ben looked out the window and occasionally asked a question. It was small talk. It seemed pointless to get into the real issues until the people who could do something about them were there. They arrived at the plant 45 minutes later and were escorted to the group president's office. Within minutes four other Dantel managers were there, and the meeting began.

"Mr. Morgan, how can we help you?" George Edwards, the group president, began. "Mr. Desposito, our marketing vice president has filled me in on some of your concerns, but I'd rather hear them again from you so I can make sure we do the right thing."

Ben explained the quality problems they were having with the microprocessors, and as he did so, George Edwards listened and jotted down several points. "You say that 1 out of 10 fails either your incoming tests or farther downstream?" George looked both astonished and concerned. "No wonder you came to us. I'm glad you did. We pride ourselves on zero defects performance. I wonder if Bill Frank, our Quality Control (QC) expert, can shed any light on this for us?"

Everyone looked at Bill Frank. He was a slight man with thick, tinted glasses that failed to hide weak, watery eyes. Fidgeting at first, obviously uncomfortable at being under such close scrutiny, Bill responded quickly nonetheless.

"Uh, I, I mean, we in QC, we inspect every unit that goes to Banyon. We test them all because they're so sensitive and expensive. I'm sure they've been passing our tests. But, well, maybe I should check into it before I say for certain."

"Weak answer," Ben thought to himself. "They say that zero defects is their policy, but we know differently."

Ben flinched as Paul began to speak. "Mr. Frank, we do another complete test of your units when they get in house, and I can tell you they don't pass. So either they leave here defective, or they're damaged in shipment."

"You do a total test again?" Bill Frank almost jumped out of his chair. "Can you tell me what you do? What kind of equipment do you use to do the test?"

Paul was quick to respond, threatened by Bill's questions. "We test every unit with a Series 254 Logic Tester."

"That logic tester is slower than our microprocessor. You aren't really testing it, and you might be doing some damage. What kind of failure patterns are you seeing?" Bill looked concerned, but he wasn't as nervous as he was at the beginning of the conversation.

"Whatever you say," Paul responded, "we're getting 10 percent defects in every batch. It's about 1 in every 10; in fact, it's usually the 10th unit that fails. Do you have an explanation for that?"

"That's not random failure, and that means that someone or something in either your process or ours is causing the problem. But we do outgoing tests. Why do you test at all? We guarantee every part shipped." The conversation was going in circles, and Bill was getting firmer and firmer in his stand.

Paul's face was getting red, eyes bulging, and teeth clenched. "I have to remember not to recommend Paul for a sensitive foreign service position," Ben thought. "We're here to get help, not to point fingers." Ben cleared his throat and turned directly to Bill Frank.

"Can you show me your QC test results? I believe you, but I'd like to get a better idea of what it is you do as opposed to what we do. Perhaps then we can isolate the problem."

"Bill, why don't you pull some information together while I take Ben and Paul to lunch." George Edwards interrupted the conversation to take control.

All during lunch and throughout the conversation on business, sports, and pleasure, Ben couldn't rid himself of a nagging fear that he wasn't going to like the answers Bill Frank would have when they returned. Paul seemed totally at ease, sure that the problem was Dantel's. Ben wasn't one of Paul's fans, but he tried to keep everything on a professional level and not to let his emotions shade his judgment.

They returned to Dantel's offices two hours later, and Bill was waiting. He had an enormous stack of computer printouts, larger than any Ben had ever seen. "Oh, oh. I don't like the look of this," Ben thought. "I think he has proof that the problem isn't theirs. And I have a feeling that I'm not going to like what I hear."

* * * * * *

The rest of that afternoon Paul, Ben, Bill, and George Edwards went over the test results Dantel kept on the microprocessors they had shipped to Banyon during the last two years. Time after time the units passed the rigorous 100 percent test with flying colors. There was simply no doubt; the problem was in Banyon's handling of the units, not in Dantel's manufacturing process. Ben was both embarrassed and angry. He tried to be as tactful as possible, but in the end they left with egg on their faces.

Hardly a word passed between Ben and Paul on the trip back to Banyon. Paul didn't have an answer for what they were doing to the units. Why were they inspecting defects in? Talk about nonvalue-adding activity, this cost big bucks. When Ben announced that he wanted all testing of the microprocessors discontinued, Paul made only a half-hearted attempt to dissuade him.

Ben was not surprised when defects in Dantel microprocessors virtually disappeared when Banyon stopped testing them. After months of detective work, the explanation itself was embarrassingly simple. The woman who ran the test equipment was a snappy dresser; she came to work every day wearing a skirt and nylons. The workstation was not in a humidity controlled area. Nylons, dry air, static electricity. Inadvertently, she was shorting out every 10th unit with a static electricity discharge. Amusing? Not to Ben.

CHAPTER 4

A SERIES OF FAILURES

The next few attempts at implementing JIT/TQC didn't go much better for Banyon. Facing failure, Ben sought a way to solve the implementation puzzle. Quitting was out of the question; it wasn't in Ben's nature. He was committed to the implementation, and he was not going to give up.

After the microprocessor debacle, the JIT committee assembled to discuss the next move. Paul did little to participate, and that was fine with Ben. Dick Williamson and Mike Gannon, though, were deeply involved and suggested several processes in the plant that would make good implementation sites. The committee decided on three areas: screw machines, molding, and final assembly.

Two Strikes . . .

Ben and Julie examined several different techniques for implementing quality improvements and finally settled on the Juran method[1] because it was simple and could be implemented with a minimal amount of training and downtime. As a result of the Dantel incident, they also decided to stick to internal processes. A careful reading of Juran indicated

---

[1] The heart of Juran's model is a "trilogy" of managerial processes that provide the keys to improving quality: quality planning, quality control, and quality improvement. The process starts with defining quality through the customer's eyes, moving on to evaluate current quality capabilities and performance, and ends with establishing the infrastructure necessary to maintain the improvements over the long run. For further information about this technique, see J. M. Juran, *Juran on Leadership for Quality* (New York: Free Press, 1989).

that the best place to start was in a "Primary Process," an area early in the manufacturing sequence that would affect the greatest number of downstream parts. Both screw machines and molding fit into this category.

* * * * *

Ben sought Dick Williamson's help in talking to the screw-machine operators about beginning statistical process control (SPC) charting on their processes. Dick seemed skeptical, and when pushed would not say why. Why soon became evident.

Ben tried several times to start a conversation with Dick, but to no avail. Giving up, he retreated into himself. Shields in place, he took command as they rounded the last corner and entered the machine shop.

"Joe, I'd like to talk to you about the SPC charting we discussed in the training seminar. But before we do, I'd like to get your feedback. Do you have any questions?"

"Just one, where would you like to start? The class talked about setting up charts on every major part and process. Do you have any idea how many machines, parts, multiple operations, and tools we deal with back here? So, pick one. I'm willing to try, but you do the picking." Joe had a way with words; he gave Ben a headache faster than anyone else.

Ben paused a second before replying. What was wrong? The entire JIT/TQC project was turning into a bigger challenge than he had anticipated. Maybe he had chosen the wrong path at the crossroad. "As Frost said, the 'road not taken' forever remains in the past. I can't go back now, not if I want to stay with Banyon." Ben kept his doubts to himself, responding calmly to Joe's baited question.

"Wait a minute, Joe. You know this area better than I do. Where would you start? Remember, this process is built on employee involvement, not orders from the top. Who or what would be the best candidate?"

Dick broke in; the conversation was going nowhere. "Ben, Joe is right. But I think if we went over to machine number three we could narrow this down a little. We use that machine for longer runs; Mike's guys only set it up two or three times a month. Want to see what the operator says?"

Ben and Joe agreed, and they walked toward the machine. The operator watched them as they approached, a look of apprehension on his face. "Hi boss, or bosses. Ah, what can I do for you?"

Ben took the lead and explained the plans to start SPC charting on the number three screw machine and asked for input. Input is what he got, too.

"I'm game," the operator began. "But you said I could ask questions. OK. How are you going to change my rate? I can't possibly make my old rate, and I sure don't want to lose my piece-rate incentive bonus. I depend on that for Christmas. So, how are you going to do that? If you can give me a good answer, I'm willing to help."

Ben didn't have an answer. He hadn't even thought about the problem. "Those are good questions. Tell you what, I'll work on the incentive question and look at your current rate and earnings, and then we'll get started. Thanks for the input and cooperation."

Ben walked Dick back to his office and continued on to his own. Julie was busy, and he didn't stop to talk. She looked up briefly, but when she saw the look on his face, she ducked her head and continued working. It was the right move. Ben was in no mood for conversation.

Ben had stumbled twice. Dantel was forgotten, but this problem wasn't going away. How was he going to handle the incentive issue? He had no intention of changing every rate in the plant. It didn't take much thought to know that would mean lower productivity or higher costs. "I knew it was going to be expensive to meet the new quality demands, but I can't change every rate. I'll have to come up with another solution."

The First Attack on Setups

The implementation team had targeted both quality and setup problems in their planning meeting. The quality effort had stalled, but Ben persevered. The next morning, undaunted, he went back out to the factory floor with Mike Gannon, whose responsibility was setups. Together, they went to the molding department.

Molding made a three month supply of components at one time, and contributed substantially to work-in-process. Since inventory reductions are one of the key benefits of JIT/TQC, it seemed appropriate to tackle areas were inventory was a problem.

"Mike, I'm excited about the prospect of cutting down inventory in molding. It should reduce operating costs and improve quality by decreasing the number of bad parts made when something goes wrong. Thanks for suggesting this one." Ben paused outside the molding department, waiting for Mike's response.

"I'm glad you think it'll work, Ben. Let's see. I brought the records for last month. It looks like setups take about 4 hours each. But we don't do very many. And the number of parts per setup is quite large. This looks like a good candidate for setup reductions."

* * * * *

There was a hole in the bucket in molding, too. Ben and Mike had not fully grasped what setup reduction meant in a JIT setting. It *did not* mean running fewer parts per setup. It meant increasing efficiency, reducing setup time. In fact, reducing the number of pieces run per setup actually reduces capacity unless it is accompanied by an offsetting reduction in setup time.

There was an additional problem at Banyon. Workers were paid for total time which included process and setup time. If more efficient setup procedures led to idle time, machine operators would lose pay. Once again Ben was stymied by an incentive system that rewarded the wrong behavior.

* * * * *

After talking with the molding foreman, Ben instructed him to begin running only one month's worth of parts at a time. All agreed that this was a good number, maintaining some economies of scale while greatly reducing inventory on an ongoing basis.

It took a month for the walls to crumble. Late one Friday afternoon Ben went to molding before heading home. He was attacked as soon as he got there. The second shift foreman was livid. "Mr. Morgan, do you realize how far behind we are? I've got people yelling for parts, and I'm spending most of my time doing setups. Instead of meeting demand, I'm holding up the rest of the plant! I don't like it. Either you get us more machines, or let us go back to the old way. I'm not going to take the heat on this one!"

Ben went over the outstanding work orders with the foreman and quickly saw the problem. Why hadn't any of the JIT books or seminars forewarned him about this? "Damn, by doing more setups, I'm stealing capacity from the department. And if what the supervisor says is true, they can't meet the specifications either. We've never been able to meet them. What a way to end a week. Now I've got to put this department on overtime to catch up. Something isn't right in the way I'm going at this. What am I missing?"

The molding department implementation had failed. Ben did not give up, but he was getting frustrated. He called another meeting of the implementation task force, and everyone put their heads together.

The Monday Morning Blues

Ben and Julie left the meeting. It had gone well, even though Paul had chosen this meeting to announce his resignation. "No big loss," Ben thought. "I'll never get through to him anyway; this way I don't have to fire him. Cut our losses and move on!"

"Ben," Julie broke in on Ben's daydream. "When do you want to get started in assembly? I think we should set up a group meeting out there because they share jobs as well as opinions. If you single out one or two people, it may cause problems."

"Good thought. Set that up for first thing tomorrow morning before they get started. And Julie, call the local paper and place an ad for Paul's replacement. We have to move fast because I need someone in Quality Assurance. Put SPC skills in the ad so we don't get applicants who aren't qualified. I'm going to corporate for the afternoon to update them on our progress."

With that, Ben left. Julie stared after him, wondering how he maintained any enthusiasm at all. He did let down in front of her, but the other managers only saw his positive side. "Well, there's not much I can do but follow through on details. Maybe we just don't understand what JIT/TQC means to this company."

* * * * *

The next morning Ben and Julie met with the assembly group. The meeting started out well. Then one of the older workers, Sara Wright, raised her hand and dropped a bombshell. "Mr. Morgan, I have a question. You're asking us to improve quality by charting what we assemble against the specs. That makes sense, but what are we going to do about faulty parts that come from the screw machine and molding areas? I don't want to cause trouble, and I appreciate your asking us what we think. I'm just a bit confused about this."

Ben didn't have an answer. Sara was right. They could chart the assembly process and succeed only in demonstrating that "garbage in" meant "garbage out." He could sense he was losing the group, so he adjourned the meeting, saying that they would start up in the near future. Until then, he told them he wanted them to think about how they could improve quality in their area.

After returning to the front office, Ben asked Julie, Mike, and Dick to join him for lunch. They had put in a lot of effort, and nothing was working right. And, he was afraid he was losing credibility with the work force. For that reason he needed to talk to his key managers away from the plant. If anyone had a hand on the pulse of the factory, Mike did. Dick was essential because he understood the processes. Julie was essential for moral support and her knowledge on the details of JIT.

"I feel awful. How am I supposed to be the champion of

excellence when I'm riding a sway-backed warhorse? This project may be impossible. Or, maybe, I'm just not doing things right. I need some help, and I'm not sure where to get it, or what to do with the help I have. If we could only come up with a winner; that would do it. It may be time to start over."

* * * * *

The answers would come, but not easily. The straightforward implementation plan Ben had developed based on his readings and attendance at seminars as well as on Julie's research wasn't working. The problem was, of course, that the books and seminars described successes, not failures. Ben and Banyon faced the chasm separating theory and practice; the bridges were missing in the stories of others' successes. The path to success is littered with the debris of failure.

A FRESH START

Ben was relieved. When Paul tendered his resignation, he feared that the implementation of JIT/TQC might have to be put on hold. Knowing that momentum is 95 percent of action, Ben knew that stopping would be deadly. It would take 10 times more effort to get everybody on board a second time. The problem never surfaced; Paul's replacement was found the day after the ad appeared. Banyon was lucky. The new QA manager was skilled in SPC and familiar with implementing TQC.

* * * * *

"Julie, this is great. I wasn't sorry to see Paul resign, but I didn't think we'd find a replacement so quickly. What do you think of him?"

Ben was happy, and that made Julie happy. Before answering, she took a moment to look at him; she preferred Ben's smile to his grimace. "I think Jim will work out fine. I felt a lot better when he described the successful quality improvement program at Excel and his role in implementing it.

Our track record is awful; maybe we can improve it by drafting a veteran. It can't hurt."

"Julie, we're going to get it right this time. It's only a feeling, but it's good to feel positive again. I was beginning to feel like Custer at his last stand. Especially after the disaster in molding. If it were any worse, I'd have less hair than I have now!"

"Now Ben, is that possible?" Julie chuckled. Ben was, well, bald. She didn't think anyone could prize a hairless scalp, but then she really didn't know.

"I left myself open for that one. If we keep at this, Julie, you may go bald too. I can see it now, 'Woman Loses Hair Battling Machines.'" That said, Ben made a quick exit, ducking flying rubber bands.

For the next two weeks Ben and Julie held JIT "awareness" classes. Rather than try another start-up without the help of Jim Andrews, the new QA manager, Ben thought it would be better to work on education, on greasing the wheels for change before using them. He hoped that spreading the gospel would make the next implementation effort more successful.

The employees enjoyed the classes on quality control and were eager to start. Ben ended each class by asking the workers to think about ways to improve the quality of the products they made.

* * * * *

Jim Andrews and the first snow of winter arrived on the same day. Ben glanced out his window and saw the flakes settle gently on the cars and dust the evergreens bordering the parking lot. He was sure the snow was a positive sign. Lost in daydreams, he came back to reality the moment he saw Jim walk toward the building.

"Julie, Jim's here. Why don't you meet him, start the paperwork in Personnel, and bring him back here. I'd like him to spend the first couple of days with Mike Gannon, Dick Williamson, and Paul. Also, schedule the next implementation meeting for Thursday."

Julie left to meet Jim, and Ben went back to the reports

on his desk. Corporate was not happy with recent performance, but that wasn't new. The next days passed without incident as Jim learned the ropes of his new job.

Within two weeks of his arrival, Jim made the first of many observations that would lay the foundation for JIT/TQC success at the plant. At a weekly production meeting Jim suggested that Ben look into the wave-solder process. In this process a "stuffed" circuit board passed through a bed of liquid solder on a conveyor which soldered all connections on the board at one time.

The Holis wave solder machine was new, yet it consistently had quality problems. It yielded 99.7 percent good product. However, defective product required 15 people for touch-up work, and touch-up work was time studied and rated. In other words, Banyon had institutionalized waste.

While a 0.3 percent defect rate appears acceptable, wave solder was early in the production process and produced defects in enough components that it caused major problems downstream. Final quality depends on reliability at each step in the production process. The overall result was disastrous as the following example suggests.

> Let's move from the wave-solder process, 99.7 percent acceptable product, to the rest of assembly. The board comes from an insertion process that produces 94 percent acceptable product and goes to final assembly, which yields 96 percent good product. What is the final level of quality?
>
> $$(0.94) \times (0.997) \times (0.96) = 0.899$$

This is a simple production sequence. In reality, boards passing through wave solder went through 20 other processes. The solder defect rate alone applied to more than 1,000 individual solder points. Banyon reworked virtually every board for some problem. They inspected quality into their product, a costly way to meet customer demand.

The final quality of a product depends on quality at each stage of production. It is the final quality that the customer sees and evaluates. The fact that wave-solder affected all Banyon products made it a likely candidate for improvement.

Getting Involved

Ben set up a multidisciplinary team to implement quality improvements on the wave solder process, although he was still uncertain that this was the best place to start. Since three prior attempts had failed, the group was ready to try something new.

The key member of the team was the operator, Carolyn. After two weeks of failure to find a solution to the touch-up and repair problems and in desperation, the technical and professional staff finally asked Carolyn what she recommended.

Her answer was simple. "Well, on Monday the quality is great, but by Friday it's horrible."

"Why is Monday different from Friday, Carolyn?"

"Your management procedures say to calibrate flux density only on Monday."

Sure enough when the team checked, Carolyn was right. Quality was high on Monday but fell off by Friday. The calibration schedule set up by Manufacturing Engineering was the problem. The schedule was changed from weekly to daily and led to immediate quality improvements.

In the months that followed, Carolyn pointed engineering in the right direction many more times. At one point, consistent problems on two different boards became obvious. Carolyn noticed that a few of the solder racks "just didn't seem to be the same as the others." An examination found that they were $5/1,000$ths of an inch out of calibration on one end, enough to keep one edge of the board out of the solder on its way through the process.

Several weeks later, Carolyn helped isolate the cause of another recurring problem. A gripper arm on the racks for one board was causing the solder to "wick" around one solder point. Simply trimming the gripper arm eliminated a major cause of rework.

Common sense is seldom valued in classroom or boardroom. A manager who makes decisions based on intuition often finds it necessary to justify them with numbers and logic. The process of justification is, after all, a part of corporate gamesmanship. Everyone knows it's a game and that the best managers have a knack for making right decisions. But one wonders how much inspiration comes from listening to people who work daily with the product and the process.

Ben learned to listen to good ideas regardless of their source. Figure 4–1 shows the progress made in wave solder where common sense in solving problems served to reduce total defects to zero.

Closing the Loop: Checkpoints and Measures

"Jim, we have to develop some kind of measurements to set SPC thresholds." Ben leaned on Jim's desk, looking concerned. "Who do we have that knows how to do SPC implementation? I see the logic; it's pretty simple, but setting specifications requires different skills. If we're going to stop and fix as JIT requires, we need to have good levels of quality control."

"I think Dick Williamson can help. He attends continuing

FIGURE 4–1
U-Chart Circuit Board Solder Defects

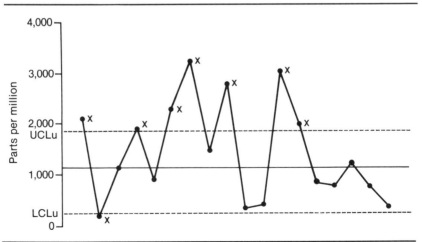

Source: Coopers and Lybrand.

education classes. In fact he brought up charting procedures at lunch a while ago. I'll talk to him."

* * * * *

Quality can be tracked many different ways. Ongoing control devices can be built into the process which result in 100 percent inspection without interruption. For example, one company combined the process of sensitizing the light meter in cameras with a test of the main circuit board. They gained a quality control check with little additional cost or effort.

Quality improvements can come from careful observation of a process by an engineer, by sampling the flow from a specific machine, or by asking machine operators where most of the problems occur. Once improvements are made, ongoing procedures need to be devised to ensure that gains are long-lasting.

* * * * *

"Dick, do you have a minute?" Jim found him fixing one of the older extruding machines at the back of the plant. "I want to talk to you about Statistical Process Control. Didn't you attend a seminar on SPC?"

Dick turned from the machine and wiped the grease from his hands. Dick Williamson was about 53 years old and had been with Banyon for more than 20 years. He was a quiet, unassuming man who did his job with pride. He spent more time keeping up with technical changes than any of the younger engineers.

"Yes. Are you ready to give it a try?"

"We're getting the wave-solder process under control, but we don't know how to lock the improvements in place with ongoing process controls," Jim explained. Never needing to be always in control, Jim found he got more done by letting the other person take charge. He guided with questions, not orders.

"Tell you what, Jim, let me finish putting this monster back together, and I'll meet you at wave-solder in 20 minutes."

Statistical Process Control

Statistical process control is a technique for monitoring ongoing quality levels. It results in a chart like the one in Figure 4–1. For each process under study, an optimum level of performance is defined. If the key level of performance is the number of defects, then the optimum is zero. In Banyon's case the desired level and the "lower control limit" (LCL) were one and the same.

The "upper control limit" (UCL) triggers the shut down of the process and recalibration of the machine. At Banyon a 0.2 percent defect level was set.

In a perfect world every part produced would be inspected. This would ensure 100 percent quality. Sampling is second best, and it may be the only cost effective way to get a process under control. If sampling limits are tight enough, critical failures or defects can be virtually eliminated.

The primary concern in the installation of a quality control system is defining the features of the process that affect final quality. It may be the thickness of a wire filament or the diameter of a tappet. Whatever the characteristic, its theoretical optimum, that is, the engineered specification, must be determined, and upper and lower tolerance levels set. From that point a sampling procedure is used to test the conformity of the process with the specification.

* * * * *

Two days later Dick and Carolyn started the charting process. They worked well together. Carolyn liked Dick, and Dick got Carolyn to open up. He didn't threaten her; he listened carefully, translating her layman's descriptions of the process into engineering terms and devising measurements. Jim spent a lot of time with them, learning to think the way Dick did, and watching how he worked with Carolyn. Jim had never gotten close to Carolyn, but then, he was new at Banyon.

"Smart lady. She knows what it takes to make good product. The words she uses to describe the process aren't fancy," Jim thought, "but she knows instinctively that it makes sense to do the job right the first time. When she was asked only for more output, she didn't see any reason to volunteer information about problems. Asking for her input is just plain common sense. I wonder why it took us so long to figure out?"

DOING IT RIGHT:
AN ONGOING COMMITMENT

Quality improvement is not a one-time program. It is an ongoing process that works everyday at every stage of the manufacturing process. Total Quality Control initiates the culture change that leads to better performance throughout the plant, a renewed sense of ownership and pride in one's work, and a means to keep the process of improvement going. Only if the improvements are locked in with a system of measures and incentives will they continue.

* * * * *

Julie went over the progress report on the wave solder TQC effort. Ben had given Jim free rein to start it, but Julie was anxious to get involved. "I'll use these articles I've read to frame the report to Ben. I like Hall's approach, it makes sense." Julie turned back to her PC, having found the quotation she wanted:

> Establish zones of quality with (a) simple rule: Accept no defects and do not knowingly pass on any defects. If defects proliferate, this rule is impossible to follow literally. Nothing would ever ship. Start applying the rule to at least some kinds of defects and keep tightening as people and processes improve. . . . Quality improvement comes from increased skill, quickly knowing what to do, and doing it right the first time—value added with minimum waste.[2]

---

[2] Robert W. Hall, *Attaining Manufacturing Excellence* (Homewood, Ill.: Dow Jones-Irwin, 1987), p. 72.

The basic theme is simple, continuous improvement. Try each day to do things better, faster, cheaper, and smarter. Julie knew that this was the message she wanted to convey and what they needed to do. Ben was under pressure from top management to get results, and few resources were available for the implementation.

Ben was banking on the dollars saved through process and quality improvements to give him breathing room. Earlier that day Ben had been candid with Julie on the matter, saying, "If they won't help us directly, Julie, I'll reinvest some of the savings to accelerate the JIT implementation. This plan has to work if we're going to survive in the long run, and I'm not going to let short-sighted management get in my way!" The words were emphatic, but Julie could see that Ben was trying to convince himself as much as her.

Ben selectively reinvested the savings from JIT/TQC successes and redeployed assets freed by increased efficiencies. Instead of allowing attrition to reduce the work force level, new workers were hired. This gave Ben flexibility to maintain training classes while meeting monthly production quotas. Some of the slack resources were used for problem solving and preventive maintenance, value-adding activities that eliminated process variances that shut down the line.

"You know, we've gone to seminars, and we'll go to more of them, but where and how do you learn to 'Do JIT?' Not think about it, or plan it, but do it? We're doing OK, but I'm not sure if it's planned, or if it's serendipity. And some days I'm afraid top management is going to push too hard."

This was the essence of the problem. Lack of top management support made Ben's effort to implement JIT/TQC all the more difficult.

Doing JIT requires more than changing maintenance schedules or moving machines. It is based on different assumptions of what constitutes optimum manufacturing. JIT/TQC is a management philosophy that cannot succeed unless attitudes and beliefs change throughout the organization. It is a system based on the value of the individual, regardless of rank in the hierarchy, and it creates an interdependent, holistic environment that violates many of the accepted tenets of traditional manufacturing.

CHAPTER 5

THE DOLLARS AND SENSE OF QUALITY

It was after 8 p.m. when Ben returned to his office. It had been a difficult day struggling with wave-solder quality issues. It had taken the better part of two weeks to learn what had gone wrong, and then it was such a simple thing!

"Thank God for Carolyn," Ben muttered to himself as he flicked on the office lights. "I wonder how many other places we're making bad product because maintenance schedules are wrong. If Carolyn knew this, why didn't she speak up earlier? Silly question; you didn't exactly make it easy for her. Live and learn."

Even after success in wave solder, Ben worried if it were possible to get the whole process under control. If every machine and every operation took two weeks or more to fix, he'd be an old man before it was all done.

"I simply need more resources. I've got to get top management on my side, to give me a little slack. But how am I going to convince them? Let's see, Probe said it was important to measure the cost of quality. If I can show management how much I can save in wave solder, then maybe they'll give me the support I need."

Ben sat down and developed an agenda for the next day. He would spend time out on the floor with Carolyn to make sure that the process was running correctly and that she understood the SPC charting techniques. But she learned fast and was probably ahead of him already. "Then to the beancounters. It's funny how that name stuck. I wonder if they ever used beans to count?"

That, as always, brought a grin to Ben's face. He had trained as an accountant, but had long ago traded his eyeshade for a hard hat and a chance to make things happen. Tomorrow he'd ask John Rust, the plant controller, to help him put together a "Cost of Quality" report for corporate. Then he would have the proof he needed.

Glancing across the hall, Ben saw that Julie's lights were on. She had been logging a lot of hours at the business school library, as well as at the plant, and her eyes and desk showed it. There were books on JIT and TQC on her desk along with a huge stack of articles from the popular press. She was trying to get to the bottom of the JIT concept, but Ben wondered if she'd ever get to the bottom of the pile of papers on her desk. If he wasn't careful, she'd become an academic, always reading, always thinking, seldom doing. The thought was amusing.

"You know, we're married to this job," Ben thought. "Taking Julie and Jim Andrews to dinner last week was a good idea; it helped relieve the tensions that were building."

Ben tried to work again, but his concentration was broken. Stretching eased some of the kinks, but did nothing to fight off the fog sweeping through his mind. Heaving a brief sigh, he began straightening his desk. As he moved papers, the immensity of the implementation swept over him. And its dangers. Without him, Julie would have to manage the change by herself; she wasn't ready. Without her, Ben would be back to fighting fires. The realization brought him back to life.

"Julie, can you come in here?" Ben called.

"Just a minute. I've got to finish this thought, or I'll lose it. There."

As Julie entered Ben's office, he looked up and smiled. "Well, our work is cut out for us, Julie. Getting wave solder online is one thing, but making the whole plant quality conscious is another. If we're going to see this project through, I need to know that you're comfortable with what we're doing. I'd like a shadow. Do you mind?"

"No, not at all, Ben. I know that this job is a lot for one person, and I'll do what I can. We've both been putting in a lot of hours, but most of mine have been spent reading books. I'd like to learn better how you manage people in the plant, but don't get your hopes up. You and I both know I'm not the leader you are."

"We learn to be leaders, Julie, no matter what folklore says about born leaders. Enough said. I have confidence in you. Anyway, tomorrow we'll go to accounting after looking at Carolyn's progress. Tonight, Julie, I'm ordering you to go home and get some rest. I can't have you collapsing from exhaustion."

The Beginnings of Trust

Carolyn quickly learned quality charting techniques. She also helped Dick and the other engineers define the specifications of the wave-solder process that needed to be monitored. She knew how to manage the process, and she was good at it. It's funny where stars are hidden.

Ben had always been friendly with the workers, but he had never asked them to help manage the plant. Worker involvement was a new concept. It was true participation. In college, a management professor had said it would work, but until now it had seemed like a pipe dream. People, Ben thought, only wanted to get their checks and go home. Well, the professor was right because at least one worker, Carolyn, was ready and willing to support the JIT/TQC effort.

* * * * *

"Julie, let's go over to accounting," Ben said. "I want to ask John about our cost of quality. If you recall, the seminar instructor at Probe said that this cost measure would pinpoint problem areas and help us keep track of our level of success."

DEFINING THE COST OF QUALITY

The cost of quality is seldom consistently measured in most companies. Banyon was no exception. When Ben took over as plant manager, he reviewed sales literature that stated that

Banyon reinvested 5 percent of its sales dollars to enhance product quality. It was this that led Ben to believe that accounting kept track of cost of quality.

Ben and Julie went to the controller, John Rust, and asked what seemed to be a simple question, "John, what is our cost of quality?"

"Our what?" he replied. So, much to his dismay, Ben had to explain quality costs to John and wait for him to calculate the numbers for Banyon.

"John, are you telling me you don't have these numbers? What do you measure? And where did the 5 percent number in the sales brochure come from?" Julie watched Ben's blood pressure rise. His face got a shade pinker than normal. This was her signal to keep quiet while Ben and John continued.

"Ben, when did you ever tell us you needed these numbers? Do we have them? You're an accountant. You know we keep a detailed record of the company's transactions, but I've never been asked to pull them all together to arrive at a cost of quality. Let's walk through this step by step, and I'll try to get an estimate for you. What's first?"

Ben thought a moment, glanced at Julie to let her know to interrupt if necessary, and began. "If what we've been told is right, quality costs can be separated into four basic categories: prevention, detection, internal failure, and external failure. Each cost raises different issues for management, so I need to know where we're spending money and how much improvement we can expect. Let's start with prevention and work our way down the list."

The Cost of Preventing Errors

Prevention means that quality checks are in raw materials and in fabrication processes to ensure that defective parts are not passed along. The prevention of error is the basis of JIT/TQC; quality is built into the product from conception.

Prevention puts the cost of quality up front for everyone to see. In the earlier example, the cost of prevention was a work stoppage to replace a defective dust cover. It also includes training machine operators to perform ongoing quality checks, examining process flow to ensure that quality goals can be consistently achieved, and setting up feedback systems so that problems are detected as quickly as possible. It means embedding quality controls within the process and the people who run it.

* * * * * *

"Let's see if I understand, Ben." John had scribbled notes while Ben talked, putting down account numbers and questions. "You want to know how much we spend training operators on the elements of quality in their jobs. We keep those costs in separate accounts, although you're used to seeing them as part of the burden rate. If what I hear through the grapevine is true, the new TQC methods you're using are going to blow this number sky high. I'll give it to you with some detail. You know, how many people were trained for how long and at what cost. Then you extrapolate to get your new costs, OK?"

Ben nodded and went on. Julie listened intently. She had taken one accounting course in her life, and this discussion was already over her head. Everything seemed to be under control and that was all she could tell.

Detection: Inspecting Quality In

Quality assurance usually involves some form of *detection*. When inspection is performed off-line by a separate group of technicians, quality is gained by detecting it in the process. Some costs of detection are easy to measure, such as people, equipment, and lost time in the production cycle. Others are more difficult to measure, such as the "quality is not my job, it's Joe's" mentality. Separating quality control from production fosters indifference to quality.

* * * * * *

"Ben, I can give you those costs right now. You're talking about the inspection department and the dollars used to support them. That cost is pulled together every month. Let's see." John opened his file, searched for a moment, and came up with the report he wanted. "You already get this, Ben. It's part of the detail we put in the back of your profit and performance report. Will this do?"

"I think so. Julie, you keep track of all these reports. Do you have them?" Ben's question startled Julie. She'd been drifting off.

"Uh, yeah. They're in the bottom drawer of the filing cabinet. I keep them, but in what kind of order is a question. Do you want me to go back and look?" Julie started to get up, but Ben stopped her with an upraised hand.

"You're needed here. We'll get them later. Let's finish briefing John on what we need. John, there's another set of costs that may be in your reports: the cost of internal failure," Ben noted. "What do you have there?"

Costing the Mistakes

Internal failure is a cost of quality. Standards for scrap and rework are often built into control systems. At Banyon, 15 people were needed to repair wave-solder defects alone, and this was caused by failure to calibrate the wave-solder process daily. Internal failure results in two kinds of losses: direct cost of parts or material lost, and time lost for initial production and rework.

Often a significant portion of rework time is spent undoing what others have done. If a mistake is made several steps before a problem is detected, effort and cost are added to the product with no additional value to the customer. This is an expensive way to get quality.

* * * * *

"I think you're after our scrap reports. As you know, we fold these costs into the final inventory value, but we do keep a running tally on them." John was back at his files, looking considerably more confident than he was at the start of the meeting. "Let's see. You only see this as a variance, Ben, but we do have the actual dollars charged off to scrap. Rework costs? We keep those, too, under a separate account. I can pull those together, if you can give me an hour or so."

"So far so good," Ben responded. "Let's define the fourth cost, external failure."

Quality Costs Outside the Plant Door

External failure is a quality cost. The direct financial impact of external failure is warranty and repair costs. The indirect, and by far the more important, cost is the loss of customer trust. A customer who exercises a warranty right may be grateful for the warranty, but will not think better of the product. Failure in the market damages reputations and hurts future sales. It is not an easy cost to measure in the short run, but it can spell disaster in the long run.

Banyon's Cost of Quality

The answers to Ben's questions were not encouraging. As seen in Table 5–1, quality costs were 12.2 percent of sales. And this was not the whole picture. If calculations were based on cost of goods, not sales, the number jumped to a dismal 24.4 percent. Almost one fourth of Banyon's total production cost was devoted to forcing quality into a process out of control.

* * * * *

"Julie, have you seen these numbers John put together? No wonder this plant isn't making money, 25 percent of our costs are going down the drain."

"We can't compete like this. How are we going to tackle this? When top brass told me to get the plant going, I thought it would mean pushing more product out the door, not tackling a mountain of mistakes."

Julie was worried. Ben seemed discouraged, and that was a bad sign. The numbers were high, so high they had shocked her at first, but when she thought of all the problems in the plant and with customers, it made sense. Quality

TABLE 5-1
Cost of Quality, 1981 ($ thousands)

Detection	$ 795
Prevention	923
Internal failure	704
External failure	628
Cost of quality	$3,050
Percent of sales	12.2%

Source: Coopers & Lybrand.

issues had kept her busy, but she hadn't thought of it as waste until now. It was job security through building mistakes, not a good long-term strategy.

Julie moved closer to Ben, putting a hand on his shoulder. "We can handle this. Look at the progress we've made in the plant already. If you accept these numbers, you can see how much we'll save just by putting Carolyn in charge of her own quality. If she can get her defects down, we'll save the downstream costs. Let's see if we can put some figures together that will give us an idea of the savings we can expect."

Ben glanced up and paused. Julie was right, of course. Strange, but she sounded like the manager, and he sounded like Julie.

"I think you're on the right track, Julie. We went to John to get ammunition to push Herman into freeing up resources to help us. If these numbers won't convince him, I don't know what else we can do."

* * * * *

A company cannot survive in a competitive marketplace with quality costs running at 15 to 20 percent of sales. World-class manufacturers' quality costs are 2 to 3 percent of sales. This does not mean quality does not exist, just the opposite. Quality is built in, minimizing costs, for example, prevention, detection, and internal and external failure. Their focus is on doing it right the first time.

Banyon had an excellent reputation for quality products, but they had a long way to go. Quality was being detected in, not built in as part of the production process.

RECAPPING THE QUALITY MANAGEMENT PROCESS

Shortly after putting SPC in place in wave-solder, Ben asked Jim to attend a quality seminar at Probe. Ben wasn't sure what to do next, and Jim had exhausted the information available at the business school library.

The seminar began by defining the five major steps involved in reaching a mature state of Total Quality Control:

1. Identify areas for improvement.
2. Define the existing process, the controls in place to monitor it, and establish a process flow diagram/analysis.
3. Set up an improvement team consisting of the machine operator(s), process engineers, quality assurance, and supervision.
4. Isolate the reasons for the quality problems. This process requires the involvement of all team members. The answer can be deceptively simple.
5. Develop a method to eliminate or minimize the "cause for pause," and establish an ongoing maintenance schedule to keep the process under control.

Quality is as much a part of a company's overall strategy as its pricing and distribution policies. While it may not show up in the five Ps of marketing, it is an inherent part of a product's market value. It is a value set by the customer, not by the company. If the customer wants a disposable product, durability is not essential. If the customer wants durability, flimsiness is unacceptable.

* * * * *

"A quality strategy begins with an understanding of the customer's needs." Jim listened attentively to the Probe manager leading the session. "It requires an analysis of the company's competitive position. If the goal is to be the high quality producer in the industry, then it is essential to know how the competitor's products perform."

"We don't do this," Jim thought. "We do market research, but it's geared toward finding new customers rather than toward understanding our competition. Probe says that our Japanese competitor was turning out zero defects. I wonder how?" Jim returned his attention to the speaker, but not before making a note to check the competition.

The instructor's next slide was Figure 5–1.[1] The message was that quality issues can be addressed from the perspective of the customer as well as from an analysis of the production process. Quality is more than making the product right; it's making the right product.

FIGURE 5–1
Quality of Design and Quality of Conformance

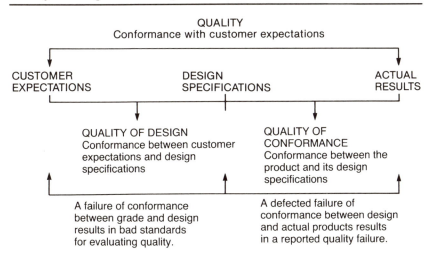

---

[1]This figure originally appeared in *Measuring, Planning, and Controlling Quality Cost* by W. J. Morse, H. P. Roth, and H. M. Poston. The monograph was published in 1987 by the National Association of Accountants.

Breaking the Production Mentality

Traditional industrial firms are beginning to understand the critical role played by market research. While consumer product marketing has always measured the consumer's pulse, industrial marketing has consisted of little more than order taking. The mentality has been, "We produce it; marketing sells it."

This doesn't work in a global marketplace. There is no assurance that a product will be salable unless it meets a customer's needs and expectations. Product design means meeting customer demands, not pushing the product a plant can produce.

New competitive quality strategies may encourage companies to reduce the range of products offered. Variety is the enemy of a controlled production environment. If many different products are made using multiple raw materials and routings, it is difficult to gain the understanding of process and product that TQC demands. Do customers really demand cars in more than 200 colors, or would 15 be sufficient? Providing what is wanted, and only what is wanted, means that too much is as bad as too little, whether in variety or in engineered characteristics.

* * * * *

With this the day's session ended, Jim went to his room, and took a shower. He needed to relax before going to dinner with a couple of people from the seminar. While Jim appeared outgoing, it was more performance than reality. Hot water washed away the stress of the day. Refreshed, he left for dinner.

"There they are." Jim walked across the dining room to join Todd and Ruth. Todd Jantzen was quality assurance manager at a local firm, and Ruth Blake was Jim's counterpart at Process Technologies, Inc. Both were there for the same reason as Jim, to learn how to meet Probe's new quality demands.

Jim sat down across from Ruth. "Hi, guys! What do you think? Today's session sounded more like a marketing lesson than a quality seminar, but then I never thought about competition the way it was described today."

"Well, all I know is that the people at Probe must be off their rockers to expect us to meet these demands." Todd was on his third drink and was venting a lot of steam. Ruth was quite uncomfortable.

"Todd, we don't have a choice. We've tried SPC at Banyon, and it seems to work. If anything, it's stripped away the misperception that we've been doing a good job all along. Have you made any progress?" Jim tried to placate Todd, but to no avail.

* * * * *

Dinner over, Todd went to his room, and Jim and Ruth went to the bar for a nightcap.

"Jim, I was interested in what you said to Todd about SPC. I didn't want to get into it at dinner, but I'd like to share our experiences with you to see what you think." Ruth told Jim about the changes they were making at Process Technologies. They were further along to TQC than Banyon. And, as is often the case, Jim learned more over a drink than he had all day at the seminar.

They left for their rooms about midnight. Jim sat at his desk for another hour, trying to recall as much of the conversation with Ruth as he could.

"This makes sense. If what Ruth said is true, they jumped into a quality project at Process the same way we did. Ruth said she wished they had a better plan, because after a few successes they had to stop and rethink the whole process. Ben already seems to have hit this barrier. She said we needed to do more training up front, so that everyone knows what we're doing. That makes sense. I'll see if we can do something about this when I get back."

Jim flicked off the light and turned in. He slept fitfully and morning came all too quickly.

A FRAMEWORK FOR ACTION

The next day's seminar discussed the use of quality cost analysis to identify areas for improvement and to meter progress. At no time did the topic of gathering data come up. "Don't they know that these numbers don't exist?" Jim thought. "Do they think the accounting department even knows what 'cost of quality' means?"

Ben, remember, had assumed that his controller kept track of the cost of quality. It was an invalid assumption. Few companies gather this data. Accounting systems tend to bury most of these costs in overhead pools, spreading them out over all products indiscriminately.

"Well, we were able to get these numbers from John. My guess is that most controllers can pull them together once they know what it is they're supposed to collect. Ruth seemed to know what they were for her company."

"I wonder why we didn't ask for them before? John was ready to help, once he knew what we wanted. Good thing, too, because without those numbers, it's impossible to move forward." Jim was tired, and he was having more trouble staying alert than understanding the information being presented. That is, until the discussion turned to pinpointing problem spots.

Identifying Problem Areas

Once a cost of quality analysis is available, the next step is to identify those areas which need improvement. Banyon did not do the analysis first; they relied on common sense and input from quality assurance. And they had failed three times before achieving their first success.

* * * * *

"I wonder if they could add any more buzzwords to the list?" Jim's thoughts wandered back to Banyon and the reasons why the wave-solder quality improvement efforts had worked.

* * * * *

Defects in wave-solder had a major impact on the cost of quality: scrap resulting from bad units, the cost of rework, and internal and external failure arising from solder problems in the circuit boards. Total costs exceeded those directly identified by scrap tickets. They included upstream costs, such as the value-adding time prior to solder, and downstream costs caused by defects. The wave-solder process at Banyon was running at 99.7 percent effectiveness, yet it was the first candidate for improvement. It was a critical step in the assembly process, and it affected both upstream and downstream costs.

The development of an effective quality improvement plan depends on understanding the process, its capabilities and constraints, as well as how to monitor the improvements with a minimum of charts, paperwork, and interruptions of the process flow. This requires a careful balancing of demands and an honest assessment of trouble spots.

* * * * *

"We started out in the middle, I'm afraid." Jim thought back to the meetings with Carolyn and others. "We put together an improvement team at the right time, but I'm not sure we ever defined the process the way it existed. Dick spent a lot of time out there, but the knowledge he gained is all in his head. When I get back I'll ask him to document the old flow so we can see where we're going and what assumptions we're making along the way."

* * * * *

If TQC is begun with little verified knowledge of the process itself, quality improvement will be an uphill battle against extreme complexity. It requires active participation by everyone at all levels and a willingness to work together to isolate problems. Without a clear understanding of the manufacturing process, any attempt to improve quality or to reduce costs will result in few, if any, improvements.

Making Quality a Design Issue

Design constraints of a product and of the machines on which it runs limit improvements which can be made on the plant floor. If, as many suggest, fully 75 percent of a product's ultimate cost is set in its design, then the real issue is designing products appropriately. Quality can be managed on the plant floor, but it begins with design.

* * * * *

Jim was taking notes as fast as he could. If he understood the lecture correctly, design engineers would have to be involved. "They don't get along very well with Dick's people. In fact, the design group is isolated; they create products the way they think best based on customer or marketing specifications. I wonder if they ever stop to think whether we can make them or not? Ben talked about breaking down boundaries between functions. It looks like he'll have his hands full with this one."

* * * * *

"The purpose of a design review is to ask a simple question: 'Can we change the way a product is built to eliminate quality problems without losing essential operating features?'" The instructor was at the board summing up the discussion on designing quality and talking about success stories.

"The desire to design products for manufacturability is reflected in the snap-on printer cover used by Raynard Computer. If you think about it, I'll bet each of you knows where changing the design of a product could help you make it better and faster."

"This is a team effort, because making the highest quality product at the lowest possible cost requires the active participation and commitment of everyone involved, starting with marketing and flowing through design, manufacturing, and service. Total Quality Control is a companywide commitment that doesn't stop with quality charting on the plant floor."

The seminar ended, and Jim began the long drive home. He had learned a lot during the last two days, and he felt he could now help Ben put some structure into the quality program.

BANYON'S TQC RESULTS: FINAL NOTES

The efforts at Banyon paid off. Cost of quality dropped from 12.2 to 4.2 percent of sales in less than four years, a 69 percent reduction. Other results included decreased lead time, as more product was shipped without time lost in rework. Product failure fell dramatically, while mean time between failure went from 1 million to 40 million counts without design change or material substitution. The product was made substantially more reliable because of the quality improvements achieved under the TQC program.

Defects in wave-solder dropped from 3,000 to less than 50 parts per million. Warranty costs and returns dropped 50 percent. Finally, and most important, Probe remained a solid customer. Banyon had risen to the quality challenge, but this was only the first step on the path toward manufacturing excellence.

* * * * *

"Ben, can you believe these results?" Julie exclaimed. "I know you said we were on the right track, but I thought you were nuts when we tackled wave-solder first. Who would have thought that so many problems would have been caused by such a simple error in process design?"

"We learned a lot, Julie," Ben replied. "But something tells me this was the easy part. Remember when you came back from visiting Regent? The manager, John Boyer, said to do quality first, that it might not be the best place to start, but that we'd get results. He was right; we did. But we still have late orders and irritated customers. Quality is there, but not process control. I think it's time we get back to the books and put together a plan for implementing JIT."

INTERMISSION

Ben had told the quality improvement stories, and was warming up for the main part of his talk on JIT/TQC. Julie continued to listen, sometimes carefully, often distracted.

A lot had happened at Banyon during the early days of the JIT/TQC implementation. Most of the changes, though, had been simple to implement once the right candidates had been identified. Many proved to be common sense; wave-solder was a prime example. Time after time machine operators identified the cause of the problem, not with fancy language or even precision, but specific enough to get engineers and managers to pay attention. "And I should be paying attention to Ben," mused Julie.

"We started out trying to do just-in-time," Ben explained to the conference audience. "But we were detecting quality into the product. Yes, we had a reputation in the market for outstanding quality, but we achieved quality by sorting it, good, bad, good, good, bad, and so on. Now we're building quality into the product."

"High levels of quality are a prerequisite for JIT. In fact, one of the first steps in implementing JIT is doing something called a quality map. A quality map identifies quality controls in the system based on current quality procedures. It identifies where the process breaks down by examining scrap and rework. For JIT to work, you have to be able to catch all errors all the time. This does not mean more inspection. It means doing the job right the first time, not building mistakes."

"When we started just-in-time, we wanted to increase our responsiveness to the market, to continue to improve quality, and to reduce our lead times. We also wanted to contribute to the self-worth of our employees. We found that employee involvement was inspiring people to give us ideas, and that we could devote our technical resources to those ideas to get improved productivity. We were now in for another surprise."

Ben was right on that one. Julie recalled the day she and Ben discussed where to go next with JIT. As they had on the first day, she and Ben went out for a quiet lunch. They both loosened up when they were away from the plant, and Julie would give Ben the truth, both barrels sometimes, but the truth nonetheless.

They had just started on their second drink when Ben asked Julie, "What do you think John Boyer would say about our success? He confused me when he said we should have an overall plan, and that quality was the easy part. I hope it doesn't get much harder; there were days when I thought we were losing the battle."

"Ben, he wouldn't have said it if it weren't true. I've been charting our progress and reading what the experts have to say on JIT/TQC implementation. They say we started wrong, that we needed top management support, a plan for total process improvement, and a devotion to continuous improvement. If we sit back satisfied after the gains we've made, I think we'll be losers in the end. We did OK, but why did we do so poorly in the first place? What other things are screwed up? And when will other problems crop up? Just saying the words 'employee involvement' won't erase years of conflict and crossed swords."

Julie talked on, pausing every now and again to wait for some sort of response from Ben. None was forthcoming. So, she stopped and waited. Shadows passed across Ben's face as he fought invisible demons. There was little Julie could do but wait for the battle to end, which it did with a start.

"Sorry, Julie, my mind was wandering. I think it's all the hours at the plant. I don't know about you, but I'd like to take a breather before we tackle any new projects. We've done well with the quality program, and the training classes that you set up are working beautifully. Everyone seems to enjoy the new system. It's almost Christmas, and I need a little time with my family. Do you have any plans?"

The time waiting for lunch passed quickly as they discussed holiday plans and the wondrous presents that they had bought for their families. Ben's enthusiasm made Julie laugh; he was like a child, all full of surprises and anxious to share them.

Lunch arrived, and conversation returned to business. Julie kept insisting that they needed a good plan if they were to go any farther, and Ben kept asking, "What is JIT?" He thought he understood TQC, but the next step was fuzzy. Maybe Julie was right, a plan would be a good idea because at some point they had to know where they were going if they were ever going to get there.

* * * * *

"We made a lot of progress with TQC. Now it was time to plan the next stage of the implementation. We assumed, as many do, that the principal task ahead was moving the machines into the right cells. We had a group of engineers headed up by Dick Williamson, our top mechanical engineer, start to chart product flow and to look for similar production paths and assembly flows. Progressing to JIT seemed pretty easy, and we got good results up front. But before we get to that, I'd like to walk you through the first steps of our JIT implementation." As Ben began to weave the tale, Julie's thoughts faded back into the past.

CHAPTER 6

JIT: THE HARD FACTS

Ben could barely wait for the closing remarks of the day. The seminar had featured Richard Schoner, the reigning guru of JIT/TQC, who had given a rousing speech on the benefits of the new manufacturing concept. His topic was "Eliminate the Cause for Pause," a simple idea that was proving to be a challenge to Ben and his company nonetheless.

"Mr. Schoner," Ben tried to get his attention. Not being the first one to the podium, Ben waited for a few moments before getting a chance to ask a question. "Mr. Schoner, I'm Ben Morgan, plant manager at Banyon Corporation. We're putting in a JIT system, and we're running into some major problems. Can you tell me how to put JIT in place when the plant has an individual incentive system?"

"With great difficulty," said Schoner, who then turned and left the room.

Ben's jaw dropped. "This was the wisdom to take back to Banyon? 'With great difficulty?' Thank heaven the rest of the seminar was a bit more informative," thought Ben.

"There's no escaping the problem. Well, no one else heard the answer so I can always pretend Schoner was of some help. I wonder how much they pay him to give one-liners?"

* * * * *

Banyon had been working on JIT for almost nine months. They had spent the time getting process quality in several vital areas under control and learning how to make progress with the people rather than in spite of them. They were now ready to move into the next stage, the creation of a JIT cell.

Ben knew from experience that the first step was to educate his own management team. So, back from the latest JIT seminar, Ben began a series of staff meetings to reach consensus on the next step in the implementation.

* * * * *

"We've got a quorum, so let's get started. Each of you has a booklet on JIT in front of you. Open it to the first page, and I'll take you through the key points in the next stage of the implementation. This is going to take some time, and we all know that it's trickier to put in place than it sounds. Once we all agree on the concepts, we'll try to isolate a pilot site. Be thinking about the characteristics of a good pilot and likely candidates as we go through the basic information."

Dimming the lights, Ben began to move through a series of slides on JIT. "To begin, we should put one thing behind us, JIT is *not* an inventory management technique. I know that much of the material we've read focuses on 'zero inventory', but having talked to many people, I can say that reduced inventories are the outcome of JIT, not part of putting it in place. So we need to stay focused on the process and ignore inventories for now. They'll go down if we do everything right."

"Ben, can you define JIT the way you see it, you know, give us an idea of what you're thinking?" Julie seldom broke in. The fact that she did meant Ben was putting the cart before the horse.

"Thanks for bringing up that point," Ben responded. "To me JIT is a process of continuous improvement. It sounds trite, I know, but that's the principal concept. It means never being satisfied, always challenging the assumptions under which you work, and eliminating the 'cause for pause'. JIT is this philosophy put into action by removing variance from the process, eliminating buffers, and linking the steps in the production sequence. It's holistic manufacturing."

"It's important to keep the objectives of a JIT system clearly in mind as we progress. First, we must increase the responsiveness of the production process and its ability to meet customer and market demand by providing such things as customized products. Second, we must lower manufacturing costs. Probe told us that the new method will make us more cost effective. We'll see. Third, we must continue to improve quality. We've already seen the benefits there. Finally, we must provide all employees with a sense of contribution and self-worth. This last one is important, as we all saw when we got Carolyn on board."

"Okay, Ben, I think we have the picture. So, what are the physical characteristics of JIT, and what changes do we have to make in the plant to get it to work?" Julie was playing a great straight man.

"I happen to have a slide on that. I must be attending too many seminars. If I start telling bad jokes, take my travel cards away."

That got a chuckle from the group, and they relaxed. Ben continued, using diagrams he got during the last Probe training class. The slide Ben used to describe JIT is reproduced in Figure 6–1.

A TECHNICAL VIEW OF JIT

The basic themes of JIT are visible and synchronized manufacturing. Banyon, like most managers adopting JIT, had a grasp of the technical part of the process. Focused on the benefits that had been so enthusiastically described, Ben was concerned most with the technical characteristics. While he knew the buzzwords, he had only a superficial understanding of what they meant.

When Ben thought of implementing JIT, he considered three basic steps: (1) redesigning process flow, (2) identifying the root cause of errors and taking corrective action, and (3) using setup time and lot size reductions to shorten lead times and lower inventory levels. These were technical changes, where in reality JIT modifies both the human and the technical. Balancing the demands on human and technical systems is critical to a successful JIT implementation, a point seldom explained.

**FIGURE 6–1
JIT Target**

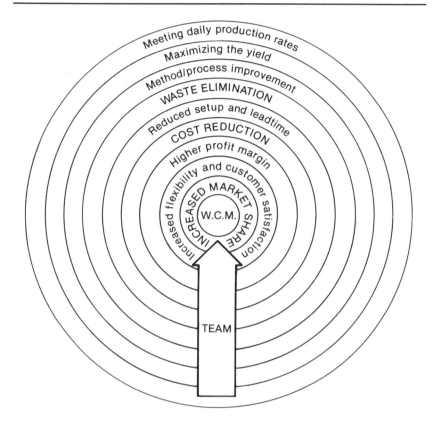

Uniform Plant Load: Marching to a Beat

Ben concentrated on technical JIT. He didn't understand the four major subelements: (1) uniform plant load, (2) Kanban inventory controls, (3) selection of a good pilot site, and (4) using performance measurements to make the change process work.

Uniform plant load is a simple concept. It means daily production equals daily sales. It means dividing total output into equal 'buckets', leveling production by removing variations in daily plant load. Most companies, for example, when beginning the implementation process, have found that taking an average month's output and dividing it into equal daily lots is the easiest way to start.

Obviously, some months more or less needs to be produced. Ben discovered that increases or decreases in total output had to be considered, not by asking each person to work faster, but by adjusting the capacity of the plant and by adding more resources.

JIT creates a cadence within the manufacturing process, a drum beat, and changing capacity is the only means of adjusting output volume. It is this disciplined, regularized flow of product through the plant that characterizes JIT manufacturing. It is the regularity of an assembly line, without the loss of autonomy by the individual worker, that solves so many long-run problems.

RT&I is an example of a company that is putting this concept to work. Using $2^1/_2$ minute intervals called "beats" to move product through the assembly process, the company has reduced from 60 days to 4 hours the total throughput time for their personal computer. Of the remaining 4 hours, 75 percent is move or queue, suggesting that there is still room for improvement.

A well-balanced line resembles a precision military drill team; each step synchronized, no movement wasted. It is a system running at an optimal stress level. It can't be stressed more to respond to demand swings. More output comes from increasing the capacity of the line, perhaps by adding stations or machines to the process. The discipline required is present in most companies; whether they are willing or able to accept it is another matter.

Kanban: Simple but Effective

Kanban systems are an integral part of JIT process flow. They are racks or physical spaces used to trigger production. Kanban devices are used to reduce the amount of work-in-process inventory to the minimum level necessary to prevent a break in the underlying cadence. Arriving at the right type and size of Kanban is a trial and error process. Too little buffer will frequently stop the entire line; too much will hide problems.

This view of the Kanban is fairly traditional. The important issue is linking the Kanban to the cadence as well as to suppliers and customers. While synchronizing buffer to cadence is straightforward, companies fail to realize that Kanban links individual processes. This is the essence of the "pull" system, forcing flexibility and reliability into the process.

The supply process will produce excess inventory unless it is tied to the cadence of the line it supports. Conceptually, this linkage is not troublesome. When implementing JIT the harsh reality of process constraint, as well as upstream and downstream ramifications, becomes apparent. "Pull" doesn't solely mean producing to demand; it means synchronizing multiple processes to make a balanced whole. Bottlenecks are the central focus; they constrain the entire plant. In Chapter 7, this concept will be examined in depth as the story of Banyon's first JIT cell implementation unfolds.

* * * * *

"Now that I've laid out the basic concepts of JIT, there are two issues to resolve. We've made progress in quality. Now we must address production output so that we can move to the next challenge, setting up cells and a Kanban system. None of us are experts here, but Jim, you seem to have a sense for these new technologies. What are your ideas on approaching 'Uniform Plant Load'?"

Ben had caught Jim offguard, but he was quick to recover. "Hmmm, the easiest way might be to take our monthly production and cut it into even buckets. Simple, but effective."

"Right. But what about seasonality, the fact that all months aren't the same?" Ben was looking for something, but the others weren't helpful.

"Let's see," Jim stalled for time. "Well, I guess we should use an average month, and pick up the balance through inventory for now. It's not the best way, but there's so much more to think about, like balancing the line itself. I know! Let's flex the Kanban to give us some room." Jim smiled, sure he had hit a solution.

"I'll have to think about that, Jim. Somehow it doesn't sound like JIT, but then, this is reality, not a textbook. For now we'll try it your way, but we'll have to spend some time looking at just how seasonal we are to determine the best way to manage those problems." Ben turned back to the slide and moved his pointer to "Method/Process Improvement" pictured in Figure 6–1.

"We all know cells are the key feature of JIT. You balance the flow of the production process by linking machines. This leads us to some other issues. When we put the machines in the cell, they become dedicated. We have to be careful. If we lose a machine serving many different lines by dedicating it to a cell, what do we do with remaining demand? And where do we start? What kind of cell structure do we want, a 'U', an 'L', or a straight line? Any ideas?"

"Ben, I think you should delay the decision on the layout until we see the process and talk to the workers. I learned a lot from Carolyn, and I have a feeling that this will come up again." Dick Williamson was right, of course. Without knowing what line was going to be changed over, it was impossible to talk details.

Selecting the right cell was an area about which Ben was particularly naive. He was less naive, though, than when he had approached quality. Remember, in trying to force change Ben faced three failures. Selecting the right cell would come from understanding the change and how the company could reap the maximum benefits from it. Banyon found that a product using the now high-quality circuit boards in the start-up phase of its life cycle was a good candidate. The final choice was left for the implementation team, not dictated by management. In Banyon's case, they just happened to agree.

Vendors and Measurements

Ben began the JIT implementation thinking that vendor relations were critical and measurements were not. After working through the implementation process, he realized vendor relations were secondary, while measurements were critical. Why? Because people respond to numbers used to evaluate them. If the performance measurement system is not changed, it is unlikely that a solution to any problem will be implemented, especially if it downgrades performance on existing measures. Banyon ran into this problem as its individual incentive system continued to undermine the learning process.

Banyon had a long history of using individual incentives to motivate its work force. Employees could make a lot more money by beating the rate. Now think about JIT, about uniform plant load, about synchronization. They mean uniform output levels, no overproduction and, hence, no bonus. Beating the rate means that the system is not properly "stressed" and that potential exists for building waste, for example, exceeding demand. This is not a minor issue.

If everyone is asked to produce at a defined rate, how do you evaluate performance and reward excellence? If the goal is zero defects, there is room for penalties, but none for rewards. Obviously, the incentive system has to be changed, otherwise people will have little incentive to improve. Ben radically changed Banyon's incentive system by instituting a "gainsharing" system that splits profits arising from improvements in productivity between the company and the employees. Both benefit, and both are motivated to improve.

Supplier partnerships are an extension of the manufacturing process. The goal is to minimize disruptions to downstream processes without increasing the total cost of production. Some companies use long-term contracts, others keep inventories of all but an "A" list of raw materials. "A" items represent the 20 percent of components responsible for 80 percent of the cost. They are the reason for inventory reduction and vendor partnerships. The rest of the inventory is subjected to cost/benefit analysis. If the cost of maintaining the inventory is less than the combined cost of worrying about it, moving it, and risking the shut down of the line, keep it on hand. Nothing is more ludicrous than stopping production because of a shortage of penny screws.

Technical? It's Logical

Most books concentrate on the technical side of JIT. The human side can't be narrated; it has to be learned. JIT is difficult to implement, not because of its technical characteristics, but because it calls for massive changes in the human system.

The technical side of JIT means engineering the process flow to respond like a single machine instead of many. It is developing a clockwork movement of man and machine across functions and departments so that material flows through the plant like water through a pipe. In the United States, where technological solutions to problems are always preferred, this side of JIT is embraced because it's logical. The other side, people, is often overlooked, or managed inappropriately. Challenges and dangers are hidden in the simplicity of the technique.

CHOOSING A PILOT

"Julie, got a minute?"
"Maybe. What have you got in mind?"
"I'd like to go over the notes from today's meeting."
"Why?"
"I'm uncomfortable. Why did we finally decide on the President's line?"
"Good question. Can I get my notes?"

Not waiting for an answer, Julie left Ben's office. She was back in a few moments holding a few tattered pieces of paper. Settling into a chair across from Ben, she visibly sighed as Ben handed her another pile.

For the next few minutes she read through the notes, nodding at times and wrinkling her brow at others. Ben waited. Reaching the end, Julie paused before responding.

"I've been turning the issues over in my head, too, Ben. Let's see what you think. Basically, I went back to one of the handouts from the Probe seminars about choosing a pilot, then matched our process against it. My notes look a lot like

TABLE 6–1
Implementation of JIT in an Area

Start in a small area that is easy to control and implement the program. Pick a downstream area
Communicate the plan to all employees prior to starting
Establish a team
Appoint a coordinator
Establish communication channels—for within and outside the team
Conduct an in-depth study in the area
Document conditions
Establish list of projects, prioritize, establish goals and schedules
Implement changes
Track results
Communicate success !!

Source: Coopers & Lybrand.

yours, although I don't agree with a few of your comments. Anyway, let me get the diagram (Table 6–1) I dug out of my files. I think it may help." Julie dashed into her office, grabbed the diagram, and returned. Handing it to Ben, she sat down across the desk from him.

"I'd forgotten about this diagram, Julie. It looks like a good template. Jim Andrews talked about the same concepts. He constantly surprises me; he comes up with insights into our problems and suggests workable solutions. I keep wondering how he does it."

"He's a good listener, Ben. The rest of us circle around the issues, throwing out idea after idea. He listens, notes the key comments, and organizes the whole discussion into a sensible outline. That's one skill I'd like to learn. When he flavors it with his knowledge of people dynamics, he comes up with a solution. Amazing? Yes. But I'm glad he's here to help."

"And he keeps such a balanced perspective, Julie. Yesterday he came into my office at noon, handed me a pair of jogging shorts and shoes, and dragged me out to run. After I recovered from the shock, I really enjoyed myself. And I felt better the rest of the day. He has great ideas, he may keep me from going off the deep end with this implementation."

Ben was right. Jim Andrews was a balanced person. He worked hard, but limited himself to 10-hour days; then he joined his family. Ben and Julie were desperately in need of the balance Jim brought to the JIT/TQC effort. Julie was thinking about her outside life again, and Ben was making room for himself and his family once more.

"Let's see now. Following the Probe sequence, I begin to see the logic of the JIT implementation process. Let's match this against Jim's list and see if we can come up with a clearer sketch of the task ahead. That will help us explain it to the others." Ben motioned Julie to pull her chair closer to the desk so they could work together. Before long they were lost in discussion, and the hours passed quickly.

Eleven Steps to Success

The key factor in implementing JIT is site selection. The best choice is a small area, one that is easy to control. Often a downstream area is best because of the total impact JIT has on a system. Remember, the JIT cell forces both suppliers and customers to match its beat. If the initial cell is downstream, it can be set up using buffers to separate it from the rest of the plant while line balancing and learning take place.

If you look at the list of JIT success stories, most take place in the assembly process. Hewlett-Packard uses JIT almost solely in final assembly, so do Wang, AT&T, and Harley Davidson. The final assembly may not be product for the retail market, but final for the plant. Stanadyne Diesel Systems is somewhat of an aberration; they use it on subassembly production processes because that's where they get the benefits of disciplined, standardized manufacturing.

Ben and his staff spent three days looking at the characteristics of JIT and developing lists of potential candidates. In the end the President's line was chosen. The reason was quite simple. First, it was a small volume product early in its life cycle. Second, even though current production took 30 days, process flow diagrams and common sense indicated that it required less than one day of real process time. Finally, the President's product line used the improved circuit boards coming from wave solder where quality was under control. On the line? Well, there were enough quality and process problems to keep a team busy fixing mistakes. Improved feedback, arising from better communication, would help isolate problems where they were occurring and support rapid improvement.

Communication: The Essential Element

People view change with suspicion. What does it mean to them? How will it affect their jobs and their security? In the never-ending battle between management and labor, distrust and lack of communication often lead to failed implementations. JIT is especially people intensive, and therefore especially vulnerable. Unfounded rumors circulating in the labor grapevine feed the anxieties of the work force. If they learn that a JIT implementation in a local plant put out workers, they are unlikely to welcome the new system with open arms.

If you recall, Ben developed employee involvement seminars long before he was ready to put JIT/TQC into place at Banyon. So employees were aware of what was happening. In fact, they were watching and waiting to see what was going to happen next.

The remaining steps in the implementation guide are important. Many of them are indicative of what Banyon did, some are not. In approaching JIT, Ben was ready for action; he had grappled with the quality improvement program for two years, and now he wanted to see some results. This time he was bound and determined to work with the people and that meant giving discretion to the implementation team. But getting workers on board was easier than getting middle management to give up the authority they wielded over the process.

* * * * *

"Julie, you've got to be kidding. Are you telling me that corporate is sending a bunch of consultants in here next week to sell us their services? They don't give us money for this. I wonder whose nephew it is? Maybe we can't avoid it, but set up the schedule to keep them safely contained."

Ben was not a fan of consultants. Most of the time they tried to fit their solutions to your problems. But he had also learned to be open to opportunities. The consultants' visit would be one such situation. But that's getting ahead of the story.

Choosing the Team

"Julie, there are more than 30 people in electronics. How are we going to pick the eight needed to get the JIT pilot underway?"

"Ben, you've got 30 volunteers. You know the gripe. The people in electronic assembly have higher skill requirements and educational levels than average, but because the work is more complex, they can't make their rates as often as others in the easier entry-level jobs. A good entry-level person can make 160 percent of rate within a month. The best workers in electronics struggle to hit 110 percent. Guess the standards are too tight, but that's tough to prove."

Julie was right. The complaints were understandable. But this didn't help in selecting the criteria for screening volunteers. Pay was usually the main issue, so it might be a good place to start. "OK, Julie. Let's think about the incentive pay question, because it's going to come up. I suggest we offer them their average weekly pay during the implementation, fix their pay so it doesn't interfere with the learning process. What do you think?"

Julie thought for a second before replying. "That might work. It'll sure cut down the number of volunteers. What are we going to offer so we don't lose them all?"

"We're offering them the chance to keep their jobs. Probably not a good thing to bring up, though. So, say they're being given a chance to grow with the company. We'll give them some new training, guarantee their pay, and promise to listen to their ideas. I think we need to start listening whether they believe we are or not."

"Ben, listening is a good idea, but what's going on?"

"Let's say I'm undergoing a 'life change', Julie. I'm starting to see that I may be a roadblock because I'm afraid to let go of the reins, to relinquish authority to make things happen. Every time I think about controlling this change, I think back to wave-solder and Carolyn. Without her, we would have accomplished little. We'd probably still be back there scratching our heads."

Julie knew it was time to leave. She also knew that Ben expected her to line up the meeting, to find volunteers, and to get back to him as soon as everything was ready. But once they had the people, where would the training come from? She wasn't ready to play expert. The consultants might provide an answer, but Julie was as doubtful as Ben.

A Light on the Horizon

Later that week the consultants arrived. They reminded Ben of the Three Musketeers. "I can't believe it. Two out of three know nothing about JIT. But the third, Ron Eddy, might work. I'll spend a few moments with him and send the other two packing."

Ben asked Julie to take Ron back to her office, while he escorted the others to the door. He could hardly wait till they were gone. "What bores. I can't believe those two got approved by corporate. Well, I'm not buying. Now, let's see if this last one has any merit."

Julie and Ron were talking about Banyon and its recent quality improvements as Ben walked in. Not saying a word, he sat down next to Ron and gave Julie a wink. "Mr. Eddy. Let's talk straight. I usually have little time for consultants, but I'm willing to listen to you. When we were on the plant tour you seemed down to earth. You appear to know JIT, and that's important right now. So talk to me."

Ron Eddy smiled briefly, then turned directly toward Ben. "Mr. Morgan, in many respects I'm a wolf in sheep's clothing. I spend most of my time behind a desk with students on the other side. I know academics usually rank below consultants, but if we can get past that, maybe we can agree on something."

"An academic. I should have guessed. You didn't seem as slick as the other two. Well, to make a long story short, Mr. Eddy, we need some training materials, some way to get facts about JIT to the people who have volunteered to work in the pilot project. Maybe being an academic isn't so bad after all."

This time it was Ben who smiled. Julie kept watching. This was Ben's job. If he could get Ron, she wouldn't complain. He was a small man, an Indian, and quite bright. And he smiled a lot. Julie liked that.

Ben was waiting for Ron to respond. He knew his budget was small, and after getting the bid from the consulting firm he had been told to use, he was hoping for a miracle. There was no way he was paying $90,000 just for software. He wanted a person with experience and patience.

"You know, Mr. Morgan, I think I know your position. You're on a tight budget, that's easy to see, and you want value for your dollar. Why don't we start this way. I'll come in two days a week for as long as you want me. I'll put together a training class and materials. You pay me if you use me, but you're under no obligation beyond basic cost recovery for my upfront expenses. Does that sound like what you wanted?" As Julie had guessed, Ron was bright.

Ben liked the idea, enough to approve it. With the JIT pilot ready to start, they agreed that classes would begin in 10 days. A daily fee was set, and the meeting ended.

Using Consultants:
Sometimes Yes, Sometimes No

There is always a concern about how best to use consultants. Some firms use them all the time, others not at all. Ben used consultants to help him leap hurdles that he might otherwise leap only after rigorous training, and he knew that training could slow down the implementation.

Consultants can't solve people problems, such as developing new incentive systems, unless they take up residence. In academic research there is a concern that researchers get close enough to understand a culture, yet remain distant enough to maintain their objectivity. Learning the nuances and the structure of a company takes a lot of time. It can mean huge fees without developing programs that employees will embrace.

JIT requires employees to take ownership and pride in the system. Continuous improvement assumes that everyone wants to pull together to get better. While a plan developed in house may not be elegant, it may be implemented more quickly.

Consultants are invaluable when a company is sailing in unfamiliar waters. They depend on being up-to-date. They can analyze current problems and suggest whether certain solutions will work. They've seen many implementations, and they usually know how to train people. In short, they can help avoid rocks lying beneath the surface. They're outsiders, therefore employees listen differently to their messages. Consultants can be useful.

Ben learned this in earlier jobs. He knew that Ron Eddy could prove invaluable if he could get the employees on line quickly. It was minimum risk with maximum potential, a comforting prospect.

* * * * *

"Julie, do you think Ron can deliver? I like the fact that he's a teacher because what we need is education, not a sales pitch. I like the fact that he's willing to be judged on his merit without a guaranteed number of days on site. But I made the decision with very little evidence except a strong feeling that he's our man."

"I like him too, Ben. There's no way you can tell a person's capabilities until they start to work. Look at Jim. We thought he'd work out, but he surpassed our expectations. Ron is intelligent, likable, and calm. Those are good qualities to bring to the table. Anyway, we'll know more next week when we see the training materials he develops."

"I'm relieved to know you got the same impression of him as I did, Julie.

"What do we have to lose? Without help we're floundering, maybe with it we'll continue, maybe we won't."

"That doesn't ease my concerns in general."

"Nor mine. But, I'm tired. Small problems look big at times like this. I'm going to head out. Do you want to join me?"

"Wish I could. But, some of this just won't wait. See you in the morning."

"Right. Don't stay all night. Promise?"

"Promise."

CHAPTER 7

INITIATING THE CYCLE OF SUCCESS

"Ben, this is the way I've set up the program." Ron Eddy was back at Banyon less than a week after his first visit. He had obviously designed training programs before; the materials were compact and complete, and his discussion, convincing. "I'd like to structure the classes into three hour-long sessions, two for classroom work and the third for a formal presentation by the class. They will learn the features of JIT and how to use them. It won't be sophisticated. It will be a discussion of useful concepts; knowledge, not beauty."

"I like that," Ben was flipping through the diagrams Ron had brought. "Now tell me about their presentation. What could they possibly present after a few classes?"

"Something simple, a case study. I want them to take a process that was converted to JIT, discuss it in a presentation for management, and put together a brief report of the learning experience."

"Ron, these are line workers, not college students. But then maybe you can get them to do it; education is your specialty. It's all new to me; but that doesn't mean it won't work. I'll have to trust you."

Ron paused for a second and took a breath. "Trust, Ben. I'd like to talk about trust for a few moments. I only walked through your plant once, and I talked to just a handful of people, but I got the distinct impression they feel management doesn't care. They said communication was poor. They said they send in suggestions and ask questions, but the suggestions are ignored, and the questions are unanswered.

Even if their comments aren't completely accurate, the attitude they convey will be a problem in implementing JIT. This class may help you turn this around. You have to do it, one way or another. JIT requires dedication from everyone."

"I trust them." Ben looked irritated. "Changing to JIT means I have to change, too. I know it. I hold fewer staff meetings and I spend more time in the plant. But establishing real trust will take time."

"I'll say one more thing before I leave. How you respond to this class is critical. If you believe in them, they'll believe in themselves. You can set up a positive environment for the future and reap the same results you did when you listened to Carolyn. Also, I want you to attend the presentation and present each worker with a diploma. You and I will sign them. Put them in a frame, and you'll really make an impression. It's a good way to build confidence."

Teaching the Basics of JIT

Ron's first task was to build team spirit among the participants. JIT is a team-based technique; linking functions and machines also means linking people. Beginning with a disjointed group, the objective is to develop group loyalty and openness among team members.

There are four basic characteristics of early team structures: lack of trust, stiff interaction, dependence on a leader, and need for structure. At this stage no one is comfortable with other individuals or with his own role in the group. In Banyon's case team members already knew each other, but that can be a mixed blessing. Existing personality conflicts come with them. Compounding this problem is the uneasy relationship that exists between management and workers.

Moving beyond the first awkward moments, the team begins to take shape, though progress may seem to be misguided. Conflict and unbalanced participation erupt, as individuals begin to press issues in a desire to influence the group decision and attain personal recognition. Yet through conflict, team spirit begins to emerge. People accept solutions and plans that they have helped to develop. This is the essence of participation; it is building commitment. It is a negotiating process that requires a free give-and-take of ideas and opinions. The role of the leader is to encourage discussion, not answer questions.

Finally, a mature team exhibits intense group loyalty, a high level of trust, and acceptance of the merits and shortcomings of individual members. This provides a constructive environment for making decisions. It is stable, capable of rapid response to challenges. Over the long run, problems can arise, such as "group think,"[1] that decrease the effectiveness of the group. This suggests that maintaining a productive team environment is in itself a challenge, a balancing act between stability and willingness to change.

* * * * *

The class was held the following week. It went better than anyone could have imagined. Ron began by describing the basic elements of JIT manufacturing, such as line balancing and synchronizing individual steps in the production process. Kanban techniques, the key to effective coordination, were described in great depth, leading to long discussions of optimal lot sizes, and the development of a usable Kanban system.

To Ben's surprise, the team members grasped the difficult concepts rapidly. Ron's goal was to involve each person in the process. He introduced the JIT case early the first day, using it to shed light on the more difficult issues.

Cause and Effect:
Ishikawa Fishbone Diagrams

Once the basic concepts were understood, Ron turned the group's attention to the case analysis. He started out by asking them to complete an Ishikawa cause and effect diagram.

---

[1]*Group think* is the term used to describe those situations where individuals stop questioning the group's decision, even if they have serious reservations about it. The Cuban missile crisis, and the Kennedy administration's response, is often cited as a prime example of this phenomenon.

The case was about a company that makes personal computer disk drives that faced a "zero defect" ultimatum from its parent company. It had a long way to go to trim 12 percent defects to zero. Ron had chosen the case because of product similarities, thereby keeping confusion and guessing to a minimum.

The Ishikawa cause and effect diagram identifies basic causes of quality problems: methods, machines, materials, and man. The purpose of the exercise is to take apart an existing process step by step and to identify areas where faulty materials or poor procedures cause downstream errors and waste. While the technique was developed to analyze quality, it is a useful exercise in many other settings.

Figure 7–1 is the diagram created by the class. While

FIGURE 7–1
Cause and Effect Diagram

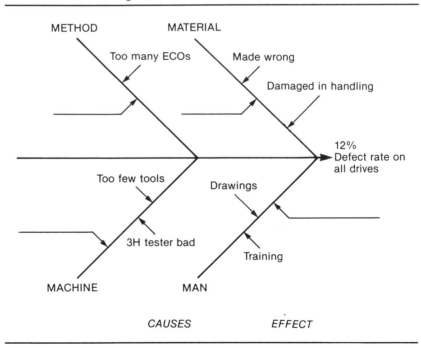

Developed as a quality control tool by Dr. Ishikawa, Japanese quality expert. Useful for detailed group analysis of causes.

Ron helped them get started, the exercise soon caught the enthusiasm of everyone. Some of the problems were easy to pinpoint, such as a faulty test device and problems in material handling. Other causes were more deeply rooted in the organization, such as lack of training and proper tools.

Converting Ishikawa's logic into a more general framework results in a diagram similar to the one in Figure 7–2. Individual problems, such as the inability to meet schedules, are analyzed for root causes. The principle question is "why?" "Why are deadlines missed?" Each of the explanations given is then subjected to the same questioning to search for root causes and solutions that will work. Once the thinking pattern is mastered, everyone becomes a source of solutions. Ben discovered that instead of a small handful of engineers, he now had an entire workforce capable of doing detailed process analysis and problem solving. It was a solution with no losers.

Defects: Diamonds in the Rough

The final exercise for the team was the development of a pareto analysis. First they analyzed a process to determine the potential cause of defects, then expanded the analysis to determine the reasons for other process-based problems; now Ron wanted them to go one step further. He wanted to focus the team's attention on the root cause of defects and prioritize them. The objective of the exercise was to help them learn how to identify those areas where their efforts would result in the greatest gains. Combining the pareto analysis with the related cost structures served to create a basic cost/benefit analysis. Figure 7–3 illustrates the pareto diagram for the case.

Facts in the case suggested that more than half of total product failures were caused by sheet metal problems. In most companies, the individual making the product probably knows that some raw materials, or a specific batch of materials, cause problems. Only by analyzing the problem to the level suggested by these techniques do true costs emerge. In this case, the biggest problem was caused by an external

FIGURE 7–2
The Focus Diagram

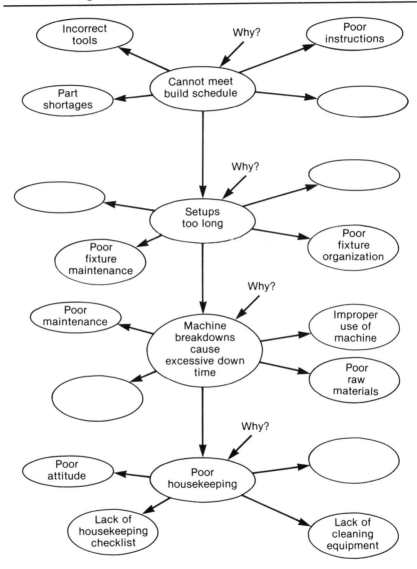

FIGURE 7-3
Pareto Analysis Example

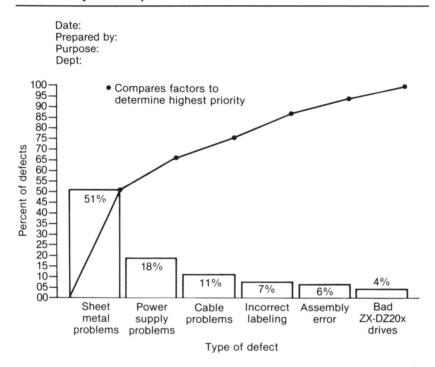

supplier. The solution? Require higher quality standards from vendors.

* * * * *

Ron spent the last day of the three-day education program helping the group develop a formal management presentation. It was not a technical process, but rather a reinforcement of what they had learned. In putting together the program, individuals had to talk about the concepts and what they meant. Everyone had to be able to define and discuss the issues and bring what they had learned to the analysis.

Pleasant Surprises and Good Beginnings

The end of the presentation brought a heartfelt round of applause from management. Ben almost had tears in his eyes, though only Julie noticed. When the applause ended, Ben began the recognition ceremony. The team members were beaming, even more so after receiving their diplomas with compliments from Ben. Julie arranged for pictures, and they were posted on the employee bulletin board the next morning. Copies were given to all the team members.

After the ceremony Ben invited everyone to attend a small party in honor of the graduating team. It was complete with cake, ice cream, and good feelings. Ron stayed out of the limelight, simply watching and smiling. Finally everyone left for home, and Ben walked Julie back to her office.

"You know, Julie, they're really excited! Such a little thing this recognition ceremony, but they're ecstatic! It's the simple things that matter, just telling people you're proud of them. I know how it makes my kids feel, but I never stopped to think of it as something I should do here."

"Ron knew it. Good teachers know how to motivate, and I'd guess Ron is as good in his classes as he was here. I have a good feeling about the whole implementation; I think it's going to work."

"I hope your intuition is right, Julie. We have a high-risk situation for everyone in the plant. There's no more time for false starts. Corporate is breathing down my neck to get profits up or trim staff. They're pushing me, but not providing any resources to meet the Probe and GRI demands. I've talked until I'm blue in the face, but to no avail. We've got to succeed, and soon."

"Ben, you talked last week about personal change, that you had to learn to delegate more responsibility to employees and to trust that they'll perform. It looks like this is a good time for the new Ben to take over. They're going to do it, they're smart, they care, and now they know you care. Now, I'd like to buy the boss a drink, if he's willing. I can't stay late because I promised to go to a movie with a friend, but there's plenty of time for my best friend of all." It really wasn't a question; Julie's tone made it clear to Ben that it was a command. He happily acquiesced.

PUTTING JIT TO WORK

The next day got off to a brisk start. The graduates were ready to cut their teeth on a real project and looked to Ben to point them in the right direction. Ben called the group together and the questions began.

"Mr. Morgan, where would you like us to start?"

"I don't know. What do you think? My only concern is that it's an area or product with which you're already familiar. If you already know the process, you won't have to spend as much time getting prepared."

"OK. Well, we were thinking about the President's line. It has problems, and we feel comfortable that we know the cause of some of them already." Brenda, the area supervisor, was talking, but one look around the room convinced Ben that this was a group decision.

"I think that would be a great place to start. When we were first talking about potential candidates, that one was high on the list. It's comforting to know that we're thinking the same way. Brenda, this project belongs to the JIT team. When do you want to start?"

"Today."

Ben was surprised, but kept it to himself. "All right. Well, I'm ready to give you a half hour every day off your regular jobs plus one full day each week until you come up with a plan. I need you in production, but I also want to give you enough time on the company clock to start the project."

"Fair enough. Now, we have some more questions."

"You do? What are they?"

"Can we move machines?"

"Yes."

"And we can work on this during business hours?"

"Sure."

"If we give you a plan, you'll review it and approve it or reject it right away and tell us why?"

"That's fair. Sure."

"Can we distribute work among employees?"

"Yes."

"What will we be paid, and how will we be measured?"

"Fair question. You'll be paid your average weekly take home pay during the experimental period. As far as performance measurements, we've been thinking about productivity, but how would you like to be measured?"

"We don't really know."

"Then we'll work on that together."

* * * * *

The newly formed team of four operators, one supervisor, one technical member from manufacturing engineering, and two alternates, was on its way to setting up Banyon's first JIT cell. Their product was the President series counter/controller; it is shown in Figure 7–4. It is a small programmable counter, 5.8 inches wide, 5.9 inches deep, and 3.04 inches high. Each of five basic models features two independent count inputs and three separate six-digit count registers, each independent of the others. Each count register has its own preset, output, inhibit, reset, and recycle capabilities. It can also send or receive data. A sophisticated counter, it is used to control numerical control machines. The counter is in a growth market with a projected life cycle of three to five years.

A Rapid Response

Less than two weeks had passed when Brenda called to schedule a meeting. She said the team was ready to start implementing JIT in the President's line, and her tone told Ben she meant it. He agreed to a meeting the next day, and asked if it would be all right to invite his immediate staff.

"Sure, as long as you are the one who makes the decision. I don't want to answer to more than one boss." Brenda and Ben agreed on a time and format for the meeting.

FIGURE 7-4
Durant® President Series

After the conversation, Ben couldn't focus any longer on the work at hand. "Julie, can you come in here?" Ben often resorted to yelling his messages to Julie; it saved time.

Julie arrived a few moments later. "You know, Ben, you're going lose your voice yelling for me. What's up now?" Julie's tone was anything but cross. In fact, she could barely keep the smile off her face.

"Who knows? Anyway, can you set up a meeting for tomorrow at 3 P.M.? Don't take 'No' from anyone. Brenda's group is ready to talk over the JIT implementation, and I want to show her we're behind them. And, it won't hurt to have everyone understand what's happening."

"OK, boss."

"Boss? Julie, I'm not your boss, and you know it. We're a team, we're partners in crime, the crime of turning a company around. Our sentence? To be chained to a desk. I'm going home. It's a beautiful day, and my concentration's gone."

* * * * *

Brenda McKee, the supervisor, began. "Mr. Morgan, we're ready to start. As you can see from our plan, we've decided to use a straight line setup for the President's final assembly cell. We've identified four major operations, and we've balanced the work among them. This plan should minimize queue and eliminate shortages that stop the flow unless something unexpected happens."

"As you can see from the report, we believe we can reduce the lot size from the current level of 500 units to a Kanban of 4 given the way we've paced the line. And, because of the product's ongoing quality problems, we're going to self-inspection. Everyone has agreed to be responsible for quality at his own station. Finally, we're going to cross-train everyone so we can deal with absences and vacations."

"Our goal is to find the problems and fix them right away. Our calculations show that the proposed line will reduce lead times and increase quality. We're not as sure about the impact on cost, because we didn't have the numbers to work with. Well, what do you think?" Brenda paused and looked directly at Ben, waiting for an answer. She was searching his face to see if he would be good to his word about supporting their decisions.

Ben was surprised, but not dumbfounded. Glancing around the room, he saw that his entire staff was horrified. That brought a smile and made responding to Brenda a pleasure. "You've figured all this out already? Are you sure you've covered all the bases, that you can meet the daily production quotas? We set that at 40 counters a day, if I remember right."

Ben's tone told Brenda everything she needed to know. Relaxed and smiling, she replied. "We don't think it will be a problem, Mr. Morgan. One more thing, we would like the authority to stop the line and fix mistakes as we find them. That's not what we do now, but it just doesn't make sense to make bad product. Once again, Mr. Morgan, what do you think. Is it a go?"

Ben really wasn't sure what he was approving. It was the first cell, and there was a tremendous amount of uncertainty. But, he knew that he had nothing to lose. Management had made enough false starts in the quality efforts to make Ben willing to let someone else try. So, his response was brief. "OK, you're on. Now, what do you need to get the cell in place and production under way?"

"Your signature so we can get the machines moved. Thanks, Mr. Morgan, we'll get to work on this right away." Signature in hand, Brenda and the team left.

While the departing group looked visibly relieved, the remaining one did not.

"Ben, I can't believe you did that," Jim Andrews blurted out. "You don't have any idea what you're approving. I'm all for progress, and I'm willing to let line workers help us get to the right answer, but you've written them a blank check. How could you do that?"

Ben thought carefully before answering, knowing this was a crisis. "Well, Jim, we know one thing, and you've pointed it out countless times since you arrived. The President's line just isn't working. If it's already broken, what else can happen? Quality is low, and we have to become cost competitive. It has to be fixed, or this product launch is going to have a very short life."

Dick Williamson spoke up next. "Ben, what do line workers know about machines? We could be months getting things straightened out. I'm really uncomfortable with this."

"Dick, if you think back to Carolyn, I think you'll agree that people on the shop floor have better ideas than we do on how to make product. So, I'm going to let them move forward until I think they've gone off the deep end." Ben waited for a response, but got none. Shortly afterward, the meeting broke up.

* * * * *

"Ben, do you have a minute?" Julie peered in, a little hesitant.

"For you, yes. Come in. Sit down." Ben set aside the report he was reading.

Julie entered and sat, looking down instead of up.

"The last meeting didn't end on a good note, Ben. I know you said that the staff would warm to the idea. Well, I'm concerned that you've misread them. They say you've lost it. You're letting lunatics run the asylum." Julie's eyes still did not meet Ben's.

"Is that all?"

"No."

"Well?"

"I'm also a bit concerned . . . not a bit, a lot. Where will this all end? Is my job safe?"

"Is that all. Of course it is."

"But if the workers are running the plant, what use is there for management?"

"The same as always. To help them do their jobs, to get the supplies and equipment they need to succeed. To mediate conflict and point the way. To be leaders, not wardens."

JIT: MORE THAN TECHNIQUE

In describing the company's transformation over the past six years, the Chairman emphasizes the importance of developing Total Productive Maintenance and QC before going to JIT. He also explains that strong leadership with a rigorous, company-wide people focus is the key to their rapid JIT conversion.

Tokai calls its JIT system "JSK" which stands for the Japanese words for autonomous production control. In describing the system, Mr. Nozaki explains that the operators themselves are responsible for controlling the process. He emphasizes that Tokai considers a high level of worker involvement and autonomy to be key prerequisites for successful implementation of the "pull" system.

Mr. Nozaki offers some advice for other organizations wishing to achieve a similar conversion. He stresses that there is no absolute set of rules or steps to follow in every situation because no two companies are alike. However, he offers a basic procedural principle and an interesting metaphor to illustrate it. "When you're fishing, you must have your hook at the right level all the time. If you place your hook too close to the fish, they will swim away; if you put it too far away, they will not be tempted by it. Therefore, we must follow the procedure of always keeping the hook close to the fish. If we want to raise the level, we must do it one step at a time." This metaphor illustrates the importance of taking small, practical steps in any conversion process involving people. Where and how upper management places the hook is of utmost importance. The best approach is to encourage an attitude that compels continuous improvement by raising the level of performance incrementally through moment-by-moment coaching in terms of target adjustments, enforced problem solving with people recognition, and a measurement system of physical goals.

Mr. Nozaki feels that the ability of his employees to find joy and value in small, everyday things is another basic factor in the success of his company. "Developing the kind of attitude that makes this possible is a matter of practice," he points out. "It takes a special effort to find impressive things in the ordinary. It takes careful looking." As the Japanese poet Basho wrote: "If we look carefully, we can see a tiny flower under the fence."[2]

Ben closed the book about Japanese manufacturing and sat quietly. He was changing from needing to be in charge to allowing others to grow and take command. It was not easy.

---

[2]P. Johansen and K. J. McGuire, *Continuous Improvement: A Close Look at Japanese Manufacturing* (Simsbury, Conn.: Manufacturing Excellence Coalition, 1986), p. 24.

He had spent sleepless nights after giving the reins to the JIT team, but he knew it was right. "Power comes from the respect of others, not from discipline and punishment. But trust, a willingness to take a chance on others, that's the scary part. Well, there's no turning back."

* * * * *

JIT is more than a technical system or a new way to design work flow in manufacturing. It is a people intensive system, yet it is a balanced system. Technical improvements are enhanced by the people, and the people learn by applying the technical. While Ben was comfortable with technical JIT and its benefits, the people dimension was new.

In the past the factory had been run like most U.S. companies. Decisions were made in large committee meetings, often with a kind of pseudo-participation; the top manager would state a position and ask for a consensus. Top down, autocratic, and distanced from the common worker, management learned to deal with the organization as a set of numbers on a balance sheet rather than as a group of people.

That organizations are machines or loose collections of physical assets is an error. A willing accomplice, accounting has played a major though unplanned role in supporting this incorrect belief. People are not recorded as assets.

The failure to attach any value to people in the reporting system, except as a cost of converting product, has led to frustration and ambiguity. Managing means people and taking an active role in guiding them. In social institutions, such as business organizations, managing is people.

Numbers result from actions taken by people. A manager cannot manage numbers; a manager can only manage activities and people who perform them. Numbers are the results. To set about managing numbers is to confuse the ends with the means. The ends are numbers, profits, or organizational survival. The means are people. The ends are achieved by actively managing the means, people, who may use simple words to get their thoughts across. It also means trust.

The Multiple Dimensions of Control

Ben was learning how to manage people better, letting them take control of their own jobs. In management literature three main controls prevail: results, action, and personnel.[3] Control can be achieved by carefully monitoring results. Control can be achieved by monitoring actions, by setting goals, and evaluating performance against them. While these controls are effective, personnel controls are by far the most effective.

Personnel controls are people-oriented. They are the self-control people bring to the job and their desire to do a good job. In a large organization, personnel controls include the formal, established patterns of interaction; and the informal, the "grapevine," group dynamics, and peer pressure. If an organization relies on formal controls, which are specific procedures and policies, it is called mechanistic. Traditionally, repetitive manufacturing firms are mechanistic.[4] If an organization relies on informal controls, which include the grapevine, group dynamics, and peer pressure, it is called organic. Interestingly, JIT relies on informal controls. The life change that Ben described reflects the transition of the organization from mechanistic to organic; a culture change, not an easy task.

* * * * *

"It's hard to let go of the reins, to let someone else take command and make decisions. But every time I do, we get better. Carolyn feels like she owns the wave-solder process

---

[3]The source of this approach to control is K. Merchant, *Control in Business Organizations* (Boston, Mass.: Pittman Publishing Co., 1985).

[4]This observation is based on a review of work done by Joan Woodward in the early 1960s that focused on classifying control systems in different manufacturing settings. She found that large batch production was related to established routines and a more pronounced bureaucracy than small batch and process manufacturing systems. These thoughts are further developed in a working paper, C. J. McNair, "Within Context: The Implementation of JIT Manufacturing and Its Impact on Management Accounting" (Kingston: University of Rhode Island, May 1989).

now. She's not going to let any bad parts come from her machine. Brenda's group is rearranging machines and redesigning work flow as well as their own jobs.

"It's frightening, really frightening. If it fails, I lose my job, and they keep theirs. So here I am, completely exposed, with ultimate responsibility but little direct control. I hope I can keep it all in perspective and not let uncertainty push me backwards."

It was Ben's life change, learning to trust the workers he had been trained to believe were lazy and unmotivated. Change is never comfortable. It brings increased uncertainty and threatens both job and role security. Uncomfortable? Yes. Necessary? Without a doubt.

CHAPTER 8

SURPRISES AND SUCCESSES

The JIT line had been up and running for a week. Ben stopped by frequently to offer encouragement, but seldom stayed more than a few minutes. Wanting to prove to Brenda that he trusted her, Ben stayed out of the way and hoped for the best.

* * * * *

The phone startled him. Ben had a tendency to daydream in the morning, a habit he attributed to his college years and a particular accounting instructor. Whatever dreams remained after the jarring ring dissipated when he realized who was calling.

It was Brenda. She asked him to come out to the line as soon as he could. Not volunteering any details, she hung up. Ben was sure something had gone wrong; indigestion was his clue.

"Julie, Brenda wants me to come out to the President's line. Do you want to come along?"

The worry in his voice was evident. Julie guessed he was feeling the need for moral support. "Sure, But why? Did she say they're having problems?" Julie joined Ben as he raced out the door. She was wearing shoes with lower heels nowadays, one of the many lessons to be learned in the fast-paced world of business.

"She didn't say. That's what has me worried. She sounded confident, not upset, but that's not enough to keep my ulcer from working overtime."

As they rounded the last corner, Ben stopped dead in his

tracks. The line was down, and Brenda was sweeping up around the machines. "Damn, what now?" was Ben's unspoken thought.

"Brenda," Ben was moving again. "Brenda, how's the new line working?"

"It's working fine."

"But it's down!"

"We've finished production for the day."

"Finished? We have to make 800 counters per month, that's 40 a day. You've already made 40?"

"Yup. Here's today's production slips."

"But you've only been running for four hours!"

"That's right."

Ben couldn't think of a thing to say. Julie noticed his consternation and made some small talk with Brenda. He recovered quickly. "Brenda, can you do me a favor? Since you've got the line under control, can you put together a report on the team's progress and present it at a staff meeting in the morning? You're doing a great job, and I'd like everyone to know it."

"Sure. It won't be fancy, but I can bring in some of the charts we've been keeping and fill everyone in. What time?"

"Eight o'clock. And thanks, Brenda, to you and the entire team."

Ben walked back to his office without further comment. Julie remained quiet, giving Ben a chance to grasp the progress he saw in the JIT cell. It was unbelievable. They had never hit the quota on the President's line. The power of JIT manufacturing was being felt. No one had anticipated that implementing JIT would result in idle capacity, at least not so fast. In fact, Ben had built some cushion into the monthly projections because he was sure that the start-up would hit major snags. Now his problem was success.

Back in his office, Ben called an impromptu meeting with Jim Andrews, Mike Gannon, Dick Williamson, and Julie. He wasted no time; as soon as they arrived he shut the conference room door.

Ben looked carefully at each face before he began. "Does anyone know how the President's line is doing?" Blank stares suggested that they didn't. "We should be drinking champagne, or we've been using loose standards. We may have found gold, but hopefully not fool's gold. We've never been caught up on the President's line, and yet Brenda told me they're finished for the day. At 11 A.M.!"

Ben described what he had seen, and told them what Brenda had said. Jim and Dick looked smug; they were sure that there were problems, the obvious outcome of giving workers control. They were goofing off. Mike and Julie looked puzzled. After a few minutes of discussion, Ben asked Mike and Julie to check out the situation and report back.

"Even though Mike and Julie are looking for answers, that doesn't let anyone off the hook. Tomorrow morning Brenda may be able to shed some light, but filling up the idle capacity, if we truly have it, is management's job, not hers."

* * * * *

"As you can see from these charts, once we got the machines lined up and everyone got comfortable with his job and the new setup, we really picked up speed. We found we could make a counter about every 12 minutes. We were surprised at first, but when we actually looked at the tasks, that's all the time it took. We'd like you to give us some more work if you could. That's why I asked to see you yesterday, Mr. Morgan. What product can we work on next?"

Brenda had done a good job presenting the facts. Jim and Dick had lost their smugness. The logic of the product flow was overwhelming; there was no question that the team had reached unanticipated levels of efficiency and effectiveness. They were doing the right job the first time.

"Brenda, you've given us a lot to do. It's our job to find more work for you, and we will. For now you can use the spare time to work on preventive maintenance and cross-training. I promise we'll be back to you as soon as we figure out what to do next. And, tell everyone I'm delighted with your progress."

"OK, I think we can keep out of trouble. If nothing else, we'll pitch in and help in other departments. I don't want to sound too pushy, but when you're looking for a solution, maybe you'll want to consider other electronic counters. They're pretty similar to the President's. Just a thought."

Understanding JIT

The President's team had made amazing progress. It was now time for Ben to accelerate the JIT implementation to cover the entire President's line and eventually the entire plant. But he was unsure of the next step. He hadn't thought beyond getting the line in place because of the nightmares of the quality improvement start-up. Ben was sure that Ron Eddy had played a major role in the success; he was the only variable in the equation.

* * * * *

Julie and Mike took their assignment seriously. They began digging into the papers and pamphlets she had picked up at various seminars. Julie was sure the answer was there.

"Julie, I can't believe this. This desk is a fire trap! If we ever find what we're looking for, I'll buy you dinner, your choice of restaurants." Mike was nursing a paper cut.

Julie found what she had been looking for. In the back of her mind she had remembered a detailed description of an implementation plan. And here it was, wrinkled, but usable.

"Mike, I found it. This brochure is our ticket to success. Look here. There are pages and pages on the ABCs of implementing JIT/TQC. And it has the steps." Julie was ecstatic. Finding the brochure meant that she and Mike could quit sifting through piles of paper.

"Good. I say we take it in to Ben before we develop a plan." Mike was in no mood to waste time. If he were in charge, Julie would learn how to file. "She's a good manager, but in desperate need of a secretary. I wonder if she searches like this every time she has to find something? A little housekeeping wouldn't hurt this office."

Ben immediately recognized the brochure. "This is it. I couldn't remember where we got this information." He glanced through the pamphlet looking for key points and suggestions.

* * * * *

There are six steps in a JIT conversion: performing a diagnostic of the target area; putting together a conceptual design of the work flow and floor layout; planning the implementation; preparing for the implementation; doing the implementation; and monitoring the implementation continuously. Banyon had skipped over the formal diagnostic, relying on common sense and team participation to make the site selection. The actual implementation analysis had been completed by Brenda's team with little interference from management. Conceptually, Ben was at square one. He didn't have a clear idea of past performance, nor the full potential of the improvement he could expect.

While the process covered six steps, Ben thought they should focus their efforts on the first two. Scarce resources could be best used in new JIT production. They had more success than they had expected in the cell, so he felt no real need to focus directly on its performance. Besides, the diagnostic would reveal areas where actual results were significantly below accepted benchmarks. To simplify the analysis, Ben asked Mike and Julie to concentrate on inventory levels, value-added time, travel distance, lead time, space utilization, and staffing. Given the initial result in the President's line, Ben was sure that similar successes could be achieved elsewhere in the plant.

A Multidisciplinary Team

Mike and Julie looked at the mountain of work in front of them. It was discouraging. "Mike, I think we need some help with the diagnostic. If I understand it correctly, an engineer has to do some of the analysis. I think we'd better ask Ben to assign a few more people to this."

Mike agreed. Together with Ben, they went over potential candidates. Given the scope of the project, they focused on people who were open to new ideas; people who represented a cross section of key areas in the plant were essential. The final list included Mike, Julie, Greg Philips, Jim, and Brenda. Greg was a design engineer who had helped manufacturing in the past. Having Mike and Brenda on the team would ensure employee support.

Ben wanted rapid feedback, so he asked the team members to find replacements for their daily activities. With the details behind them, the team got started.

Ben and Julie were thrilled with the enthusiasm with which the team members tackled the expanded JIT project. Like the initial President's team, the JIT task force had concerns about time and spending commitments. Ben assured them he would give them whatever they needed to get the job done. Within four weeks the team completed the diagnostic in electronics. It included the remainder of the President's family, as well as other electronic products that captured the volume, variety, and complexity of their electronics business. Data gathering completed, they worked on their analysis to prepare their presentation for Ben.

THE PRESIDENT'S LINE DIAGNOSTIC REPORT

> Two hundred seven thousand six hundred printed circuit boards are produced each year using large lot size job-shop manufacturing practices. Of the total units produced yearly, 70 percent of each product family is made up of no more than two to four catalog items.

Ben began to read the diagnostic report prepared by the JIT implementation team. They had done a thorough job; now his task was to ensure he understood the implications of their findings. The first table in the report (Table 8–1), detailed the yearly volume of printed circuit boards and completed units for products coming from electronics. The current JIT line was making 9,600 President's units. Several of the catalog products, though, were quite similar. Putting those volumes aside, the Probe counter looked like a good candidate for JIT. Ben made a note of this and read on.

TABLE 8–1
Banyon Product Volumes

Product Line	PCBs	Units
Xerox	48,000	24,000
President	38,400	9,600
Other OEMs	35,700	12,100
Catalog products	31,500	12,700
Interdivisional	24,900	
Controllers	29,100	5,820
Total	207,600	

Source: Coopers & Lybrand.

Value Added: Disheartening Results

    The President product family exhibits some seasonality in the spring and fall due in part to promotions.

    The President products travel over 4,450 feet from the receipt of raw materials to packaging/shipping. This travel distance excludes retesting of defective units. Higher volume Presidents have 47 minutes of value-added time in the completed units; the units with additional features contain 52 to 57 minutes of value-added time.

    The present lead time for a President is 46 days, or 9 work weeks. The 46 days break down into 10 days for making the printed circuit boards, 5 days of assorted testing, 18 days in subassembly, 3 days of final assembly, 8 days of final test and burn-in, and 2 days of packaging/shipping.

"This is unbelievable! This report says that of 46 days in the plant, we add value to the product for 47 minutes. That leaves 45 days and 7 hours of nonvalue-adding time. I can see where this is leading. Let's see. Are there charts or tables that summarize this?"

Ben turned to the back of the report to Figure 8–1 and Tables 8–2 and 8–3. Figure 8–1 was a "Spider Web" diagram, with each major stage in the production process aligned on an axis. Value-adding minutes are plotted on one axis; nonvalue-adding on others. The figure displays the sum of all axes or total time, 265 minutes, against value-adding

FIGURE 8-1
Spider Web—Value Added versus Nonvalue Added

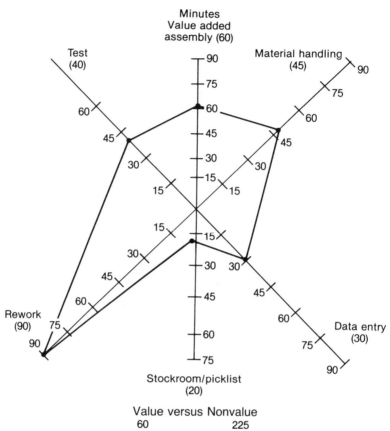

time, 47 minutes. Rework time exceeded production time! It's hard to compete with numbers like these.

Table 8-2 detailed the steps in the current production sequence for Presidents. Out of 138 steps, only 33 could be classified as value-adding. Forty-one percent of the activities added value, 59 percent did not. All other steps in the production sequence were waste in a true JIT sense. In Table 8-3, activities were extended to represent minutes of assembly time, about 52 minutes of value-adding time per unit.

TABLE 8–2
Banyon President Process Analysis

	Inspect	Delays	Stores	Operations	Value Added
Receive	2	3	1	4	1
Picking	1	7	1	42	14
Build	7	20	5	20	11
Test/ship	4	6	1	14	7
Total	14	36	8	80	33

Total steps—138
41% of operations are value added.

Source: Coopers & Lybrand.

These numbers were not unusually high. Most American manufacturers are in similar situations. Because factories have grown around functional units, such as machining and assembly, the complexity of individual product process flow has increased exponentially as units zigzag their way back and forth across the plant. At Banyon, the Presidents traveled *almost one mile* from entry of raw materials to exit of finished products.

Ben read on, disturbed. With the success on the plant floor to guide him, he knew that the report had to be correct; they got too much improvement, too fast, for any other expla-

TABLE 8–3
Banyon Value Added Time (Excluding Test)

	Minutes
PCB—display	4.5
PCB—MPU	5.6
PCB—power supply	6.2
PCB—terminals	3.7
Molding	1.1
Relay	3.7
Final assembly	25.4
Label/packaging	2.2
Total	52.4

Source: Coopers & Lybrand.

nation to hold. "If these numbers get to corporate, they'll fire me. How did we ever get into such a mess? Didn't anyone ever question process flow?"

Most factories maintain process flow diagrams for existing products. They serve as outlines for constructing detailed bills of materials and for routing products through the plant. No one, however, has ever questioned paths that products take or the logic behind assembly sequences. Simply reclassifying existing information can lead to startling and discomforting revelations. Ben was glad he knew the truth, but it didn't make it easier to accept.

"I wonder what other bombshells are in here; it's a testament to careless growth and failure to question basic assumptions in plant layout. Good, inventory is next." Ben didn't have to read it to know it was bad news.

Inventories: Compensating for Mistakes

Staffing for all Presidents, to include molding, wave solder, etc., totals 10 full-time employees. Capacity imbalances between processes exist at axial insertion, molding, functional test, and burn-in. Each of these processes have both varying setup times and run speeds. The capacity imbalance is accentuated by differing lot sizes, varying from three days for burn-in to three months for molding. Lot sizes are based on economic order quantities; excessive in-process inventory has resulted from varying economic order quantities for the various President parts.

Work-in-process inventory is significant; periodic samples from manufacturing indicated an average of 52 days in process and 8 days in test. Various components with quality problems had higher levels of in process inventory. These included PCB's (printed circuit boards) 78 days, power supply units 82 days, and relay assemblies 89 days. Part shortages, evidenced by manufacturing orders issued short, indicated 5 days of Dantel 8031 microprocessors, 9 days of Novrams, and a stockout of control panel labels.

WIP is accounted for through manufacturing work orders. Through detailed labor reporting by operations, order status can be obtained. However, multiple orders for the same part exist on the floor with rejected lots falling behind newer orders. Units from one lot are added to another lot to speed flow of needed material. These conditions make detailed problem solving and process improvement difficult.

Present performance measures of labor efficiency and utilization, overhead absorption, and material price variance do not motivate desired behavior. Concentration on labor efficiency and utilization rewards quantity over quality, and discourage desired "stop and fix" problem solving. Overhead absorption is encouraging production in excess of demand, leading to increased inventory levels.

Ben wasn't surprised by this information. The chart included in the report (Table 8–4) merely confirmed what his intuition had told him; inventories were being used to hide problems. The plant floor was in chaos; orders were handled randomly with no clear sequence or scheduling of shipments. The MRP system released orders to the floor, but once there they sat for months in corners plagued by parts shortages and rework problems.

"I knew this problem existed, but it's distressing to learn that some orders are sitting because we're out of labels. No one is even thinking about them! 'For lack of a nail, a shoe was lost. . . . ' This horse is missing more than a few nails."

A Solution: The Conceptual Design

Ben turned the page and brightened. The bad news was over. The team put together a conceptual design as a basis for directing improvements. He read on.

CONCEPTUAL DESIGN

To meet the President demand of 800 units a month, or 3,200 PCB's, a mixed model, one shift operation is recommended. The uniform plant load needed to meet customer demand is 11.2 minutes, derived as follows:

$$\frac{8976 \text{ minutes per month}}{800 \text{ units per month}} = 11.2 \text{ minutes per unit}$$

TABLE 8–4
Banyon Raw, WIP, FG Inventory

	President— Days on Hand
Raw	45
Assembly	52
Test	8
FG	27
Total	132

$$\text{Days} = \frac{\text{Total units}}{\text{Average daily sales}}$$

Source: Coopers & Lybrand.

A single final assembly process, "U"-shaped line with three workstations, is suggested. After line balancing has reduced Kanbans to two per station, the line should be able to absorb subassembly, test, burn in, and packaging. These additional activities add one person to the line, but will require rebalancing the work for each person. For example, the packager can handle burn in, test, and material movement to and from the line. The final assembly line will be fed by three subassembly departments: molding, PCB manufacture, and relay assembly. Further work will be needed to incorporate relay assembly into the line.

Volume and one of a kind equipment prevent wave solder, axial insertion, and molding inclusion into the line.

* * * * *

"This makes sense. We should include all subprocesses in the line with the exception of those performed on equipment that is required to serve the entire plant. That's a constraint we have to live with for now. If these operations are included in the line, how will we synchronize the production process?" Ben didn't have to read far to get his answer.

Kanban in Action

Within the line, a wooden box holding four PCB assemblies will be the Kanban signaling system. Initially two Kanbans per workstation will be used, dropping to one Kanban per station as problems are solved. Reducing the Kanban quantity will further stress the process and uncover additional problems for resolution.

A two-bin Kanban signaling system will be employed between final assembly and each subassembly/primary-/feeder cell. Final assembly will have two bins. When one is empty, material in the second bin will be used, while the first bin is returned to subassembly to be refilled. This will link subassembly to final assembly via Kanbans. Later, an overlapped movement should be employed, eliminating the Kanbans.

For primary operations, such as molding, initial Kanban quantities should equal the economic order quantity (EOQ) quantity. As setup time is reduced, the Kanban quantities will be reduced to the number of units needed as buffer for setup and run times plus a management confidence factor. Ultimately, single minute exchange of dies will support daily production in place of current runs of three months of inventory.

* * * * *

The report indicated that lengthy setup times in subassembly departments were the cause of excess inventory. But because of process constraints, some inventory was inevitable. Linking the JIT cell to subassembly through Kanbans would expose excess production; for now, the Kanban system would signal replenishment of the JIT line, but *would not* trigger production from subassembly. Failing to put the Kanbans in place, though, would work against continuous improvement and the need to recognize problems. With a properly designed cell, Banyon could accommodate changes in feeder areas without missing a beat. Without this accommodation, future change in subassembly procedures might lead to changes in the JIT cell's configuration.

"If we're going to put the cell together, we might as well do it right. By making subassembly problems visible, they'll get attention and be resolved. Otherwise, we'll be facing the same mess." Ben was encouraged. While he was sure the conceptual design was optimistic, it did set process capabilities, given current equipment and product assembly characteristics.

Synchronized Movements and Plant Design

Problems that disrupt synchronous movement of material within or between lines must be dealt with quickly by "on call" support personnel. The support personnel include an electronics technician, a quality engineer, and a maintenance employee.

The final assembly line should be located immediately next to the stockroom to reduce shipping travel distance. In order to reduce travel distance further, the following processes are to be relocated next to the final assembly line: PCB test, relay subassembly, burn in and test, and packaging.

The final test after burn in should be part of the final assembly cell. This move would improve communication between final assembly and test, and foster improved quality. Currently, final assembly tests the product and then Quality Control runs the same test. By incorporating the test within the line the redundancy can be eliminated.

We found no evidence to support the 48-hour President burn in. A set of experiments should be employed to determine the proper burn in period.

* * * * *

"Experiments? That means we have no idea what the optimum test time is. That's not encouraging."

Like many manufacturers, Banyon based its procedures as much on tradition as on knowledge. If in the past an engineer had recommended a 48-hour burn in, it is likely that all future products would be treated the same. Technological and product changes were ignored. Why? The manufacturing process is built on independence, it is *not* stressed. Buffers proliferate. And in a 46-day cycle time, 2 days for burn in are inconsequential.

* * * * *

"The good news is this report is thorough. The bad news is that we're doing everything wrong. Too much nonvalue-adding, too much inventory, and too little understanding of the process. If JIT requires a critical look at operations, it's no wonder that improvements are gained so quickly. In a system built on waste, a little fixing goes a long way." The results made Ben uncomfortable. The uncertainty surrounding the JIT implementation was easier to accept than the harsh facts about the current situation.

Matching Schedules to New Capabilities

> Components for final assembly should be stored at the beginning of the cell. This will significantly reduce material handling. To eliminate the problem of an increasing number of work orders as lot sizes are reduced, the backflush technique will be employed instead of detailed bill of material tracking. The materials department will provide a weekly final assembly schedule using the current Master Schedule. As good units are built daily, a backflush transaction will move them to finished goods and relieve raw-in-process inventory.
>
> We suggest a change from the current one month frozen schedule to one week. The improved lead time expected from incorporating the JIT technology in the cell eliminates the need for manufacturing to respond to any schedule changes. After the line has been synchronized, the frozen schedule time can be reduced, and the finished goods inventory safety stock can be brought down to a level consistent with the cell's output capabilities.
>
> From the President pilot of 33 percent productivity improvement, to date, it appears that a full 100 percent improvement is possible. This means that cell staffing can drop from 10 to 4.7, as indicated by the following calculation:
>
> $$\frac{\text{Value-added time}}{\text{Uniform plant load}} \text{ or } \frac{52.4 \text{ minutes}}{11.2 \text{ minutes}} \text{ or } 4.7$$

* * * * *

Ben looked at the last table in the report (Table 8–5) that summarized data gathered on the President's line. The findings were striking. He could see countless dollars of waste and potential for significant improvement. If every product family revealed similar patterns, it was a wonder they were still in business.

"Is this possible? We've been fairly successful. Business is good. We've been making a profit. Our products aren't

TABLE 8–5
Banyon President Conceptual Design (Summary)

	Diagnostic	Conceptual
Days inventory	132 days	14–37 days
Value added	47–57 minutes	47–57 minutes
Travel distance	4,454 feet	500 feet
Lead time	46 days	2–4 days
Staffing	10 employees	4.7 employees
Space	10,000 square feet	2,000 square feet

Source: Coopers & Lybrand.

overpriced. But with all this waste, I can't see how we've made it. Part of me wants to thank the diagnostic team, and another wants to strangle it. I wanted the truth, but this is awful. I feel like burning the evidence."

"What is our capacity? We've found that JIT creates idle capacity fast. If we accomplish the goals in the conceptual design, I'll have idle people and machines. But I promised I wouldn't lay off anyone during the implementation. Now I'm faced with excess capacity with no way to fill it. If we can double output with half the resources, I've got problems!"

DEALING WITH SUCCESS

Ben didn't let the fear of success keep him from continuing to implement JIT. He knew he'd have to lobby to bring more products into the plant, but if they could out perform other plants in the division, convincing management to give them more should be easy. And if downturns came, he'd deal with them by talking with the people in the plant.

Ben began to realize that his work force was the source of solutions, not problems. Poor procedures and disorganized management created the inefficiencies. The plant was full of good people turning out good product in spite of the system.

The success of the plant can be seen in Table 8–6. Scrap and rework were reduced 75 percent, while responsiveness increased 28 percent. The decrease in work-in-process inven-

TABLE 8-6
Banyon Group Cell JIT Results

Group Cell	Results
Scrap and rework	Reduced 75%
Customer response	Increased 28%
Floor space	Reduced 60%
Inventory	Reduced 66%

tory and floor space was significant. JIT was working, just as the seminars and books had said it would. Banyon had taken a unique path to get to JIT, but then, each company is different.

Interestingly, one of the causes of continued downtime was the MRP system. It was paced to long lead times. Therefore, it judged that the line was not ready for new orders and would not release materials. No one thought to adjust it. But within existing constraints, lead time dropped from 30 days to 10.

In light of the improvements, batch sizes were halved which doubled work orders and nonvalue-adding clerical time. The MRP system proved to be a major bottleneck! This led Ben to eliminate work orders, a change that would have been suicidal a few months earlier.

Learning the Meaning of Group Technology

It was obvious that idle capacity on the President's line had to be filled. After a brainstorming session between management and the JIT team, they decided to include all 20 models of the President's line as well as subassembly and packaging. The different models used similar parts and subcomponents with only minor variations.

Banyon discovered group technology, production geared to product families, common assembly paths, flexible inventory, and machining techniques to accommodate different operations and components. General purpose machines with low setup times are the means of implementing group technology. It also relies on "smart" product design, often discussed under "Design for Manufacturability."

JIT cells are similar to dedicated assembly lines. Traditionally, assembly lines require a standardized process, and changing products is seldom done because of high setup costs and difficulty in sequencing operations. In JIT, standardized subassemblies increase flexibility. It is made possible by the computer, both in design and in numerical control devices, that facilitates changeovers. In the "Age of the Smart Machine,"[1] people put the computer to work to simplify non-value-adding tasks, not to dehumanize the process.

* * * * *

"We've got our work cut out for us. If this report is correct, we have to redo every process in the plant. The potential for improvement is overwhelming, but so is the task ahead. I wonder if I would have started down this path if I had known where it would lead? I thought we'd have the plant straightened out in a year. Instead, we've been at it for two and a half, and we've barely started. I wonder if Julie and Mike are still here. I need to talk this over with them before I go home."

Julie and Mike were more than willing to leave the day behind to join Ben for a drink. He listened intently as they talked about the work ahead and ordered a second round. This brought the laughter they all needed. As life slipped back into perspective, the conversation turned to lighter topics.

SUCCESS AND NEW BEGINNINGS

The JIT cell's idle capacity was used for the assembly of all 20 President models. Ben was happy, and the workers could see their success. The team was used to managing its own

---

[1] The source of this term is S. Zuboff, *In the Age of the Smart Machine* (New York: Free Press, 1988).

affairs, which led to more requests. One day while out in the plant, Brenda approached Ben. She appeared to have been waiting for him, which made Ben apprehensive.

"Mr. Morgan, how are you today?"

"Good, and you?"

"Great. I've been meaning to talk to you about a few things we'd like to do out here. Do you have a minute?"

"Sure. What's up?"

"Well, we've all been talking, and it seems that we need to start training some alternates for the cell. You know, get some backup in place."

"Why?"

"The usual, Mr. Morgan. We all get sick once in a while, sometimes we lose someone to motherhood, a death in the family, and some of us are planning vacations!" Brenda was smiling.

"You have a point there. Why now, though?"

"We have the line under control, and we're ready to spread the learning around. Before, we were still balancing the line and learning each other's jobs. Now we're all cross-trained, and it's the next logical step. And if you were serious at last week's meeting, you'd like to start JIT in other areas. We can take some time out of the process by sharing what we've learned with others."

Ben agreed, and Brenda solicited new recruits. He had learned to trust her judgement. She knew how to pick people who would work with others and who were supportive of JIT rather than against it. The trainees could also spread information about the technique to the rest of the work force.

Ben intended to use two people from the existing line to "seed" a new JIT cell. After a lot of discussion with Brenda and his management staff, Ben decided to pick an area: the Probe counter. Brenda's idea, therefore, fit with the emerging implementation sequence. It was a step-by-step plan, even though it bore little resemblance to Ben's original plan.

* * * * *

"You know, Julie, we may not be as lucky the next time around. This cell worked because of the people. Brenda's been invaluable, pulling the team along, soothing egos, and making smart choices. When we move to the next cell, we have to deal with new players. I think it could be a problem. Joe Woods is not another Brenda. What do they call him? Oh yeah, 'Little Hitler.' I'm worried."

It was after 8:00 P.M. Ben and Julie shared a pizza while they plotted strategy for the next cell. Everyone else, with the exception of Mike Gannon, had left for the day. Mike, interested in the next implementation, was working on the plans in his office.

"Ben, we should call Mike and ask him to join us. He'll forget to eat otherwise."

"Call him, Julie. You and I are both due for a lecture from Jim, and Mike is next on the list. It'll give us a chance to compare notes and unwind."

When Mike arrived, the conversation turned to plans for the new cell, then to the world outside of Banyon. It was a pleasant break from routine. Eventually, the conversation wound down and the three went their separate ways, each preparing for the next round.

CHAPTER 9

THE HUMAN SIDE OF JIT

Is a product late? Culture held it up. Is market expansion behind schedule? Culture got in the way. Is a plant slow to adopt new technology? Culture is the mother of resistance. Is a new division head unable to command the loyalty of the division's old hands? Culture is the mother of intransigence. Is it hard to get full discussion of unpleasant facts? Culture is the enemy of truth. Is effective follow-up an infrequent visitor in executive ranks? Culture holds the door shut against it. Nary a corporate sparrow falls without disappearing into the La Brea tar pit of culture.[1]

Banyon was in the midst of a massive culture change, and Ben was at its center. It went deep, altering his view of management and his role in the organization. The successes achieved on the plant floor proved it was right, but the right approach is seldom easy.

The JIT cell kept improving. While building all President counters in the cell employed excess labor for the moment, before long there was idle time again. Keeping everyone busy became a problem in a plant where on-time shipments were once rare.

* * * * *

"Julie, call Mike and ask him to come here. I want the two of you to look at capacity on the JIT line again. It's a high-class problem, but we're unprepared for it. We've gone

---

[1]A.M. Kontrow, *The Constraints of Corporate Tradition* (New York: Harper & Row, 1984), p. xi.

from expediting orders to scrounging for work. We're producing higher volumes than ever before, and we have to resolve capacity before it becomes a problem. We promised there wouldn't be layoffs, but if we don't do something, we'll have a *clean* plant and an underemployed work force."

Julie called Mike, and a few moments later he was there. An easy-going man, Mike was never in a rush; he was always ready to spend the time needed to get an answer. Between Mike's quiet competence and Julie's improving managerial skills, Ben was able to delegate greater responsibility.

"OK. We've tried to keep the JIT cell busy, but it keeps beating all our productivity expectations. What do we do next? They're out of work again."

"Ben, have you watched a clock? It's boring. You'll have happier employees if they have enough to keep busy. If anything, the JIT cell proves that workers aren't naturally lazy."

Mike waited a moment before speaking again. "We have a bunch of overachievers. We can live with that. You know, group technology has progressed down its logical path, but we never factored in the process improvements the workers would make, like the joint effort between Brenda's people and the design engineers. Through design changes and experiments, they found a way to reduce burn in from 48 hours to 16 with no decrease in quality."

"I know, Mike," Ben replied. "Why isn't Brenda here? She should be. Julie, call her and see if she can free up an hour."

Brenda joined the group shortly, and Ben brought her up to date. "Brenda, we're trying to keep all of you busy. You're doing such a great job, we're running out of work. Can you think of another product similar enough to President's to work on the line?"

Ben was becoming a facilitator working with his employees to write a JIT success story. Since the beginning of the meeting, he had voiced no opinions, only asked questions. So far he had no answers, but he had the best people in the plant working to find them. He'd put his money on them.

"I'll have to think about that, Mr. Morgan. Let's see, the product has to use the same machines and processes, otherwise the training and everything we've learned will be useless. There are a lot of different products, but none use the same parts as the President's line. Hmmm, same process, different parts." Brenda was thinking, and conversation ceased for a few moments.

Julie broke the silence. Looking at Mike, then Ben, she began. "This may be crazy, but the 1700 and 1800 model counters are older, simpler versions of the Presidents. They're not as fancy, but the real difference is in the components. While there are few common parts, the assembly sequences are basically the same. They just might be close enough. What do you think, Brenda? Mike?"

"They may be close in process, but how about the different parts? Do we have to reset the entire line? That's not a step in the right direction." Brenda had internalized JIT, and she was right. Extra setup time would not maximize value added to products in the cell.

Mike's face lit up. "Do you remember the spinner that your mothers used at Thanksgiving to hold the pickles, olives, and other goodies? I wonder if that concept could work here? No new setups, just turn the wheel."

"A lazy Susan, of course! That's so practical it has to work! Mike, can you work up a sketch?" Julie was excited and had taken the lead.

Ben simply watched. He was learning more from listening than from talking. They were on the right track. So, when Julie took charge, he settled back in his chair with a smile.

Mike drew a sketch, and soon Brenda was loading the spinner to match the process flow on the line. Within two weeks the JIT line was making both product lines.

That's not to say there were no problems. While the spinner could be loaded to match the new product flow, time needed to perform various steps in the production sequence differed significantly; the line was not balanced for the 1700 and 1800 series models. But this is where trained alternates excelled. They filled in where needed, balancing the line, not to perfection, but well enough to start the new process.

Participation: The Basic Element of JIT Management

Solutions were coming from the work force. Ben became the coach, sending in strategy and hoping his players would score. He didn't abdicate leadership; he empowered individuals within the firm to expand their duties with Banyon and participate in its future success. In a recent book, Rosabeth Moss Kanter describes the keys to participative management:[2]

> Participation would appear to work best when it is well managed. 'Well-managed' systems have these elements: a clearly designed management structure and involvement of the appropriate line people; assignment of meaningful and manageable tasks with clear boundaries and parameters; a time frame, a set of accountability and reporting relationships, and standards that groups must meet; information and training for participants to help them make participation work effectively; a mechanism for involving all of those with a stake in the issue, to avoid the problems of power and to ensure for those who have input or interest a chance to get involved; a mechanism for providing visibility, recognition and rewards for teams' efforts; and clearly understood processes for the formation of participative groups, their ending, and the transfer of the learning from them.

Participation means change through people, not in spite of them. It requires a clear definition of roles and expectations, and power sharing through participation in decisions. It means well-defined, focused participation. Ben had always been willing to listen, but now he trusted his employees to take the reins. In the years to come, he would refer to this as his "life change."

Mastering Change

After the first round of training, Ben asked everyone to think of ways to improve the quality and performance of

---

[2]R. M. Kanter, *The Changemasters* (New York: Simon & Schuster, 1984), p. 275.

their jobs. A few weeks later he was surprised and disappointed to learn that no real change had taken place. Discussing the problem with Jim Andrews, Ben learned that freedom needed bounds. No one knew where to start, so they did nothing. Without clear direction and specific expectations, no one knew what Ben wanted. Ben later described the situation as follows:

> If you have an expectation, you have to tell people what you're looking for, give them the tools, such as education, and some direction to get them rolling. Also, most people will look for problems in someone else's area. It's easier to suggest that someone else should change than that you should change yourself. . . .
>
> One thing to remember is never to give an answer because when you do, you are spoon-feeding the person. My dad taught me to answer a question with a question, because only when someone figures out the answer for himself does he really learn. You are not in command nor the all-knowing individual, you are a facilitator. You have to set up a risk-taking environment and be willing to live with the small mistakes in return for the major successes. Because, in the long run, there is no such thing as "wrong." There is only experience and learning.

Ben began to understand the worth of people. When putting in the quality programs, he allowed total discretion to the workers as a first step. Nothing happened because no one knew what to do. He then changed his approach letting the central staff make the decisions. Errors and misfires abounded. Finally, Ben allowed participation by everyone affected. In the process he became a leader instead of a boss. Success, first in wave-solder and then throughout the JIT implementation, was the outcome.

JIT IMPLEMENTATION: EVOLUTION NOT REVOLUTION

Learning took time. It is important to remember that it took nine months to complete the implementation of the first JIT cell, and to get the process under control once an acceptable level of quality was achieved: time to develop the trust and mutual respect necessary to support the change to JIT. JIT cannot thrive in a traditional top-down, controlled atmosphere. It requires managed participation.

Creating the Learning Organization

Hayes, Wheelwright, and Clark, in their recent book,[3] describe the development of organizational dynamics that support responsiveness to change in the environment. Much like Kanter, previously cited, their concern is with the management of change in organizations.

Since the publication of *Future Shock* by Alvin Toffler, the management press has focused increasingly on change, its accelerating pace, and the need to develop people systems to deal with the problems created. Rules, regulations, and formal procedures, the tools of management, are harmful in fast-changing settings. They can cause paralysis and death of organizations. Anyone who deals on an on-going basis with large bureaucracies, such as state or federal agencies, understands lack of motion where tight formal controls prevail.

Hayes, Wheelwright, and Clark discuss the key assumptions underlying a continual improvement model. They are:[4]

1. All employees are responsible, thinking adults who inherently want to do their best.
2. Human resources are too valuable to waste or leave untapped.
3. Creative talents and skills are widely distributed at all levels of an organization and society.
4. Workers will surface important problems and concerns if they feel the organization will respond appropriately.

---

[3]R. Hayes, S. Wheelwright, and K. Clark, *Dynamic Manufacturing: Creating the Learning Organization* (New York: Free Press, 1988).
[4]Ibid., 250–52.

5. Work is more interesting when people are challenged in performing it.
6. People take pride in training others.
7. Better performance occurs when artificial differences in how people are treated are removed.
8. Real responsibility motivates high performance.
9. People make better decisions and implement them better when they work together.

After examining this list, many of the changes made at Banyon make sense. Perhaps more by intuition than by understanding, Ben facilitated a culture change necessary for ongoing success.

Management by formal control was successful in the past. Since people use precedent in making decisions and take actions based on previous success, it is easy to understand why many managers fail to make the changes necessary to make JIT work. It also explains why many successful implementations take place when companies are under siege, or facing crises that makes change necessary. The alternative is paralysis, decline, and death.

SUCCESS: SETUPS, JIT, AND BALANCE

Early in the implementation process, Ben tried to reduce lot sizes in the molding department. The project failed because setup times had not been improved. Now that JIT was running, he was ready to tackle setups again. The area picked for improvement was the axial insertion process.

Reducing setup time increases the capacity of the machine, line, and plant. To reduce setup time, the setup process must be studied. External setup, activities that take place while the machine is running, are separate from internal setup, activities that take place while the machine is down. Adjustment, calibrating the machine to get good product, must be monitored. Internal setup interrupts process flow, and adjustment results in scrap. Therefore, internal setup and adjustment are the focus of improvement efforts.

Once again Banyon used a team, including machine operators, to improve the setup process. Steps taken were to move material necessary for the setup close to the machine, to do the external setup while the machine was running, and to use a more stable printed circuit board changeover process.

* * * * *

"Ben, do you have a minute?" Mike Gannon was at the door.

"Sure. What's up?"

"Well, I've been out at the axial insertion machine with Dick Williamson and Dan, the operator, trying to find a way to reduce downtime. We were wondering about something, and thought some input might help."

"I'll bet you already have a solution in mind. What is it?"

"It's quite simple, really. We're using a PCB fixture that has to be screwed into place and requires a lot of adjustment to get centered. What do you think of a fixture that can only go in one way and clamps down?"

"That makes sense. You want to use clamps? How are you going to make sure the fixture settles in? Do you have some way to get it seated?"

Mike thought for a few seconds, his face lit up, and out came the answer. "It's so simple! We can use guide pins to do the job for us. Once seated on the guide pins, the PCB fixture will be positioned correctly and no further adjustment will be necessary. And when the clamps are turned, the fixture will be locked in place. Dan will love not having to lift it. It's heavy!"

"It should work." Ben was pleased, but not surprised that Mike had the answer. He was long on common sense, the key element in the continuing success the plant was coming to enjoy. "Work it out with Dan and Dick, and see if it can be done. If it can, go ahead. I trust your judgment."

"Thanks! I hope it works because we need more output and reducing downtime is the only way to get it."

Mike left, and Ben went back to work. He was involved less and less in the changeover, and that was good. Unless the changes were accepted and the workers dedicated to the new process, the implementation would die down the road. There was enough proof around to show that the entrepreneur had to know when to let go. And much of what was happening at Banyon was entrepreneurship. It had begun with a push from Probe, and now it was taking on a life of its own. The implementation process was picking up speed.

The results were impressive; a setup requiring 38 minutes was reduced to 19. The setup time ultimately dropped below 15 minutes. (See Figure 9–1.) That meant that the number of setups could be doubled with no loss of output.

The axial insertion process at times caused the printed circuit board to flex, resulting in mis-insertions. Improvements resulted in less scrap, less costly setups, and more flexibility on the production line. As setup times declined further, the cost of changing from one product to another also declined. This allowed for variety with no additional cost.

Success was extraordinary in molding, scene of the first ill-fated setup reduction project. Here, each setup required

FIGURE 9–1
Setup Results

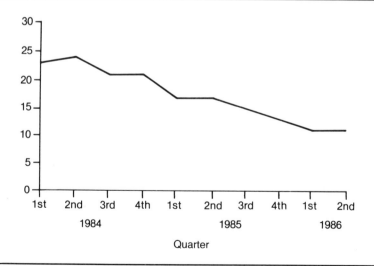

Source: Coopers & Lybrand.

from 45 to 75 minutes. This severely limited the capacity of the line and led to a proliferation of work-in-process inventory. Based on lessons learned in axial insertion, employees found three different ways to speed the process: (1) a fast-on/fast-off water hose disconnect; (2) preheating the die; and, (3) using a gravity feed mold slide without bolts in place of a mold with 18 bolts. It resulted in a dramatic reduction from 45 minutes to 35 seconds.

Expanding JIT to Other Lines

Success on the President's line added tremendous momentum to the JIT project. Time was ripe for implementation in other areas. While the team could be seeded from the first line, Ben knew he would have to give control to the people in the new cell if it was to be a success.

* * * * *

"I've asked all of you to meet with me to discuss changing the Probe counter line to a JIT cell. Each of you has an interest in this, therefore, your input is important. This is your line, you're in control of the process, and you know it best. I hope that we can find a way to use what we've learned in Presidents to speed the process. Who would like to start?"

Ben looked expectantly around the room. The team chosen had already gone through the training class, and given the success of the first efforts, he believed that the team would be ready. One factor he failed to consider was the power of a line supervisor to influence the workers' views.

Joe Woods, the area supervisor, responded. "Mr. Morgan, we've talked about this, and we don't understand why we need this new fangled JIT idea. We're getting orders out on time. Our quality is high, and overall, we think the line is fine just the way it is. Don't all of you agree?"

Ben looked at the other faces. Joe had an interesting way of gaining consensus. When he asked for agreement, it was an order. "Oh, oh. There's going to be a problem here." Ben kept his thoughts to himself, trying instead to break down the walls of resistance.

"Joe, your group does a good job. That's not the issue. You're getting work out, but at high cost. Everyone here works long, hard hours whenever a problem occurs. Julie and I had the same misconceptions when we started, and I think that you're succeeding in spite of yourselves. You're spending a lot of time and energy expediting and making sure orders ship." Ben paused. The atmosphere in the room was strained, and Joe's temper barely contained. Since he wasn't getting anywhere, Ben let Joe simmer for a while.

"I'd like you to think about how you could use the concepts from the training class to make the process in your area run a little better. To help you, I'd like you to take a half hour a day on company time to work on the implementation. We'll meet again in a week."

Joe's face was purple. He was upset by the implications of Ben's comments, and he wasn't about to let his people sit around for half an hour every day to talk. They needed to be pushing product out the door and meeting schedules. He didn't say a word, but if looks could kill, Ben would have died on the spot.

After the team left, Ben, Julie, Jim Andrews, and Mike Gannon got together. He briefed them on the meeting and asked for help.

"Sounds like a casualty, Ben," Julie said. "You know Joe's nickname, don't you? 'Little Hitler.' There's a big problem there, but no one will stand up to him; he's fired people for less."

"How long has he been here?" Ben asked.

Julie thought a moment. Ben watched her and detected an ever so slight movement of her fingers. He had to catch himself to keep from laughing. "Got an answer yet? Or do you need to take off your shoes?"

"What? Yes, I do, and I need a few of your toes! If I count right, Joe's been here for 25 years or so. He must be doing something right."

Mike spoke up. "I know he has a bad reputation with the workers, but he's really loyal to Banyon. And he's no spring chicken anymore. He's given the company his best years, and I for one would hate to see him turned out."

"I agree. We owe it to Joe to bring him around. We'll

have to transform him from pit boss to cheerleader. But don't tell him I said that!" Even though the meeting had gone poorly, Ben was in fine spirits.

Meeting over, Julie waited to talk to Ben. Things were going so well that they were back to regular hours; they hadn't worked late for weeks. "Ben, do you think we should work on this together? We could save a lot of grief with a good action plan. I'm free tonight, if you are."

"Do we need to? Well, I'd rather do it over dinner than in the office. I'm tired of these four walls. Make reservations, and we'll leave at six. OK?" Ben turned back to his desk and missed the skip in Julie's step.

Success: It's Even Better with Effort

Julie might have been ready to celebrate, but there would be a long wait before Joe would be brought around. Nine frustrating months passed, and many times Ben came close to firing him only to talk himself out of it. Joe learned his bad supervisory habits at Banyon. He had never worked anywhere else, and Ben kept Joe even though his entire staff asked for his head.

In the end, Joe went along with the JIT project and became one of the plant's best supervisors. No one had ever taught him the difference between demanding consensus and asking for it. He had a need to be in control, and letting the team take charge threatened his view of himself and made him uncomfortable with his job and his place at Banyon. As he let go of the reins, he began to see results. Other members of the team began to work with him, not against him. It was no longer "him versus us"; it was simply "us."

THE DANGERS OF JIT: MANAGEMENT BY STRESS

The JIT implementation continued to spread to other areas and products. One year after the start-up of the President's line, the project began to unravel. Not because JIT didn't work, but because it worked so well. Everyone could see the massive improvements in productivity and quality, and the workers wanted a share of the increased profits coming from productivity gains.

*****

Brenda waited for Ben to finish his call. He had waved her in just moments before, not wanting to leave her standing at the door. She looked around, her eyes stopping now and then to examine a productivity chart or profit projection on the office wall. Making mental notes, she listened to Ben's closing remarks.

"Right, Mr. Randolph. If you'll look at our real performance and not the standard reports, you'll see that we're doing better than ever. Our productivity is at an all time high even though the labor efficiencies don't capture it. We're getting more product out with less rework and scrap. Could you come down so we could talk this through. Then I could show you around? Next Monday? Great!"

Ben hung up and took a deep breath before turning to Brenda. It had not been a pleasant phone call, and Ben had a feeling something else was about to go sour. "Sorry about the delay, Brenda. What can I do for you?"

"Oh, nothing today, but I'd like to talk to you for my group about our incentives. We've been working on our average pay for almost a year now. Outside of merit and cost of living increases, we've seen little extra take home pay for the extra work we're doing. So, we'd like to talk to you about returning to the incentives at a low enough rate to guarantee bonuses if we keep up the current pace."

Ben couldn't believe his ears. Not two hours earlier he had told Julie the individual incentive system would likely die of natural causes. He had no intention of returning to it; it would destroy everything that had been accomplished. And there weren't any extra dollars to give. Every penny from productivity and quality gains was needed to reduce prices, improve profitability, and accelerate the JIT implementation. Corporate wasn't willing to fund the project; they kept increasing profit goals.

"Brenda, are you saying what I think you're saying?

You? I thought you believed in JIT. How are we going to keep the process under control and output at a uniform level if people are paid by the piece?" Ben paused, waiting for an answer.

"Mr. Morgan, it's simple. We're producing more and we deserve more. We work for the money. Sure I support JIT, but I also support my family. I think it's something we have to think about, that's all."

"Brenda, if I could give it to you, I would. But I don't have it. What we've made by reducing costs has gone into more training. I value the efforts of you and your people. I'll think of something. Can I have a little time?"

"Sure, Mr. Morgan. We're not going to cause trouble, we just want to be rewarded for the extra effort. Is it all right if I stop back next week some time?" It was a question, but Ben couldn't say no without some downstream problems, and he knew it.

"Ah, sure. Next week. Say Thursday afternoon? That will give me a deadline."

"Fine. See you Thursday." Brenda left. As Ben settled back into his chair, Drew Pearce, Vice President of Personnel appeared.

"Got a minute, Ben?" Drew was in the office in a flash. Ben could tell by the tone of his voice he had something to say.

"Sure, why not? It's been that kind of afternoon. What can I do for you?" Ben didn't want to know, but that wasn't an option.

"I just talked to Corporate. Human Resources studied the pensions and benefits that companies in the area offer. It wasn't good news. We're behind on key benefits. Anyway, I'd like to improve the pension plan especially if we're going to do away with the incentives as we implement JIT/TQC. That may help employees to accept the changes and prove to them we know the cost of living is going up. It's critical that we do something about the benefits package if we're going to stay competitive in the labor market." Drew paused, waiting for a response. Ben was quick to accommodate him. Did everyone think money grew on trees?

"You're making good points, Drew. For the long-term survival of the plant we have to devise a plan that gears pay increases to productivity. Maybe not the old way because we know it causes waste in the process, but I can't give across the board increases either. We're below profit projections, and unless we come up with a miracle, I'm out of funds. Can't share what I don't have."

"Sorry, Ben, we don't have a choice. It's not a request, it's an order from headquarters. They don't want a union movement here, and poor pensions unify workers. We have to find the money." Drew's expression gave Ben no hint of his position. As human resource coordinator, his job was to keep everyone happy. Right now, everyone was unhappy. Drew was right; something had to be done.

"Drew, I'd like to find a way around these issues. Corporate isn't going to force a system on us. Let me tell you what I've been thinking. There's a kind of equality in JIT, everyone is treated the same regardless of rank."

Ben took a breath and continued. "What if we give people in the factory the same benefits as the staff? Sick days, for one. Let's do away with perks, take away reserved parking spaces and the rest. It would even things up, let the workers know we're behind them, and give us the time we need to develop a good incentive system. I don't want to make a mistake now; we've worked too hard to get where we are."

Drew didn't respond right away. Ben was looking for some indication of his feeling on the issues, but "Stonewall Pearce" was not cooperating.

"Let's see if I understand, Ben. You want to even things out by taking privileges away from middle management and office staff. They keep their sick days, but now everyone gets them, even guys on the loading dock. It's a novel approach. But I think the problems it solves on one end will cause problems on the other. It may work for now. The real issue remains, though. How do you propose to respond to the pay and benefits shortfalls?"

"Through compromise and discussion with the people in the plant, the same way we've done everything else in the past two years. I'm hazy on details, but I'm working on them.

I know there's an answer, and together we'll find it. I'll need everyone's help, especially yours, Drew. Can I count on your support?"

"Of course. I'll make a few calls, and get back to you. Thanks for the time to talk this through, Ben, I appreciate it." Drew was up and out the door before Ben could say a word. That made Ben uneasy, but he had to trust his people.

Hidden Dangers

The basic features of JIT make it a tempting solution to the problems facing American manufacturers. When implemented with the people, it can be successful. Before moving on to the next stage of Ben's story, it is important to pause and recap the key issues facing Banyon and its JIT implementation, and in changing its culture to match JIT.

JIT requires the participation of each member of the organization; each must be free to make suggestions and have confidence that management will listen. Based on trust, the group improves the process, cutting slack from their jobs and providing detailed information about how they do their work.

The downside of JIT is surfacing at the Nummi plant in California. When at its optimum, JIT is a *stressed system*. The goal is to run the line at capacity within the constraints of the process. Each step in the assembly is synchronized, timed to the second, to eliminate the cause for pause: it is the joint efficiency of man and machine.

It's successful unless the man or machine has an off day. JIT makes the process visible. Every worker and every step in the manufacturing sequence can be observed. In theory, this suggests that workers can signal for help when they need it, and the necessary resources will rush to their aid.

If only human nature were not at issue. "Us versus Them" pervades American manufacturing. At Banyon these walls were breaking down. But at Nummi, the climate is not so pleasant. Workers who shut down the line are considered to be problems. The stress this causes can be readily imagined. Think of not being allowed a down day because your problems now affect the entire company, not just your own job.

There is no reason why this has to be the case, but it can happen. JIT's true fate lies in the hearts of the managers who implement it, in trusting the work force, and in believing in each person's rights. The team is an extension of its members. If the members are treated properly, the output of the team will exceed that of individuals. If treated poorly, disaster can lie ahead. Oppressive managements breed revolt. In the end, as with all organizations, the answer lies in the people who use the tool, not the tool itself.

Crisis in the Management Ranks

In addition, JIT breaks down barriers between manager and worker. Ben contemplated the elimination of the perquisites of white-collar workers. They were, in fact, eliminated. The changes went beyond a redistribution of benefits. Office jobs, once seen as plums, were attacked. Ben needed teams to work together.

As development of the cells progressed, Ben realized he needed staff people closer to the plant. To accomplish this, he assigned an industrial engineer and a cost accountant to each cell. Other support personnel, not tied to a specific cell, were moved into the plant to improve communication.

These events were not greeted with enthusiasm. Several good people quit because they couldn't accept the loss of their offices and privileges. They weren't forced out, but Ben didn't try to stop them. JIT/TQC is built on participation, equality, and trust; everyone plays an equal role in the company's success. If management gives only lip service to this philosophy, then JIT can lead to even greater problems downstream. It is an effective, but fragile organizational structure.

BANYON'S JIT IMPLEMENTATION: A SUMMARY

Before moving to the final hurdle in the implementation, the development of an acceptable incentive system, it may help to recap the story to this point.

Banyon, having received 11 annual awards for manufacturing excellence, began to implement JIT/TQC after getting ultimatums from its major customers to improve quality. Quick to respond, Ben and Julie embraced JIT/TQC as the only acceptable solution. Decision made, problems began. Because they viewed JIT/TQC as a technical system rather than as a management philosophy, they met with failure. Only when they listened to workers and used their talents, did the situation begin to turn around.

The first success was in wave-solder. With Carolyn's help defects were reduced and problems solved at their source. But it took two years to get this far. Ben's plans allowed nine months for the entire implementation. After grasping the true nature of JIT, the implementation picked up speed.

The first cell was fully operational in under nine months. Subsequent efforts took less time. A learning curve was involved, but not in the usual sense. Ben had to learn first. With the help of his staff and input from Ron Eddy, he began to realize that JIT/TQC was management, not a technical process. The key element in the implementation was employee acceptance, garnered through awareness, education, and involvement.

The plantwide JIT kickoff took place in January 1984. The first cell was created in February, the second in April, the third in June, and the fourth and fifth later in the year. Each cell was based on a separate product family; for example, the second cell made electronic controllers such as the Probe key counter. Occasionally failures occurred, but they no longer created intense anxiety. Answers were available, if the right people were asked.

In the end Ben and Julie's formal plan didn't resemble the ultimate implementation. They planned, but until they embraced the underlying philosophy of JIT management, their efforts would not be long lasting.

* * * * *

"Ben, Mike and I are here to take back the green eyeshade we gave you when you started. After analyzing your performance, you no longer qualify as a bean counter. We know this is a shock, but there's no alternative. Hand it over." Speech delivered, Julie began to laugh. It was infectious, and all joined in.

"Is this a promotion or a demotion? And what am I now? Before I give up my security, I'd like to know what I'm getting." Grinning from ear to ear, Ben picked up the eyeshade. He kept it on his desk, at first as a gesture of humanity, later because of it.

"We've elected you the 'Leader of the Pack.' Vroom! Vroom! Here's your helmet. You know how hard it is to find old leather helmets?"

Mike spoke up. "After you set up the roundtable, a few of us wanted to get you a sword, but Julie vetoed it. She said this would be better protection in staff meetings." Jim made a late entrance.

"You're in on this, too? I thought you were balanced. All of you belong at that bar in Chicago where they sing oldies, 'Lawrence of Oregano's.' You'd fit right in!" Ben was happier than he'd been in a long time. The award meant a lot to him, especially now. It had been hard on everyone to give up their "perks," but they had done it, and without making Ben resort to authority. He listened to them, and they listened to him. Banyon had come a long way in the two-and-a-half years since Ben had become plant manager. He hoped they would never return to old habits.

"Ben, we have one more gift for you, a pair of steel-toed sneakers. When you're on your morning plant walk, you can stride in comfort and safety. Is hot pink your favorite color?" Jim pulled the shoes from behind his back, hot pink with chartreuse laces! Ben didn't think shoes were made that ugly. Someone in the shop had made steel casings and attached them to the soles.

"How did you know, Jim? This is my favorite color. I'm going to put them on right now." Ben changed shoes, then leaped to his feet. "I'm ready for anything. Thanks, guys. Now I'm taking my favorite cohorts out for beer." With that, he took the helmet from Jim, put it on, and grabbed Mike and Julie by the arm on his way out the door. "Jim, shut off the lights and follow your new leader. 'My folks were always putting him down, down, down. . . .'"

INTERMISSION

Ben had described the basic characteristics of JIT, answering questions as he went along. Julie wanted to interrupt a few times for the sake of accuracy, but thought better of it. "Much of the truth really doesn't matter; we had some difficult times, especially when the incentive issue reared its head. I think that's when Ben began to think about leaving. That, and the high-handed way that Corporate dealt with him. But, we're not here to bare souls or share intimate secrets." Julie returned her attention to Ben.

* * * * *

"Through JIT seminars we learned to identify value adding activities. An example is the insertion of a component into a circuit board. If I make a kit of parts prior to insertion, that's not value adding. Neither is inspection, nor excess handling. We were shocked to learn that 50 percent of our routings were not value adding. Think about that. Industrial engineers established rates, and accountants had to cost these nonvalue-adding operations, all for the sake of control and precision. We got precision to the second decimal point, but it was useless because we were using general allocations in accounting. We knew what the costs were, but we didn't know what they could be or should be, or what caused them. As we got farther along in the implementation, the accounting system became a real problem. Why? Because the workers wanted a bonus for improvements, but there was no way to connect the plant's profit & loss (P&L) to daily cell operations."

"We then looked at the problem on a macro basis. Henry Ford did repetitive manufacturing. Our problem was that we were more of a job shop, and we weren't sure if we could use repetitive manufacturing concepts. We found out we could because the employees showed us how. We set up a cell using four operators and a small support group. We then asked the operators to design the work flow for that cell. Not only did they do it, they did it well."

"Being practical people, the employees used inexpensive material handling equipment: plain wooden boxes. Only four circuit board assemblies fit in that box. An industrial engineer, a supervisor, even a controller can now see the queue and where quality problems are because they're visible. Moreover, it's impossible to generate scrap of 250, 500, or a 1,000 parts, which we used to do. Now, only four parts can be generated before scrap is detected."

"Here are the results. Scrap and rework were reduced 75 percent. By cross training, by getting everyone involved in the work close to the cell, and by eliminating work-in-process inventory, quality problems can't be hidden. Four defective units is the maximum. Customer response improved 28 percent because lead time was reduced; the product flowed like water through pipe. Floor space was reduced 50 percent. After we refined the process further, it was reduced 75 percent. Best of all, inventory went down 66 percent, and it didn't take long. Inventory on the President's line dropped from $200,000 to $20,000 in six months. The reason it took so long is that we had to shut off the flow of incoming inventory."

* * * * *

Once again Julie drifted back to earlier days. There had been good times and bad. The night they gave Ben his helmet had been the best! They didn't stop laughing all night, nor for days after. And Ben wore the silly shoes till the end. She was sure they were packed in his suitcase right now.

"When we asked Susan to leave her office in engineering to work in the second JIT cell, well, that was one of the worst times. It caused a lot of bad feelings in engineering. She was well liked, but a rule is a rule. Ben had more trouble with the staff than he had with people in the plant."

The biggest problem, though, was the incentive plan. It took forever to reach agreement, and then everyone sat with their fingers crossed while the results were tallied. Even though it was the last formal step of the implementation, there was no doubt about its importance. Ben had convinced her that you "get what you measure." If the old system had been left in place, old behaviors would have returned.

* * * * *

Laughter brought Julie back to reality. "Darn, I missed a joke! Even if I've heard them before, I always like Ben's jokes. Pay attention, Julie!"

The crowd quieted, and Ben continued.

"Now we were ready to do setup reduction, the next logical step in reducing lot sizes. I started with the axial insertion machine because I had an appropriation request for another. Setup time was 38 minutes; we were able to reduce it 50 percent in one week without any tooling changes."

"The first step was to put material closer to the machine. We stored resistors, transistors, and capacitors in the stockroom at the other end of the plant. Why? For control. Even though resistors cost a nickel, we kept them in the stockroom. When we asked the Controller, he said there was no reason why they couldn't be next to the machine. That saved time because we organized them to match process flows."

"Then we went to molding. We had old machines with setup times of two, three, and four hours. It was time-studied, costed, and placed on a routing. The operators were on bonus because they were beating the engineered rate. Reducing the setup time would have reduced their bonus; we had an impasse. They were, in effect, in business for themselves because of the individual incentive system. Their goal was to maximize take-home pay, not tighten setup standards."

* * * * *

Julie walked into Ben's office arm in arm with Mike Gannon. Ben raised an eyebrow, "Now what happened?"

"Au contraire, monsieur. We've been following the Probe

audit team. Carolyn blew their socks off!" Julie was beaming as if Carolyn were her child.

"Tell me before that grin cracks your face!" Ben waited and waited. Julie was teasing him and succeeding.

Mike spoke. He sat down across from Ben and assumed a too casual posture. "They wanted to know how deep our change process had gone, you know, were we just putting on a show to stay out of trouble. So, they walked up to Carolyn, casually, and started a conversation."

"And?"

"And she surprised me. Their first question was simple. 'What do you do?' Carolyn answered, 'I manage the process.' That took them aback. So then the big guy says, 'Describe it,' trying to catch her. Well, Carolyn spent 50 minutes going through her job routine, starting with prepping the machine and board test, through the SPC charts, and on. Then she dragged them to the PC, and showed them the reports she keeps. After that they just nodded their heads. They really thought they'd find problems somewhere."

"Then they left, right?" Ben was relieved they had passed the audit, but it seemed they still had something to tell him. "We passed, right?"

"Not so fast, Ben." Julie said. "They thought maybe Carolyn was a plant, so they say, 'Let's see the molding operation you've bragged about.' In we go."

Mike broke in, uncharacteristically. "These two go to Andy and say, 'Your manager tells us you can set up this machine in less than 30 seconds.' Andy says he can. Then without waiting for them to react, he shuts down the machine and grabs the die for the next job. Down the slide it goes. Pop, pop. He's done. In 27 seconds. I know he was showing off, but even I was impressed. Anyway, then we passed. They simply shook their heads, signed the forms, gave us a copy, and left."

It was great news. After the mishaps with the incentive system, Ben was convinced that life was taking a turn for the worse. Maybe it would all turn out okay. They were now a preferred vendor for Probe. It was an honor; one they'd worked hard to achieve. It was a sign that a battle had been won at least for now.

"Now I know why you looked like Cheshire cats when you came in. That's the best news yet; you've made it happen, not me. I'm proud of everyone in the plant. We've actually met the Probe challenge, but can we keep it this way?" Ben was relieved, but he knew it was too early to consider the war won. A battle was behind them, but there were more ahead.

CHAPTER 10

PUSHING INDIVIDUAL INCENTIVES OUT THE DOOR

Banyon became a preferred vendor for Probe and GRI. JIT/TQC was now well beyond initial implementation. Instead of putting cells in place, Ben now proceeded to restructure the organization to match the new technology. Unless the incentive system used to motivate employees and the performance measures used to evaluate that performance were changed, the gains would be short-lived.

The major challenge was responding to Brenda's request for fairness, sharing the gains arising from the redesign of the manufacturing process. The plant was located in Wisconsin and its work force descended from Germanic and Scandinavian immigrants. Traditionally, they emphasized equity, not individual wealth. In their minds every person in the plant had a right to share in proportion to their efforts and abilities, and this belief became the basis of the incentive system Banyon developed. It was tailored to the work force, its expectations, and ultimately, the environment in which it all took place.

The existing incentive system set everyone up in business for himself. This ran counter to the teamwork and interdependence of JIT and prevented company goals from being embraced by employees. The old system had to go and a new one developed to protect the improvements made and lay the groundwork for future success. Change was the critical element in moving from the old system to the new; participation and compromise would forge an agreement that everyone would support.

The design of an incentive system, more than any other aspect of JIT/TQC, is unique to each company and plant. Organizations are not the same. They serve different markets and consist of different people from different backgrounds with different goals. The solution to Banyon's problems was to address business needs through employee involvement.

* * * * *

"Julie, when I think back to Schoner's remark about putting JIT into a plant with an individual incentive system, I get worried. 'With great difficulty.' That was helpful. Have you dug up anything?"

"I think so. There's something here about a seminar on incentive plans. Where did it go? Here it is!" Julie smiled, handing a crumpled paper to Ben. Julie's desk was not getting neater. It was a barometer of their progress; piles of paper rose as the implementation progressed. How high could they get?

"This looks like it's been through a blender, Julie. I understand why Mike wanted housecleaning to visit your office. What's buried in these stacks? Never mind, I don't want to know." Ben smiled, although the message was clear. Julie was not setting a good example. "Back to business. This looks good. Has Drew seen it? It's a seminar he should attend."

"I agree. He sent it to me. He said it was being offered by the Human Resources Association of Greater Milwaukee. Since we don't know enough about incentive systems, this may be a good way to find out." Julie's desk might be a fright, but as long as she remained informed, Ben couldn't fault her.

"I agree. Make reservations for you, Drew, and me. It's next week. OK?"

In a few moments Julie had confirmed places at the seminar and at the hotel. Things were looking up. "A potpourri of incentive systems is just what we need. I don't know what we're up against, but if we don't get the full support and understanding of everyone in the plant, we'll fall flat on our faces. I hope the seminar lives up to its promotional material; we need alternatives, not euphemisms."

The Shortcomings of Individual Incentives

The problems in the plant were flat productivity, employee rate problems that defied solution, and with the exception of the JIT cell, poor attitudes toward management. Since JIT/TQC requires participation, teamwork, and flexibility, as well as delegation of decision making to line operators, these problems could not be ignored. And Ben felt most of the problems were due to the individual incentive system.

The effectiveness of an incentive system is determined by the responsibility employees take for the work they perform. Figure 10–1 suggests that traditional incentive systems discourage employees from accepting responsibility. It indicates the nature of these forces and the merits of various incentive schemes.

There are three critical dimensions to consider when redesigning an incentive system within JIT:

1. Pay must be linked to productivity.
2. It must be fair to everyone.
3. The system must encourage behavior that supports teamwork and continuous improvement.

Productivity is, simply, a ratio of output to input. The goal is to get more output using the same input, or the same output with less input. Linking pay to gains in productivity aligns the system with continuous improvement.

Trust and equity are critical features because teamwork is necessary. The goal is to achieve total participation. Each individual's opinion, value, and contribution is important. If this rule is violated, the system becomes a political tool for anointing the chosen, and sets up a caste system that discourages others from joining the effort.

At each stage the impact of the incentive needs to be considered. No other formal control has such an effect on individual and organizational performance. Blending incentives that reward teamwork with those encouraging individ-

FIGURE 10-1
Incentive Systems

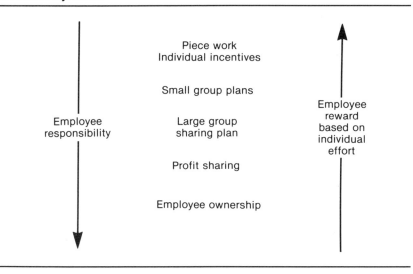

Source: Coopers & Lybrand.

ual excellence is a challenging task. Quite challenging as Ben was to learn.

* * * * *

Ben, Julie, and Drew arrived at the hotel at 8:30 P.M. on the evening before the seminar. They used the evening to discuss the objectives of the trip and unwind. Brenda's request weighed heavily on his mind. The lounge was sparsely inhabited, and they took a table at the back.

They talked quietly, pausing every now and then to listen to a song, or to watch those entering and leaving the bar. They talked about upcoming vacation plans, families, and recent events in the plant. Before long they turned to more serious matters. Impending changes to the incentive system loomed large as the three did battle with implementation nightmares, real and imagined.

The objectives were straightforward, but there was concern about setting precedent, dealing with corporate, and melding the new system with existing benefits. Drew was concerned about the ramifications of the changeover, constantly returning to the fact that the old system was working. At first Ben tried to point out the reasons it wouldn't work in the future, but gave up. Drew was going to have to see the light for himself.

Drew, somewhat annoyed by some of Ben's comments, turned in first. Ben and Julie talked for another hour. At this stage few words had to be said about the problem with Drew. A lifted eyebrow or a shrug of a shoulder conveyed the message.

They agreed they were here to get information; decisions and details would be worked out at Banyon with the workers' participation. It was comforting to know that they were on the same track. Together they could help Drew see that the final answer wasn't as important as the path that led to it.

Ben walked Julie to her room and went on to his own lost in thought. He had spent much of the evening discussing and rethinking the problem, wondering where it would all lead.

Solutions Abound . . . Which One to Choose?

The next morning came all too quickly. The three met at breakfast. While Julie and Ben seemed a bit worse for wear, Drew was all enthusiasm. After checking out, they headed for the seminar.

Three companies made presentations: Warner Electric, Mercury Marine, and Avco. Each had implemented a different form of gainsharing. Warner Electric had put in a profit sharing plan with several unique features, such as lifetime employment guarantees to 50 percent of the work force. The plan focused on sharing the profits of the plant.

Ben paid attention, but soon discounted this plan because Banyon already had a corporate profit-sharing plan. Corporate was not going to let the plant break away from it, and setting up a plant-based system that integrated with the corporate plan was impossible. As well, Ben was sure the presentation left a lot unstated, for example, how the company dealt with volume and mix changes that affected take home pay, factors they couldn't control.

Next was Mercury Marine. Their plan was "Improshare," which shared productivity gains with employees. Under careful scrutiny, the plan turned out to be a confused jumble. When questioned, the company representative revealed that two sets of standards were used, one for the incentive plan and another for setting prices and evaluating overall plant performance. Employees only shared in improvements for which they were responsible. If productivity gains came from the installation of new equipment rather than from improved work procedures, the employees did not share the gains.

Ben was concerned about using two sets of standards; it would violate the trust necessary for JIT/TQC to take hold. Employees would have little incentive to install new equipment if they wouldn't benefit from the improvements. Julie pointed out that something just wasn't right, because after a 3 to 15 percent improvement across the board the first year, the line flattened out. It seemed that the plan led to a one time productivity gain, rather than to continuous improvement.

Avco presented their plan. Ben and Julie were now concerned that they might have wasted their time coming to the seminar. Drew was engrossed, taking copious notes and enjoying the presentations. Ben hoped that he was doing more than writing; success at Banyon would require mutual agreement and adjustment. So far none of the plans fit the bill.

Avco used the Scanlon plan, sharing labor cost savings with employees. While it sounded good, the presentation broke down under questioning. Company representatives got defensive as Julie asked the same question repeatedly. She wanted to know why the plan was inconsistent, paying out bonuses one year and not the next. She kept asking, they kept side-stepping. While the plan itself looked good, Ben and Julie agreed that Avco was not a good plan to use as a model for Banyon's.

TABLE 10-1
Comparison of Incentive Systems

Incentive System	Administrative Cost	Time Frame	Performance Factors	Output Measured
Individual	High	Daily/weekly	Labor only	Individual earned hours
Improshare	High	Weekly/biweekly	Total labor hours	Total standard hours earned
Scanlon	Low	Monthly	Payroll cost	Net sales ± inventory adjustment
Rucker	Low	Monthly	Payroll cost	Value added
Scanlon multicost	Low	Monthly	All costs	Net sales ± inventory adjustment
Profit sharing	Low	Months/year	Profit before tax	Net sales

Source: Coopers & Lybrand.

The most useful outcome of the seminar was a chart comparing the various plans, their administrative costs, time frames, performance factors, and output measures, (Table 10–1). It gave them a method by which to examine the characteristics of each plan. Ben also left the seminar with a happy human resource manager.

Exploring the Scanlon Plan

Julie found a plant near Milwaukee that used the Scanlon plan and set up a visit for the following week. Ben wanted to talk to its managers about their experiences, both good and bad. He gained insight into Avco's inconsistent payouts during the visit; it was greed. With the Scanlon plan in place, Avco's management began to see huge gains in productivity. Instead of consistently and fairly sharing the gains, they changed the formula for the bonus every year. Thresholds were constantly raised, making it increasingly difficult for individuals to earn an incentive bonus. It was a strange form of participation.

This plan, though, had its own set of problems. While it was working well, there were some problems. First, the plant had a union. This radically changed its complexion. Second, Ben felt the plan had too much structure; rules, regulations and bureaucracy abounded.

Small group improvement teams reported through a chain of command to a steering committee that met once a month to review suggestions. No time limit was set on the review, and if a suggestion were rejected, an elaborate appeal process could be invoked. Its structure was needed to deal with a union. It was not the system for Banyon. Ben and Julie left more knowledgeable, but less encouraged. The Scanlon plan looked like the best candidate, but it might not work. They needed a plan that fit not only the demands of JIT/TQC, but also the requirements of Banyon's plant and corporate parent.

Setting the Stage for Change

Ben knew that something had to be done; they had to get rid of the individual incentive system. The only question was how? He wanted some form of gainsharing because he knew, instinctively, that it would be the key to maintaining continuous improvement.

After considerable reflection, Ben decided to use the company mid-year meeting to set the stage for the change. Banyon held such meetings once a year before the annual review process. The purpose was to present the company's progress toward its goals, as well as other important items, such as changes in benefits, pension contributions, and prospects for raises. Also, physical inventory and plant shutdown schedules were announced, followed by a question and answer session.

This year Ben had other plans for the meeting. Once introductions were completed, he talked about Banyon's global competition and his long-term plans to continue implementing JIT/TQC throughout the plant. After a few comments on the progress of the JIT implementation, he turned to a chart detailing the major problems caused by the current incentive system:

- It encouraged workers to resist new machines and methods.
- The system ignored support personnel, paying incentive bonuses to direct labor only.
- Maintaining accurate standards to support the system was costly.
- Management upgrades of the standards ended up restricting output.
- The system was less and less applicable in the face of continued automation of the plant.
- Old rates tended to be too loose, while new ones tended to be too tight.
- The system, in general, conflicted with the objectives of the JIT/TQC system.

Ben went through the list point by point. Again and again he emphasized how the current system hurt the JIT/TQC efforts. Operators were more concerned with the quantity of their output than with its quality, and more interested in their own pocketbooks than in teamwork. There was no time for suggestions, for SPC charts, or for improvement.

* * * * *

"The best way to change from individual incentives to team incentives is to work together." Ben neared the end of his presentation and worked on gaining consensus through participation. "If I have Julie, or Drew, or any of my staff put this plan together, it will not be your plan, it will be management's. We want to show our trust by working with you to solve this problem."

"I'm going to take the first step because we need a push to get started on something as important as changing pay structure. I'm going to do away with the individual incentive system over the next month. In its place you will be paid the average of your weekly earnings for the last six months; whatever pay you got, you'll continue to get. And, we'll stop filling out detailed time cards for accounting; simply report your total hours by cell or work center. I trust you to get to work every morning and to work a full day. We'll solve the incentive problem and find a solution together."

After answering the remaining questions, Ben and Julie returned to their offices. Mike Gannon, Jim, and Drew tagged along, with Dick Williamson not far behind. Although he hadn't planned it, Ben found himself in a staff meeting. Employee questions had generated doubts among the staff despite staff consensus to drop individual incentives.

"Ben, I heard what you said. Engineering is behind you all the way. But what does it mean to us? Are we going to fall under the umbrella of the group incentive plan? And what about labor standards? Are we supposed to stop monitoring them, too?"

Dick was sitting on one side of Julie; Mike and Drew sat on the other. The beauty and the beasts! Ben thought, then responded. "I don't know what's going to happen, Dick. Not in detail. I know individual incentives are out. I need teamwork, not entrepreneurs on the plant floor. As for the labor standards, I only meant we were dropping payroll reporting. Nothing else."

"I'm glad to hear that. We can hardly keep the standards up to date for the new JIT cell, and since we're still learning, I'd hate to drop the effort. I'm happy for now." With that, Dick conceded the floor to Drew.

"Ben, are we throwing out the baby with the bath water? How can we stop monitoring the employees? Trust? Give me a break. I've worked in factories a long time. Discipline and control are the name of the game, letting everyone know that you know what they're doing." Drew paused, waiting for a response.

While Drew's comments caught Ben off guard, Julie was quick to respond. "Drew, what are you talking about? We're not here to beat peasants into submission. I've seen what trust can do, and so have you. I agree with Ben."

There was fire in Julie's eyes, and Drew turned red. It was trouble. Ben knew an explosive situation when he saw one, and if it weren't defused quickly, the problem would fester and the plant could be hurt.

"Both of you are making valid points. Julie is a JIT/TQC convert, and you're not, Drew. It's not a surprise to find you on opposite sides. But I need a compromise, and I think it has to start here." There was no mistaking Ben's intent. He settled into his chair, ready to spend all day discussing the incentive issue if necessary. The message got through; no one made a move to leave.

"Ben, we have to keep some sort of cap on behavior. Even if 98 percent of the employees can be trusted, the 2 percent that can't have to be dealt with. I'm not proposing that we stay with the status quo, but whatever solution we pick has to leave us with a way to discipline employees when it's needed." Drew sat back, not looking at Julie.

"That seems logical, Drew. What do you think, Julie?" Ben wasn't going to let either of them off the hook.

"I think Drew is wrong. I can't look Brenda in the eye and say, 'I trust you, but if you mess up, here's the punishment.' Can you?" Julie acted like a bulldog. Ben had to redirect her.

Jim broke in, saving the day. "Drew, can you think of a way to keep tabs on a few bad apples without a full reporting system? A way that everyone will support? I'd resent it if I knew someone was slacking off and was getting away with it, and I don't think the workers would see that as fair." Jim was right, of course. It wasn't an issue of trust or control, but rather a recognition that some people would take advantage of the system. If they got away with it, real damage could be done to everyone's morale.

"Maybe we could develop an exception reporting system. A 'NAB 1' program that supervisors would enforce. They know when there's a problem, and they can tell us without damaging the team's trust in each other. If the supervisor says someone is slacking, he can request a counseling session. Three complaints and a slacker is out." Drew had a workable solution. Now Ben had to make sure everyone would accept it.

"That may work, Drew. I like the fact that discipline comes from the team, not management or staff. What do you think, Julie? Can you live with that?" Ben waited for an answer in a silence so overwhelming that the walls themselves seemed to hold their breath.

Julie wrinkled her brow, scratched her nose, and sighed. It was obvious she was fighting some internal battle. Everyone waited for the outcome.

"I'm willing to try it, although I'm not satisfied that we won't create more problems than we'll solve. What if the problem is the supervisor? We're giving them a lot of power and that troubles me. Will they wield it fairly? I'm caught in a personal dilemma. Until I have an answer, I'll go along with the group." Julie was not convinced, but she didn't have another solution.

Ben asked for further comments. Tension eased as everyone agreed to try Drew's idea. It was a good decision, as the future would tell. Over the next two years, only seven people were disciplined, and two dismissed. Another crisis had been averted through honest communication and compromise.

AN EMERGING INCENTIVE PLAN

"Each of us is beginning to understand that we perform both value-adding and nonvalue-adding activities in the plant. And we know that JIT tells us to eliminate the nonvalue-adding, the cause for pause. But we continue to have problems with standards. I'd toss them out now, but John Rust would have my hide. Do you have any suggestions?" Ben looked around the room. Most of his managers were present; accounting, engineering, and quality control. As he moved toward the new incentive system, Ben held a lot of meetings to keep the channels of communication open.

"We need some standards if we're going to cost product and report gross margins to Corporate, Ben. I know it's a pain right now, but I guess I'd insist that engineering spend more time working out standards on the new line." John Rust looked not at Ben, but at Dick. The tension between them was barely hidden.

"You seem to think we have a lot more engineers than

we do," Dick said. "I think, John, and I've said this before, that you should be using the actual costs for that cell. We have no idea what the standards should be. All we know is that they're making improvements in productivity that we'd never dare put in the standard. Won't that work?"

"A historical standard? That's not a solution. How do we support the variance analysis process? How am I supposed to explain to Corporate and the auditors that we're using different measures to evaluate the cell?" John turned to Ben, continuing his argument. "Ben, you know how important it is to have good information. What are you going to do?"

"*We're* going to support Dick for now. He and his people will work on standards when they can. What's important now is momentum; we need to keep getting better. As long as we do that, we shouldn't have to worry about the standard." Ben could see this wasn't sitting well with John, but it was the truth. "I've changed a lot since my accounting days, John, but that doesn't mean I've forgotten the basics. What I hope is that as we move forward you and I can reach some common ground. Until then, let's try running the plant by results rather than by numbers."

"But we still need the numbers, Ben. I have to send detailed reports back to Corporate, and we'll get a phone call every month demanding an explanation for the variances we report. I know where we're heading, but there's only so much I can do." John was not going to let this topic rest.

"My only other solution right now, John, is to ask you to assign some of your people directly to the cells. Let's give them the authority to develop new standards for the accounting system. It will do them good to gain a better understanding of the process, and if the workers get to know them, maybe we can improve communication in the bargain. What are your feelings, John?"

John had been boxed in. Ben didn't like to take such an active part in the decision process anymore, but there were simply times when it was necessary. Everyone responded to authority and command, especially when backed by logic. Not every decision could be participatory, especially if the parties were unwilling or unable to compromise. "I'm still the referee. But, I have to step in less and less, so there's progress." Ben's thoughts were interrupted by John's discomfort.

"You want to put my people in the factory? Tell you what, Ben, you come and deliver that news." John paused, waiting.

"John, all departments have to work together. We can't let tradition hold us back. You've convinced me we need the standards updated, and Dick's people are stretched thin already. It's a compromise, John, and I'm counting on you to support it." Ben's tone ended the conversation. He didn't want to dictate, but rather to facilitate change. Some of the changes, though, would not be welcomed, forcing him back into an older role. Ben trusted John, and he hoped he would see the logic behind the decision.

The next item was the individual incentive system. Ben reviewed the current system: everyone was guaranteed a base rate, a premium was paid for units above standard, and the standards were derived from engineering estimates. Everyone knew the standards were bad that had surfaced in the search for JIT volunteers. Some areas continually hit 170 to 180 percent of standard, and workers successfully foiled every attempt by engineering to set more accurate rates. Other parts of the plant, such as electronics, were barely able to make rate. Inequity was rife.

"I'd like to include support groups in the plan, Ben," Jim Andrews said. "I know the problems with individual incentives in my area. We want to increase the value-adding component of our work, but individual incentives lead to quantity over quality. When we put individual incentives in the QC department, we ended up with more inspection than necessary. Same in logistics. Everyone's interests need to be aligned, and we've not done that well in the past. Will these groups be in the plan?"

"I hope so. That's the intention. Also, I want to remind you why we're pursuing gainsharing. One of the reasons is in line with your comments, Jim. Today, our direct labor costs are only 7 percent of sales. Yet this 7 percent seems to control all our costs because of the incentive system. I want gainsharing because it will marry all of the employees to the goals of the company. I think it will work."

Ben then asked for suggestions on how to implement the system. The consensus was that a committee be formed of 1 person from each department on the plant floor, a total of 22, Julie, Drew, and Ben. Drew was given the task of having each department elect a representative.

Time, Time, and More Time

At each stage the actual implementation took more time than planned. Quality was allotted three to six months. It took two years. The JIT cells were only two months behind schedule. The incentive system proved to be no exception. Ben allotted three months, it took nine.

It can't be emphasized enough that the change that took place at Banyon was evolutionary, not revolutionary. It took time. Few companies are willing to stick with new ideas unless they pay off quickly. JIT, with its potential for huge gains, is especially susceptible to premature abandonment. First is the misconception that its purpose is to get rid of inventories. Too many companies, therefore, do away with inventories first. When chaos results, they abandon JIT. Not understanding why the problems occur, managers eliminate the solution, not the cause.

* * * * *

Ben barely got through the door, returning from a week's vacation, when all hell broke loose. While he had been gone, a JIT consultant had been working with Drew and Julie on the incentive plan. While he had great ideas, he lacked tact. Everyone was up in arms, and Julie got into a fight with Drew. Julie threw the consultant out, and Drew, in retaliation, went straight to Ben's boss, Herman Randolph. Before Ben got back, Corporate was there. Drew convinced them that the new plan would affect pay, and that meant corporate involvement.

It was a nightmare. Ben was not in the mood to deal with corporate on the incentive issue. As it was, every month he was on the phone for hours, explaining why the plant's performance was better than the reports said. And now they were inside his plant. Now, as far as he knew, Herman was meddling in some vital decision.

"Something was bound to happen. Drew and Julie have been fighting for a month. They both have good ideas, but they're being pigheaded. Drew is good at coming up with solutions, but his packaging leaves a lot to be desired. Julie? She knows how people think and respond to different ideas. I'll have to separate them and use each as a separate resource, not as team members." Ben walked into his office, only to find the battlefield shifted. And, as he had feared, Herman was there gloating over the malcontent.

"I've been working on JIT for almost three years, and you want to keep on doing business the old way. Drew, I don't care how much you like the current system. I've talked to manager after manager and everyone has done away with complex performance measures. I want everyone paid on productivity gains. Period. That's what we want, and that's what we should reward." Julie was mad. Without a doubt she was a changed person. The tentative, easy-going Julie of three years ago had matured. She was holding her own with Drew, although Ben wouldn't say she was winning.

"Let's just go back to the Stone Age, Julie. I want an elegant, modern incentive plan, not one from the dark ages. We can do better than simply monitor efficiency. I want us to provide a strong environment for personal growth, something you probably wouldn't understand." Drew's remark was rude. Ben broke in.

"Hold on, we can't solve this problem when we lose our perspective. I've told the people in the plant that we'll forge a plan together; we've chosen a Scanlon plan, and we'll work out the details in the committee. Now, what else is bothering you, Julie?" Ben looked at her. Julie's face was flushed, and her nostrils flared. If she had been of a different nature, she might have been hysterical. Instead, she composed herself to prepare for round two.

"I do have another issue. The labor grades. We have 75 of them. We only need 5. We're all equal; every job is necessary. It's hard to convince the work force that we're all the same when there are such major differences in pay grades."

Drew looked incredulously at Julie. Before he could sputter an answer, Ben interceded, drawing his fire. "I agree with Julie, Drew. I've done my own informal poll on labor grades, and JIT means simplicity, cross-training, and paying for skills. You know how I feel, because I took your private parking spot away and removed the walls around the executive dining area. I think we should remove the walls around pay grades as well."

"I'll have to think on it, Ben. It's a big change, and coupled with a new incentive system and changing the standards, it's too much to digest. I'm uncomfortable changing all these major personnel policies in one fell swoop."

"Drew, I want you to do a survey that may help us. Call around to the companies in the area and get some competitive benchmarks for our own salaries. I want to know the standard pay for the jobs we have, where we're high, and where we're low. If we're high, we'll have to get the rates in line. If we're low, raises are in order. I intend to keep JIT/TQC moving, and that means I need good people. I'm willing to pay up to 10 percent over market to get them."

Herman had been quietly listening to the entire exchange. Now he jumped in. "I think you're being hasty, Ben. I think Drew is right. You can't make major changes this fast. If you do, the plant will unravel around you. Slow down. Do your study, but don't make any decisions without me, and I mean it."

On that note, the meeting ended. Ben was not at all pleased having Randolph around. Every chance he got, Ben worked on ways to move him out and regain control.

Problems and More Problems

Julie was in revolt. She threatened to quit, and Ben was furious. Julie had brought in a second JIT consultant, and Drew had managed to get him thrown out, a retaliation for Julie's earlier action. And Drew refused to change any major components of the incentive system. He knew any change wouldn't be to his liking, and he lobbied overtime to keep Randolph on his side. And when it seemed nothing else could go wrong, the monthly reports came out. Productivity was off 5 percent after dropping the old incentive system. Ben couldn't believe his eyes or his luck.

* * * * *

"Julie, please reconsider. I support you, and you know it. Don't let this problem get the better of you. I need you, and the people in the plant need you. We need this incentive plan. We've gotten the workers' expectations up, but nothing has happened. I made that announcement about the Scanlon plan over three months ago. Three months. No action. No productivity. We need help."

"I'll stay for now, Ben. And, I'll see if I can find a consultant that everyone will accept, even Drew. I still think we need a JIT specialist, but more than that, we need action."

Julie was good to her word. Within a few days she had found a consultant who had helped a Two Rivers plant put a Scanlon plan in place. Ben called her.

"Hello, Ms. Washbone? This is Ben Morgan at Banyon. I wonder if I could speak to you for a few moments?"

"Sure. How can I help you?"

"Well, we're trying to put a Scanlon plan in place, and we've heard that you have experience in this area. I wanted to know if you could spend some time with us working through the plan?"

"Yes. You do know that I charge a fee. My time is not free."

"But this is a sales call; surely you don't charge for the initial visit?"

"Oh, but I do. If I spend the day with you, I forgo a paying job. If you want me for a day, you'll have to pay my fee."

"I guess I have no choice. When can you come?"

"Let's not rush. I have another question, Mr. Morgan. You're thinking about a Scanlon plan. Have you got rid of your individual incentive program yet? I won't deal with that, it's too messy, and more than that, the workers wouldn't consider me objective."

"I've already done that. The problem is we don't know how to get started on a new system. The actual change is a mystery right now, and I don't have a lot of time to experiment."

An appointment was made for a week later. When Ms. Washbone arrived, Ben was pleasantly surprised. She was bright, personable, and mature. Although she didn't have a college degree, Linda Washbone didn't need one. She had street smarts, learned in the trenches. Ben was convinced after watching her interact with plant workers during the plant tour, that she could help. Drew and Julie both agreed, a surprise and welcome result. It was the first thing they had agreed on in a month.

Linda Washbone did not come cheap. Ben gasped when she discussed her fee. It was almost double what another firm had quoted for a different incentive plan. But somehow he knew she was worth it. Plans were made to start in early October, and Ben made the announcement to the plant.

* * * * *

"Julie, I hope this works. I think we're all going to be eating beans to cover the fee, but I don't know where else to look for help. When she's here, let her pick up her meal charges. I don't want another dime of expense; she's stretched our special budget to the limit." Ben seldom brought up money. Julie didn't know what the cost was, but it had to be major dollars.

"It'll work, Ben, because it has to. We have to get past this roadblock. But do you think we'll ever see the end? Every time we build momentum, we lose steam. If we had known three years ago how hard this was going to be, I'll bet we would have given it a second thought." Julie was discouraged, there was no question about it. Ben was thankful that she'd agreed to stay, despite her continuing disagreements with Drew. His job was to make sure she didn't regret the decision.

"Julie, we would've done it anyway. I wouldn't change

what we've done. Sometimes, just for a moment, everybody gets excited and moves in the right direction. And, the moments come more and more often. I'm still convinced it's the right way to go. But the change we're undergoing, that's the key. If we can just get a handle on the process, we can handle any problem."

"Like Ackoff said, right? I still think he's on the right track, although every time I reread that book I end up wondering what's at the heart of the whole system," Julie stood up, and walked around to Ben's side of the desk. Bending over to kiss his forehead, she said, "What do you say, friend, to a quiet lunch with your favorite employee? Let's get out of here. I've had enough challenge for one day."

"Couldn't ask for a better offer. Get your coat, I'm buying."

CHAPTER 11

GAINSHARING: A COMMITMENT TO EQUITY

"The election results are in, Ben, and I feel like a reporter. The Democrat, George Bangle, is ahead in the early returns. Everyone is waiting anxiously at election headquarters to find out who their next president will be. Details at 10." Julie settled into her chair, waiting for the inevitable barrage of questions.

"Cute, Julie. Do you have the final list?" She nodded and handed a wrinkled sheet to Ben. "Not again. Every time you touch a piece of paper it wrinkles!" Grinning, Ben read the list. It was a good cross section of the plant's personalities and opinions.

"I don't think they could've picked better people, all quality. Carolyn, Brenda, even Kathy. That's a positive sign. The workers must feel the same way about JIT as we do; they've made our job easier. Once they design a plan and agree to it, we're almost assured a successful plant vote." Ben glanced through the names again, making mental notes of potential personality clashes. He'd become adept at group dynamics during the implementation, learning how to minimize bad situations and maximize good ones.

"Ben, does this mean Linda can begin the incentive plan implementation? She said we had to do three things; get rid of the individual incentive plan, sign a binding agreement with the employees, and hold the election. The agreement was a problem, but I think Linda was right. If the workers are ever going to accept it, they have to know that we'll go along with the consensus of the Incentives Committee. It looks like we're ready." Julie played with her pen as she talked.

"No more clicks, please. I've lost my hair, now you're working on my sanity! Yes, we're ready to start on what I hope is the final leg of a long journey. I'll call Linda this morning and get a starting date."

* * * * *

Linda Washbone, the incentives consultant, made a preliminary visit to Banyon in November. She assessed the situation and laid out an action plan for Ben. Linda proved to be worth her fee as her common sense and communication skills were immediately put to use. Ben used her as a sounding board for his ideas, as a facilitator when problems occurred, and as an expert witness in negotiations with Corporate.

Her first tasks were to get the elections off the ground, stir up enthusiasm in the plant, and explain the process to workers and management alike. The initial visits helped to set a productive tone for the implementation. When her official involvement with the plan began in January, Linda was well-liked and a known commodity. She was effective because she understood the process of organizational change, a knowledge she taught Ben as the months progressed.

The Elements of Change

There are four elements basic to change. First, management needs to create conditions that free workers from the fear of losing their jobs and help them maximize their incomes. Ben used part-time workers to give him the needed flexibility to offer this protection under normal volume shifts.

Second, equity in hiring, promotions, and pay must be a cornerstone of the process. Unless everyone shares equally in both positive and negative outcomes of change, problems will erupt and the implementation will fail. For example, if productivity increases after JIT/TQC is initiated, there should be a plan for some form of profit sharing. Brenda asked for "a fair share." When the incentive implementation stalled, so did productivity. The gainsharing program played a critical role in anchoring the JIT/TQC systems and in changing the culture of the organization to coincide with continuous improvement objectives.

Third, individualism is a vital aspect of change. American society is built on individualism and the right to pursue individual goals. Each worker is unique, and the workplace should be structured to allow each worker to pursue his own development. It means allowing individuals and teams to do work at their own pace and in their own way. The JIT implementation reflected this, as the team designed the work flow, not management. Ben held his ground against middle management interference, freeing the JIT team to put a process and structure into place that matched the logical assembly path as well as the strengths of individual team members.

Fourth, democracy is a critical feature.[1] The genuine and open participation of workers in the JIT/TQC program at Banyon resulted in joint acceptance of the outcome. Discussions shifted from the defensive, "us versus them," to the cooperative. It requires a shift in power, changing concepts of control, and a willingness to take risks at all levels of the organization.

It was the climate that made JIT/TQC succeed in spite of tremendous obstacles. Ben created an environment where improvement could flower, and equity and democracy were possible. He also came to realize that change, no matter where in the organization, required the same approach to succeed; it had to be implemented with people, not in spite of them. Although painfully slow to achieve at times, consensus was the essential feature. And change required leadership, not authoritarian command, to set the direction by clearly defining goals. Ben, as plant manager, was expected to set the boundaries and keep the projects moving, to facilitate and motivate, rather than to dictate.

The critical factor in Banyon's JIT/TQC implementation

---

[1]These four characteristics are detailed in a recent book by J. Simons and W. Mares, *Working Together: Employee Participation in Action* (New York: New York University Press, 1985) p. 175.

was *communication,* open-door interaction. Everyone listened to each other, regardless of rank or background. The underlying belief was that everyone was capable of contributing, and that they would and should do so. JIT/TQC demands that boundaries between functions, as well as between levels in the chain of command, be broken down. It can only succeed if true participatory management evolves, real participation by all.

Criteria for Successful Gainsharing

"Linda, come in and sit down." Ben motioned to the chair by his desk. "I'm glad you're back because we're anxious to get started on the incentive system. As I told you, the committee has been formed, the agreement signed, and we've eliminated individual incentives through a guaranteed average weekly pay. Now what?"

Linda smiled, more impressed by Ben's continued use of "we" than by the accomplishments to date. "It sounds like you're ready, Ben. Now tell me, what does the committee look like?"

"Good question. As you know, we held an election to select a representative from every department in the plant. That gives us 22 people. I've also put Drew and John Rust on the committee. With me the total is 25." Ben paused, waiting for Linda to ask another question.

"That's a workable number, although getting consensus with a group that large could be difficult. What is the mix, and are we facing any potential problem people?"

"I was worried about that myself, Linda. I've gone over the list, and I don't foresee any problems. I also checked with Mike and Julie to make sure I wasn't missing something. They agree with me, it's a great group." Reaching for the papers he had set aside when Linda arrived, Ben retrieved the list of names. "Here's the final list. You probably know some of these people already, like Brenda. Kathy O'Ryan from machining is a tough, honest person. I think we can count on her to keep the discussions moving forward. All in all, I'm pleased and confident that we can formulate a system that will work for everyone."

"I believe you. The easy part is behind us. I think we need to talk about the criteria necessary to develop an effective gainsharing system." With that, Linda turned the conversation to future challenges.

* * * * *

There are many criteria that can be used to develop gainsharing programs. The ones Linda described were based on consensus, equity, and open communication. The underlying expectations were that the plan would:

- Be fair and equitable to all employees.
- Be easy to understand, implement, and maintain.
- Be simple to administer.
- Be based on employee involvement and commitment to outcomes.
- Pay for productivity.
- Be self-motivating.
- Be supportive of JIT/TQC concepts and efforts.

The Scanlon Multicost plan was chosen because it promised to fill these expectations and objectives. The plan was based on productivity, it included all employees, supported Banyon's business goals, and would foster employee involvement if properly implemented and used.

EQUITY IS NOT EASY TO ACHIEVE

The Incentives Committee, although large, appeared to work well for the first few meetings. Using experience and details from other plans and approaches, Linda helped the group pick the main features of the Banyon plan. Problems arose when decisions had to be made, not about whom to include in the plan, but about whom to exclude. Should part-timers get a share? Only production workers or the entire company? And what about the sales force? They already benefited from a bonus plan, so any additional compensation could be seen as double-dipping.

The general consensus was to include as many as possible in order to set up joint acceptance of the plant's performance. Early on, the decision was made to exclude sales and engineering; sales because of existing incentive plans; engineering because of the structure of the plan. The plan defined the gainsharing pool using control principles: if the workers could control an expense, it was part of the base profit calculation.

The problem with the inclusion of engineering was major purchases. Engineering often bought expensive items to use in new products or in the redesign of existing ones. These purchases could distort the plant's monthly expenses and affect plan payout. They felt that resentment would build over these uncontrollable expenses, negatively affecting the plan.[2]

Fair Division of Dollars

"I know each of you has spent time thinking about how we should divide the gainsharing bonus pool. In the past only direct labor received incentives. We've already addressed that problem, but now we have to handle the hard part, namely, how should we divide the productivity gains?" Linda wanted to focus the group, so she intervened. They had been meeting for 45 minutes with little forward movement.

The initial division of gains between work force and company had been determined by management. Faced with practical constraints and using Linda's knowledge of other plans for guidance, Ben had decided that an even split was the best answer, half for the company, half for the plan. The issue here was how to split the plan's funds.[3]

Brenda was the first to speak. "Linda, I was raised to

---

[2] After the plan was implemented, a study was done of these expenditures. Instead of being erratic, they were in fact quite predictable purchases that could be accurately budgeted. Once this was determined, engineering was included in the gainsharing plan.

[3] As will be seen later in the chapter, Ben also put a constraint on the total payout percentage. Namely, 20 percent of any gain entering the pool was set aside as a buffer for bad months. This would protect Ben from paying out gains early in a year where final profits were below projections (or negative).

believe that everyone is equal, that I'm no better than anyone else and no one else is better than me. That means everyone gets an equal portion. Just take the pot and divide it by the number of people in the plan. We do great, everybody wins. We mess up, everyone loses. Equally."

"I think that's a good idea. But that raises a question. Does anyone have an idea on how to deal fairly with part-time workers?" Linda asked the question and waited. Silence. Ben glanced around the conference room, hoping someone would start the conversation. But the silence dragged on. Finally, Dan Rogers, the Shipping Foreman, raised his hand.

He cleared his throat. "Sorry, frog in my throat." Dan was slow to start. "Ms. Washbone, I don't think part-timers should be included in the plan. They don't have the same skills as the rest of us, they come and go, so why do they deserve a share of the pie?" Even though Dan asked the question, he didn't seem firmly committed to his stand.

"That's a fair question. I don't know as much about this issue as the rest of you. Does anyone else have an answer for Dan?" Linda picked up the ball and tossed it back to the committee. Ben simply watched. Linda knew the work force, full- and part-time. She was not here to decide for the committee, and so had deftly side-stepped the question. They didn't have to wait long for an answer.

"That's baloney, Dan, and you know it!" Brenda spoke directly to Dan. "Some of the part-timers are *better* workers than the rest of us. And the objective is to be fair. They're putting out effort and contributing to the gains we all share. I say put them in and give them a share based on the hours they work."

"Brenda, some of them last less than a week. I don't want to deal with people who come and go. I know some of them are permanent fixtures, and I like them, too. But I want to know they're going to work before I share my lunch with them." Dan and Brenda faced off, constructively. Locked in conversation, they debated the issues. Both knew a compromise had to be reached, and slowly a consensus emerged. Linda and Ben remained quiet, watching and waiting for the answer.

The final decision was to establish a waiting period. Part-time employees, normally hired to fill entry level positions, needed about 30 days to learn the ropes and gather the required skills. The turnover during this same period was high. It seemed logical to exclude new part-timers from the plan for 30 days to let the dust settle and establish a commitment to the company. After this probation period, part-time workers would be entitled to a share of the gainsharing pool based on total hours worked during the month. Since hours worked was the defined basis for payout, equity was maintained.

Building Consensus

Brenda's suggestions met with almost immediate consensus. Since every decision was based on consensus, one negative response could table an idea. On this issue, Ben wasn't sure he agreed, but he wasn't going to be the one to interfere with the process. "That's a pretty straightforward approach, Brenda. And from this vote I can see it's popular. We're devising this plan to establish a common destiny for all. Equality in the incentive system is a good way to start. I can't remember seeing any of the other plans doing it, but that's not important. This is your plan." Ben wanted to put his word in, but not interfere with the group process. Linda nodded, and continued.

The meeting continued for another hour before breaking up. A lot of ground had been covered and with surprisingly little dissension. It was an interesting process to watch. What made it so effective was that the employees felt comfortable with it. The representatives had been elected by their coworkers, and they had the responsibility to go back to those who elected them and tell them of progress and decisions made. Every decision could be reopened for good reason, such as negative feedback from the plant or subsequent concerns based on downstream implications of the decision.

* * * * *

"Linda, I like the way you've built team spirit, starting from the first meeting where you forced us to drop pretenses.

What was the purpose of that exercise?" Ben's question was sincere, as was his puzzled look.

"I had to get everyone comfortable with arguing a point without being wedded to it. The only way a compromise can be reached is if everyone is willing to change his mind and listen to reasonable arguments. That often means stepping out of one pair of shoes and into another. I wanted to set that tone up front. The added benefit was having workers get comfortable with disagreeing with you."

"You succeeded on both counts. The second exercise I understood, but still enjoyed. By having everyone describe themselves, you avoided the standard questions and opened up a lot of doors. I feel like I know everyone better. And when you randomly handed out the autobiographies and made everyone commit them to memory, the fun really started! I couldn't stop laughing. Ron practically had me playing a trumpet in a jazz band!" Just the thought brought a smile to Ben's face.

"I enjoy that exercise, too. It's all part of creating an environment where consensus can be reached, getting everyone comfortable and involved."

Linda and Ben continued, he the student, she the teacher. College degree or not, Linda was a good teacher and a good leader.

* * * * *

Consensus building has three distinct phases. In phase one the group is simply a collection of people in the same room. There are distrust, hidden agendas, and self-interest at play. Through continued interaction and with the right facilitation, the group moves to phase two. In this stage, camaraderie emerges. At Banyon, individuals on the committee visibly relaxed, jokes and jibes floated freely, but the group still lacked a strong sense of purpose.

Purpose is the essence of phase three. Getting comfortable with each other, the group is ready to move. One could almost see the adrenalin flowing through the Incentives Committee. There was increased after-hours socializing; during the meetings less time was spent on discussion and more on decisions and planning. This is where the group was in early January. The prospects for rapid resolution of the gainsharing plan details seemed excellent.

Communication was the heart of the process. In addition to face-to-face meetings throughout the hierarchy, the bulletin board got heavy use. Each decision was laid out in detail in memo form prior to a final vote. Everyone could read it and think about the decision and its downstream implications. While Ben was concerned that this process might lead to excess opinions, it never did. Linda made sure that didn't happen, artfully guiding the committee toward its final goals.

Issues and Answers

"Linda, I'd like to ask a few questions before we get too far today." Kathy O'Ryan had moved to the front of the room, a signal to Linda that she had items to put on the agenda.

"Okay, Kathy. Why don't you start with your points, and we'll work on the other issues later." Linda turned the meeting over to Kathy, and everyone directed their attention to her.

"Something's been bothering me this last week. Most of you know that Ed Rangley, one of the maintenance guys, passed away last week. That made me think, 'What would the plan do for his family?' We're talking about sharing, but what if someone dies? How do we handle that?" Kathy waited for a response.

"Kathy, I hadn't thought of that." Brenda was the first to comment. "I'd like to see their share go to them. Any other decision would be unfair."

"But if they die on the first of the month, they'll be getting something for nothing. I won't vote for that." Dan was playing devil's advocate, a role at which he excelled.

"But we can't leave them out. What's fair? We know if they die the last day of the month there's no problem, they get a share. The 28th? Still seems like they deserve the money. This one's hard; it makes me feel like Solomon." Brenda was pushing up against her own limits. While equality was her guiding light, it had to apply to people in the plan as well as those who were out.

It took five days to work through the issue. Discussion continued endlessly in Ben's view, but it wasn't his place to break it off. Finally, a compromise was reached. If the individual passed away in the first two weeks of the month, they were allotted a half share. Once the two week mark was passed, a full share was allotted. More difficult issues, such as a potential gainsharing deficit, were voted to be outside the realm of "death benefits." The final solution was equitable, humane, and workable.

The plan was focused on motivating the work force to make suggestions to improve both process and product. While bonuses weren't paid for ideas, gainsharing provided sufficient incentive to submit suggestions as increased profits were shared. The fact that their ideas would be listened to and acted on reinforced this behavior. Along with increased motivation came the reality of making the plan work.

Problems with No Easy Answers

"There's no way this will work, at least not in my area. Our supervisor isn't going to pass along our ideas if he doesn't like them, no matter whether they're good or bad," Ellie Gray, one of the senior purchasing agents, had started the committee down a difficult path.

"If I understand you, Ellie, it's a personality problem. We know that suggestions that improve the quality, cost, or lead time needed to make product are needed if the continuous improvement goals are going to be met. Why wouldn't the supervisor pass on the ideas?" Linda was pushing the issue, hoping to open up the discussion.

"Linda, I know you're not naive," Brenda responded. "We have good supervisors as well as bad in the plant. If an idea from one of us is seen as threatening by the area supervisor, he can simply hide it. There will always be indians and chiefs, and some chiefs are only happy if they're in control."

"Brenda, I agree," Ben broke in, a move that startled

everyone. "This issue is too important to ignore. What do you think will work? We need a solution that doesn't create guerilla warfare in the plant and that won't put the brakes on the JIT/TQC project. I'd really like to hear some ideas."

Discussion continued for several hours, and even though the meeting lasted well past lunch, a solution was found. The committee voted to set up an appeal process which any employee could use. If gainsharing suggestions were ignored by a supervisor, they could take them up a level. This appeal process could go up the ladder until a compromise was reached or the case lost.

One final issue arose: how were improvement efforts to be funded? Ben didn't have resources to fund all suggestions. Yet, it was important to support the improvement process. Linda advised that most companies provided $200 to $400 per suggestion with funds coming from the gainshare pool; Ben decided to put a $500 limit on each project. He realized that minimal funding would result in many suggestions of lesser quality and that more substantial funding would provide a better climate resulting in more worthy suggestions. The fact that the funds would come from the gainsharing pool also ensured that the suggestions submitted would be well developed.

* * * * *

"Julie, let's go out for lunch. If you want, call Mike and Dick to see if they want to join us. It's a beautiful day, and I'd like to clear my head." Ben had his coat on. He was ready to get out of the plant.

"Mike and I already have plans, so I'll call him and ask him to grab Dick on his way up. Where are we going?"

"That little Italian place on the corner. I feel like eating lasagna, espresso, and dessert. I can taste it already!"

"All right," Julie was laughing at Ben. He looked like a little boy in front of a candy store. She turned off her PC, and Ben helped her with her coat. "Mike said they'd meet us in the lobby, so we might as well go." Julie dashed out the door. Ben had made her hungry, too. As they walked to the lobby, visions of pasta danced in her head.

Lunchtime Conversations

"Ben, what's happening in the gainsharing meetings? We hear some rumblings in engineering, but I don't know if they're true or not." Dick paused, fork midway between plate and mouth, cheese stretched between fork and plate. Italian food could be a challenge.

"Dick, it looks like engineering is out of the plan for now. I thought all along that would happen because of the formula used to construct the bonus plan. The big technical purchases you make could sink the plan because of their size. Besides, Dick, I think you make more than I do!" Winking, Ben took another bite of his lasagna. He had ordered the largest on the menu and then some. Julie had groaned when it came to the table, fighting off the urge to take his fork away from him.

"I guess I understand the logic, although I hope my guys do. Downstream we might want to work on that one, especially if you want to get heavily into design for manufacturability. But I'd rather keep my paycheck over a potential bonus."

Jim Andrews joined the group at the restaurant. He'd been at a vendor working through some quality problems.

The rest of lunch was spent discussing the details of the gainsharing plan. Jim may have been late to the conversation, but as he'd done during the quality implementation, he immediately picked up on the problems Ben was facing. Before long, unfortunately, it was time to go back to work.

"Ben, how about a fish restaurant next time. I think I just may pop a button if I move too fast. It's almost as bad as Thanksgiving. Plop, plop, fizz, fizz when I get back."

"The second Napoleon is responsible for the lady's discomfort, I fear. Are you absolutely sure you don't want a third?"

Julie stopped Ben mid-sentence. "Not one more word, Ben Morgan, or you'll be sorry. And drive slowly, and don't make any fat jokes, and whatever you do, don't stop at any restaurants."

"OK, my little dumpling, we'll take it easy."

* * * * *

"Hello, Herman, what can I do for you?" Ben picked up the phone after Julie buzzed it through.

"Hate to break it to you over the phone, Ben, but you're in deep trouble."

Somehow Herman didn't sound all that concerned. "What do you mean in trouble? The plant's doing just fine. What could be wrong?"

"Let's just say that my boss, who is your boss too, doesn't know very much about your gainsharing program. And, he feels that it's out of control. So, he's asked me to have you do a major presentation for him next week, say Wednesday? We'll arrive at 9:00 A.M."

"Thanks for the notice. We'll see you next week." Ben did not wait for a reply before hanging up the phone. If he had, his temper might have got the better of him. "I can't believe it. Just when it looks like everything is going to work out, in comes trouble. When will this ever end?" Disgusted and disheartened, Ben began to list the details he'd need to take care of before the meeting. After calling home to let his wife know he'd be missing another dinner, he settled in for a long night.

CHAPTER 12

NEGOTIATING WITH CORPORATE

"Julie, I spent most of last night going over the details we need to cover in the presentation. I was irritated by the request at first, but I think it makes a lot of sense to try to get support from Corporate. If they can see what we're doing, there's a chance they may like it." Ben sounded more confident than he felt. He hadn't met John Roscoe, Herman's boss, but the stories he'd heard didn't add to his confidence

"Ben, how can you be so calm? We've been killing ourselves for over two years, we're near the end, the employees like the project, and now in waltzes Corporate. And John Roscoe? All we've seen of him since we started is red ink on monthly reports with a 'Why?' on the side. Do you think he's going to change anything? Ben, he'll stop the JIT/TQC project over my dead, and otherwise employed, body!" Julie's anger was based on a fear that Roscoe might veto the project. She was on edge, and she knew Ben was on edge as well. They couldn't handle another setback, not now when the end was in sight.

"Julie, there's nothing we can do but prepare. I think we may need Linda's help. Why don't you call her and then take a few hours off. It's almost lunch time, and I need you relaxed and focused this afternoon. Why don't you run up town and get the details of Wednesday's lunch arranged with the caterer? It'll do you good to get out for a bit." Julie agreed, and after talking to Linda left the plant.

Managing through Pressure

Ben had spearheaded change at Banyon that ran counter to established corporate procedures. He'd tried to keep the communication channels open, communicating with Herman Randolph on a weekly basis. The problem was that Herman hadn't passed the information along. For whatever reason, he'd kept the memos and the implementation from his manager, John Roscoe.

When Roscoe found out about the JIT/TQC project, he felt left out, his authority threatened. When he finally had an explanation for the problems he'd been seeing on the monthly variance reports, he re-exerted control. Ben's problem was that Roscoe didn't know how to manage. Participation wasn't in his vocabulary. He believed he had to approve or disapprove every project in his division. Ben attributed this behavior to Roscoe's Ph.D., and over the course of the next few days he could be heard muttering, "Those who can't teach, manage divisions!" Not a fair comment, but Ben was apprehensive about the forthcoming meeting.

* * * * *

"Linda, thank you for agreeing to help us give this presentation. Your communication skills will come in handy if what I've heard about Roscoe is true. I'm worried because he can stop the whole project. If he does, that will spell the end. We've worked hard to establish credibility with the work force, and he can undo it at will." Ben was more willing to share his concern with Linda than with his managers. Linda's security wasn't threatened, so she could remain objective.

"Ben, I've had to do this before. All I can say is that we'll be okay as long as he's a reasonable man. If he listens to us with an open mind, he'll be satisfied. It's working, we know it, and now we have to convince him."

Linda's words did little to comfort Ben. They continued to work on the presentation, but Ben just couldn't shake the nagging fear that everything was going to go wrong.

Narrow Minds and Ultimatums

One week later they arrived. Linda, Julie, Drew, and Ben greeted them and took them to the conference room for the presentation. Ben had decided that Linda should handle the formal discussion in the hope that her skill and expertise would add merit to the project. The plan backfired. Roscoe, not a supporter of women, was also an elitist. His assessment of an individual began with educational credentials and ended with abilities. Before Linda even started, he had dismissed her. Only half listening, he kept interrupting and turning his attention to Ben. It was obvious from his behavior that he felt that Linda wasn't his mental equal, and, therefore, not worthy of his attention.

Ben was furious. At first he tried to stay out of the presentation, turning the questions back to Linda, but before long Roscoe was screaming at Linda, and Linda was sitting quietly, smiling without comment. That drove Roscoe into a frenzy. The plans Ben and his staff had made were in danger of being destroyed in one fell swoop. Against his will, Ben took over the meeting. Saving the JIT/TQC project was more important than ego or manners.

"John, let's see if we can regain our perspective. We've been working for two years on implementing JIT/TQC, after getting clear ultimatums from our major customers. We passed the information along to Corporate, and I'm sorry that you weren't briefed in more detail. What matters now is that you understand the plan for what it is. It's a solid partnership between company and employees. We've set up a system of checks and balances with employee involvement and mutual agreement. As you can see from the charts, we've reached unforeseen levels of productivity growth. The gainsharing plan says, 'You've helped improve productivity, now we'll share the gains.' The company is the winner all the way around. Can you help me? What areas are of real concern?"

Ben sounded much more diplomatic than he felt. Briefly glancing over at Linda, he caught her nod and wink. The encouragement was sorely needed. A little more confident that he was on the right track, Ben returned his attention to Roscoe.

"I'm glad the productivity is up, Ben, but you've put the company at risk, I'm afraid. This incentive plan is a radical departure from our existing personnel practices. I don't want to be involved with it, in fact, I'd like to put a disclaimer on it that will protect the company."

Roscoe seemed to be enjoying the discomfort he was causing. Once again Ben struck out, hoping a rational compromise could be found.

"John, you have to understand the dynamics of the plan. We've spent almost three months setting up the details, meeting every week with the plant's elected representatives. Every decision has been made by consensus. To stop the plan now or to make any changes will cause the workers to feel we don't trust them, that we're cheating them. That could damage the implementation beyond repair." Ben paused, looking directly at Roscoe. His stomach was doing a tap dance, but his composure was intact.

"Ben, I'm pulling rank on this one. I'm not at all comfortable with the plan as it stands, and I'm going to have to ask you to send it to the Corporate legal staff for review. If they think the wording or promises need to be changed, you will change them. I'm sorry about this, but you shouldn't have gone this far without consulting with us. The least I'll agree to is the disclaimer, no matter what legal says. That's it. Now, I've got to get back to my office. Sorry I can't stay for lunch." Without another word, Roscoe got up and left the room and the plant. Herman followed him, but not before he stopped to tell Ben he'd call him as soon as he got back to his office.

After they left, you could hear a pin drop in the conference room. Julie was as white as a ghost, making derogatory statements about Roscoe's heritage under her breath. Drew played with his tie clip, unwilling to look up. Ben locked eyes with Linda, breaking the silence.

"I'm sorry, Linda, that he was so unprofessional. I hope it won't affect our relationship." Ben held his breath, waiting for an answer.

Totally in character, Linda was obviously unruffled by the encounter. Her reply gave Ben new hope. "Actually, it makes me even more committed to seeing this through. You and your people are working hard to make some major changes to the plant and its incentive system. No, you're not going to lose me, but I do suggest you put on your thinking caps and come up with a way to block the S.O.B. Pardon the term."

A light went on over Ben's head as Linda's message struck home. "That's it. Of course. Fight fire with fire, pressure with pressure. I'll give Walt McVicker a call. Herman and I have asked him in the past to help us handle matters with Corporate. He's in Human Relations and reports to the Group President. And he's familiar with what we're doing; he's helped us, if only indirectly, to get where we are. If he can't help us with Corporate, maybe he can see the alternatives more clearly. There has to be a way to stop Roscoe and salvage the plan."

A Glimmer of Hope

"Walt, thank you for seeing me on such short notice. It's been at least a year. You look great! How's your family?" Ben knew Walt liked a little small talk before business. He felt it broke the ice and gave him a chance to settle into the conversation before he was asked to make a decision.

"Thanks for asking, Ben. Things are fine at home."

"I'm glad to hear that. Have you been sailing lately?"

"No time for that this year, unfortunately. I've been keeping pretty busy here at work, so when the weekends come it's all I can do to mow the lawn and trim the bushes."

"I know what you mean. Believe me."

They chatted for a few more minutes before Ben steered the conversation to the business at hand.

"Anyway, enough of that. I'd like to fill you in on the things I've done at the plant since I took over, Walt. After you hear me out, I'd like to ask for your suggestions on the best course of action to take. We've been working hard to turn the plant around, but unless we get creative the whole project could falter."

Ben took 20 minutes to describe the JIT/TQC efforts, the

results achieved, and where they were on the gainsharing plan. Walt listened quietly, only occasionally asking a question or jotting a note.

"So, let me get this straight, Ben. You're in the process of changing your plant incentive scheme, and Roscoe comes in and pulls the rug out from under you. I know him, and I understand how difficult he can be. While I don't have any formal say in the decision, if you were to invite me to participate in the review of the plan, I might be able to help. I'm sure Roscoe would support my involvement because he'll see me as a Corporate person who should be involved in it directly. And, he'll count on me to support the best interest of the Corporation. That much is true, but that doesn't necessarily mean I'll agree with him."

"That would be great, Walt, and more than I ever expected. If you're on the review board, I know the solution will be fair for everyone. Is there anything we can do to help?"

"I think you should be around while the review takes place to help everyone understand the plan and how it fits into the corporate incentive system. I'd also like you to spread the word a little. It sounds like you're on to something really promising with JIT/TQC, and this company sorely needs some rejuvenation and foresight. I'd like you to plan on spending your Fridays here for the next month or so. OK?"

"I can do that, Walt, if you think it'll help. I may bring Drew Pearce, my personnel manager, along. The experience will be good for him, and it may help to have someone explain the plan who understands the issues from a human resources perspective." Decision made, Ben took his leave and returned to Banyon.

The next week Ben and Drew began the shuttle. Ben at first thought it was a good idea, but as time dragged on, he could feel that he was losing time and spending money all to educate a group of people who didn't seem interested. The trips were coming to a conclusion when Walt McVicker got transferred.

* * * * *

"Drew, can you put together a final presentation for the review board? With Walt's transfer, they're planning to wrap up the report next week. I'd do it, but you understand what they need to hear, and you can frame responses to their questions in human resources jargon." Ben and Drew had just arrived at the local airport. It was late, and both were anxious to get home.

"I'd like to give it a try, Ben. Having to explain the plan to Corporate has really given me a different perspective. I've thought of myself as an outsider through much of the JIT/TQC implementation, but not any more. The gainsharing plan makes sense, it's fair, and everyone stands to win. I'll start the outline this weekend, if my wife doesn't have a big list of chores for me."

Drew looked pleased. He'd come a long way from his early days. Now he was the plan's chief promoter.

* * * * *

Ben faced a problem that was both discouraging and likely to destroy the JIT/TQC project: lack of top management support. His story is not unique. In plants across the United States middle level managers are being given mandates to implement JIT. And they do, often quite successfully.

In the beginning stages of the project, several things can happen. In some companies for no apparent reason top management stops it. In others they take personal credit for the work of underlings. In too few, does top management support the effort.

Corporate Compromises

All this occurred while the incentives committee continued to meet. Ben didn't pass the information down because he didn't want to hurt the efforts. Buying time, he hoped that the final decision of the review committee would remove the last hurdle set up by Roscoe.

One week after Drew's presentation, the decision came down from the review committee. It was a partial success for both sides, the definition of a compromise. For Ben, no compromise seemed possible. How could he change the plan without losing credibility?

* * * * *

"Linda, what do you suggest? The vote in the review committee was unanimous, and their demands are fair, but I have to explain it to the people who wrote the plan. I don't have any cards left to play." Ben was at the end of his rope. While the committee's demands were reasonable, they didn't solve his problem; management was preempting the consensus decision.

"Ben, I think you have to tell them exactly what you've told me. They trust you, and they're reasonable people. They won't like it, I agree with you on that, but they're not going to take a chance on wrecking the plan now. Remember, it's their plan too."

Linda was right, of course. Ben scheduled a meeting of the Incentives Committee for the next day, and spent the rest of the afternoon putting together a presentation that would lay out the changes ahead.

* * * * *

"This is how it stands. Before Corporate will sign off on the plan, we have to agree to three things. First, they want us to build in what they call 'reality' into the gainsharing formula. That means a new plan formula each year. The formula will have to be adjusted annually to match the budgeted profit plan for the plant. We'll have to factor in new products, new equipment, review decisions to manufacture versus buy, and incorporate our designated profit targets for the year." Before he could continue, Ben was interrupted.

"Ben, can you clear that up for me? Who gets to participate in the discussions? I mean, is Corporate going to pass along the decision, while we simply rubber stamp it? I'm not a rubber stamp, for anyone." Kathy stopped, intent on pushing for an answer.

"Kathy, we have as much say as we've always had. Every year we get profit targets, and we've always had to get approval for major capital expenditures. What they want us to do is to make sure we stay realistic, and that we formally recognize that our markets are constantly changing. It seems sensible because we know there will be mix, volume, and capacity changes as we move forward. By uniting business conditions with the profit plan, Corporate is ensuring the ongoing success of both the plan and the plant."

"Maybe. We'll see. What other things do they have in mind?" Kathy was voicing a common sentiment. As Ben had feared, the committee felt that Corporate was dictating to them, that autonomy had been lost.

Ben grabbed the opportunity to continue. "We've talked back and forth about the pension plan. As you know, Drew and I feel it should be brought in line with the plans used by most of the local companies. Here we did hit a snag. Corporate manages the basic pension, and is willing to change the size of its contribution only if its covered by productivity; and, in light of the gainsharing bonus, they believe their request is reasonable. They didn't reject it, they simply won't allow profit erosion."

The anticipated explosion was quick to come. "What? What do they mean, you can improve the plan, but we won't pay for it! That means no increase unless it comes out of our pockets." Brenda was angry.

"What we have to understand, Brenda, is that Corporate views the gainsharing payout as a substitute for other benefits, and they won't make further contributions. We can improve the pension plan, but the additional funding will have to come from the plant's productivity."

There were a few grumbles in the room, but no comments were voiced, so Ben went on.

"There's one more thing. Raises. Corporate feels these should come out of productivity also. What they suggested is that we take half the productivity gain as a raise and adjust the formula yearly. Say we get a 6 percent improvement, rather than pay it as a gain, they'd like us to raise wages. That's actually a good idea, because your take home pay becomes more assured."

Still facing silence, Ben let the last shoe drop. "That's what Corporate wants. I think if you look at it from their perspective, you'll see they simply want to participate in the decisions we make. And, they have the right. The dollars used to set up this plant came from them, and, therefore, they have a right to some say in how the profits from those assets are used. The last thing I have to tell you isn't as logical. John Roscoe, Randolph's boss, is putting a disclaimer in the plan book. It's a bunch of legal mumbo-jumbo, but it relieves Corporate of responsibility should the plan run into trouble down the road."

The committee sat quietly. Drew fidgeted, and John Rust nervously tapped his pen. No one in the room liked the facts, including Ben, but neither were they ready to quit.

"Are you saying we don't have any options, Ben? If we don't agree, what happens?" Dan broke the silence.

"If we don't agree, we don't have a plan. This isn't a proposal; we change the plan or we don't have one. I don't like it either, but I have to take some responsibility. All along I assumed that Herman Randolph was passing the information up the ladder. He wasn't. And I didn't check it out. Maybe if we'd had a Corporate Human Resources person here all along, there could have been discussions and compromise. That's not the game we're playing at this stage." Ben glanced at his watch, hoping by some miracle that it would be time for everyone to leave. It wasn't.

In the end the committee voted to make the amendments to the plan. Everyone signed the cover page of the original document, and Ben asked Drew to send it to the printer. The decision was made to hold the plant-wide vote on the plan two weeks after the booklets were received.

A Change of Command

Ben was called back to Corporate the following week. Apprehensively, Ben agreed to a meeting with Walt McVicker's replacement, Jack Brady. Brady had been hired from the outside, so Ben had no idea what kind of person he was. He got an answer to that question right away.

"Mr. Morgan, Ben, right? I have about five minutes for you, so you'll have to make your case and make it quick. I've gone over these memos and other information on your plant's incentive plan. A little nontraditional, isn't it?" Jack Brady paused and Ben jumped right in before he lost the chance to respond.

"I don't think the plan is that strange. Maybe it doesn't look like the old one, but there are a lot of good companies using this approach. It's been proven to improve productivity and morale time after time. It's already working for us." Ben was irritated. Five minutes. He'd spent over two years working on the JIT effort, struggling to keep the plant's major customers, winning battle after battle. In return? Five minutes.

"I can see you believe in this, and I'm not one to put a stop to something if the manager *responsible* is behind it. So, you can keep doing whatever it is you're doing, Ben, but there is a rule. As long as you succeed, things will be fine. If the plant should fail, though, you fail. And, you look for another job. No questions asked. Agreed?"

Ben felt like he'd been hit with a sledge hammer. Was this support or threat? "I hope that you see we're trying to set up a climate for improvement. I believe that success comes from trusting workers, giving them the tools to do the job, and holding back the avalanche while they do it. That's all I'm trying to do, to help them do the best job possible."

"Ben, that sounds great, I mean it. Anyway, our time's almost up. After talking to John Roscoe, I agree that a disclaimer for your new incentives manual is in order. I don't want anyone confusing your efforts for corporate policy. Finally, Ben, I do reserve the right to change my mind on this. I've gone along with it because Walt McVicker spoke highly of you. It's really not the kind of project I'd like to see us involved in. We're here to make money for stockholders, not line the pockets of employees."

That was the end of the conversation. Ben was angry, but at least the plan was safe for now. It wouldn't do any good to argue. Jack Brady wasn't going to win any popularity awards, but the ball was at least in Ben's court now.

In the end, Corporate never had to intervene. In fact contrary to the message Ben got from Jack Brady, Corporate did agree to the change. Ben and Drew, by shuttling back and forth, had provided the review panel a chance to participate in the plan. Having passed on its merits, each member of the panel had a personal interest in seeing it succeed. As he had done many times before at the plant, Ben won cooperation and consensus through participation.

A NEGOTIATED PLAN

Table 12–1 presents a sample calculation format for the final plan Banyon used in implementing the Scanlon Multicost Gainsharing Plan. Simplicity was the key to its structure. There was no need to set up another set of standards to measure productivity or to bring in a team of measurement specialists to watch the others work. The plan was directly tied to the monthly closing routine.

The base for calculations was defined as net sales less controllable, that is, direct and variable, costs. It was used

TABLE 12–1
Bonus Plan (Sample Calculation)

	Bonus Earned	No Bonus Earned
1. Net sales	$500,000	$500,000
2. Inventory variation	50,000	50,000
3. Value of production (1 + 2)	550,000	550,000
4. Allowable expenses (81.5 percent of 3)	448,250	448,250
5. Actual expenses	415,250	463,250
6. Gain (loss) (4 − 5)	33,000	− 15,000
7. Employee split (50% of 6)	16,500	− 7,500
8. Bonus pool (80% of 7)	13,200	0
9. Participants payroll	165,000	165,000
10. Bonus % (8 ÷ 9)	12.5%	0
11. Deficit reserve (20% of 7)	3,300	0
12. Deficit reserve from last month	10,270	13,900
13. Deficit reserve to date (11 + 12 if bonus earned; 12 and 7 if no bonus earned)	13,570	6,400

Source: Coopers & Lybrand.

as a historical standard for gauging monthly improvement levels.

The plan called for the company to receive 50 percent of all productivity gains as determined by the comparison of actual against standard. The rest was put into the incentive pool. A holdback provision was used to protect the company in case early gains failed to result in year-end profits.

Each month there was a gain, the holdback provision put into reserve 20 percent of the productivity gain entering the pool. Ben easily convinced everyone that the buffer was a good idea when he pointed out that otherwise everyone would have to pay the company in a bad month.

At year end, 50 percent of the balance remaining in the incentive pool was paid to the employees. It kept the system fair, and it provided the chance for a Christmas bonus. The holdback provision effectively buffered the plan from mix and volume changes outside the control of the workers.

It was a novel plan, working from the costs and output each worker could control. By focusing on sales, production couldn't gain by building inventory. By using a rolling average of actual as the standard, continuous improvement was embedded in the plan. Through foresight, the committee ensured that the plan would continue to pay benefits.

Examining Table 12–1, the details of the plan can be tracked. Taking a sample month with sales of $500,000, the bonus is based on actual plant expenses as opposed to allowable. If actual were less than allowable, a bonus was paid. Conversely, if actual exceeded allowable, a bonus was not paid, and the deficit resulted in an adjustment to the buffer account.

Given a set gain or loss, a 50 percent allocation between the company and the plan was made. In case of a loss, the employees' half was credited against the buffer; if it was a gain, 80 percent of it was passed through as a bonus based on hours earned. Finally, the buffer balance was reconciled and a payout made annually as a Christmas bonus.

* * * * *

"The manual is ready to distribute, Ben. There was a last minute call from the printer about the disclaimer, but it's been resolved. The disclaimer looks unusual in front of the title page. Anyway, I think we're ready for the vote. Should I schedule it?" Julie had stuck her head in the door. She looked kind of funny, her head hanging around the corner. Ben smiled and nodded. Julie left Ben to his thoughts and arranged the formal presentation and meeting.

The two weeks passed quickly. Monday morning found Ben shuffling papers, looking nervous.

"Ben, are you ready? The meeting is supposed to start in two minutes, and everyone else is there." Julie was at Ben's door. He didn't seem anxious to go, but with encouragement he got up from his desk.

"I think so, Julie. Sorry for the delay. I have a lot on my mind these days. I keep hoping the plan goes through, because if it doesn't, I'm history. I feel like a man on death row with five minutes left to live. I know it's a good plan, but that doesn't mean everyone will like it. Well, let's get it over with."

"Ben, after the introductions, each person on the committee will give a part of the presentation we worked on two weeks ago. They've all been practicing, and they sound good. I think it'll work out great!" Julie added a last comment as they rounded the corner to the lunchroom. "It's time to meet your public!"

As Ben entered the room, everyone started applauding. Ben stopped dead in his tracks. As he looked from face to face, Ben knew why he had worked so hard. These were good people, hard working people, who deserved a manager who respected them. Waving his appreciation, Ben moved to the platform at the far end of the room.

"Thank you. No more buttering up the boss. We're here to discuss something that's very important to all of us: the incentive plan. Your committee is here to give you the details of the plan and to take your questions. So, let's get underway." Ben sat down, and like a precision drill team, each committee member took his place at the microphone and covered step-by-step the details of the plan.

As the presentation went on, Ben was visibly moved. The applause had been one thing. Now, here he was, witness to a near miracle. A traditional manufacturing company rife with discord and confusion had been transformed into a team. The enthusiasm was palpable. Wiping tears from his eyes, Ben sat and listened. He needed to do nothing more.

After the presentation the committee began to take questions. The dialogue continued for 45 minutes until finally Brenda held up her hand. As if everyone knew what was going to be asked, the rest of the group fell quiet.

"Mr. Morgan, I mean Ben, the last two questions are for you," Brenda paused, waiting for some signal.

Ben was surprised, but quickly recovered. He inclined his head while holding Brenda's gaze. "What's on your mind? I'll answer any question if I can."

"Well, sir. The first is, we'd all like to know what this disclaimer is. The words are really hard to understand, but it sounds like Corporate is washing their hands of the plan. Is that what it means?"

"No, Brenda, it's not. It's Corporate's way of protecting themselves should it not work. They're behind the plan, but they feel like it's a plant decision, not a corporate one. They have to worry about setting precedents that could harm shareholders. The disclaimer simply says that they're doing their job. I hope that answers the first question. What's the second one?"

"Can you run the first answer past me again before we move on? I still don't quite understand the wording."

It was obvious that Brenda wanted more than a "packaged" answer, but Ben just couldn't see any use in giving them a blow by blow description of the problem. "Brenda, I don't know how else to say this. All I can say is that with any legally binding document, our lawyers have felt the need to clearly state the company's liability in the plan. They believe in the plan, but don't want to be sued by us or the stockholders should something go wrong that we haven't planned. It won't affect anything we do on a daily basis, I promise. Is your next question any easier, Brenda?" Ben was hoping to keep enthusiasm up by moving the questioning to an end. The vote was what mattered at this stage, not the problems in communicating to Corporate.

"It's simple, Ben. Where is your share and the plant's

managers? I understood from Carolyn that when we set this up that all of you were in the plan. Now, well, it's just us. What does that mean?"

"It means that the plan belongs to the work force, Brenda, not the company. We wanted to share with you because it meant sharing the gain and the pain. Corporate sees it differently. They feel that managers are judged on other financial criteria, such as total profit, and that participation in the plan would create a situation where conflict of interest could arise."

Ben continued on, hoping to convey his feelings with his words. "Brenda, you are the plan; you and everyone else that's here. You can make it a success or not, because in the end it's your choice whether to accept or reject it. And as we move forward, we've got to keep our perspective. I'm proud of the fact that this plan is as close to 100 percent ours as is possible. All that's happened is that Corporate has asked us to remember that the stockholders have rights, too. And the changes they made won't affect the final payout. It's a good plan, Carolyn, and I believe in it."

* * * * *

The plan was approved by an overwhelming majority, 93.8 percent of the workers approved it. Since a two-thirds majority had been chosen as the cutoff point, the final hurdle was jumped with ease. Surprisingly, Kathy O'Ryan voted against the plan in the end. Why? Because of one insurmountable problem: supermen couldn't be rewarded under the plan. Even though a pool had been set aside for raises, there was little doubt in anyone's mind that it would be divided equally at year-end.

Kathy had always been one of the top machinists in the plant. When the gainsharing system went into place, she was a loser. This, coupled with her fierce individualism, made it impossible for her to do anything but vote against the plan. And she never changed. Throughout the years, she stayed with her job, refusing to work in a cell or to support the JIT/TQC efforts. She did her job, married to her machine and her history.

* * * * *

Ben turned and left amidst cheers and congratulations. Alone, he walked back to his office. Julie couldn't get through the crowd to join him, and no one else really thought to go along. Each was caught up in the excitement, ready to do battle with the enemy. The general? He was tired, very tired.

INTERMISSION

"We now had to address our individual incentive system. The biggest problem was flat productivity. The reason was that all employees kept asking our IEs to check the rates. 'Hey, we think this rate is wrong, we think that rate is wrong,' and you can imagine why. On an individual incentive system, you want to maximize your own paycheck. Your goals aren't the same as the company's."

"Addressing the entire work force, I said, 'We produce and sell to a global market with global competition. Either we accelerate productivity, or we watch the company fail. I'd like to reform this company, and I hope that you do too, so please help me.'"

"Productivity had been improved by adopting JIT/TQC. We now needed to adopt a gainsharing philosophy because of problems with the individual incentive system. With the incentive system, everyone was in business for himself. Quantity was almighty, not quality, new ideas, or teamwork."

"For example, workers may resist new ideas or equipment because they fear they will be replaced. In order to overcome these concerns and to make the changes necessary to survive, we needed a fair and equitable gainsharing system. Fair means that everybody participates, not just direct labor, and that everybody participates at the same percentage because it takes the whole team to get the job done."

"To put gainsharing in place, we set up a task force made up of one person from each major department on the plant floor. By election, each group picked a representative. Naturally, they picked the strongest, most vocal employee, which was fine. We had 22 hourly employees and 3 managers. That ratio is about right in terms of mix, getting their input, and acceptance of the system."

"We looked at all sorts of systems before we decided on the Scanlon Multicost plan. We picked it because it paid based on productivity. Productivity is more output from the same input, or the same output from less input. The final decision, therefore, was based on our plant and the people in it. There was no way we could ask for help from the work force if it was going to lower their pay. What we needed was continuous improvement, and that could only be gained by total employee involvement. If we wanted them to help us improve profit performance, there had to be a clear tie between pay and performance."

Ben continued, moving into the gainsharing plan with zest. It had been a difficult process, leading in many ways to Ben's decision to leave Banyon. "I thought when we started that it would take six months to implement the new system. It took us 18 months from the time a decision was made to put in a new system to the first payout. It took that long because we had to do it right; and that is the speed at which the employees agreed. They're going to be affected, so you want to make sure everybody can make the trip and get there together."

"Here are the results. With a stiff initial hurdle, we had a payout the first month; we had a payout the first quarter; the first year, we had a payout every month. We now had suggestions increasing tenfold. Instead of having a suggestion box with cobwebs, we were getting hundreds of suggestions."

"What this shows is that minds are like parachutes. They work better when they open. Before, the employees believed they were giving ideas to the managers, but the managers were offended. Now we had employee involvement that translated to major productivity gains."

* * * * *

"If management's response to the gainsharing program had been more favorable, we might still have Ben with us."

Julie turned to whisper to Jim Andrews, who had just arrived at the conference. He'd been back at Banyon working on a major problem, but had finally got free. "Missed you, Jim. I was starting to feel like the last Mohican. It's hard to think of him leaving."

"I don't know. That's not what I heard."

"What do you mean by that?"

"I saw you trying out Ben's chair when you thought no one was looking!"

"What!"

"Come on Julie, you can hardly wait to start ordering us all around."

Julie gave Jim a hard poke, so hard he had to bite his tongue to keep from letting out a sound. "What did you do that for? Cripes, can't a guy have a little fun?" Jim was, despite his words, obviously enjoying himself.

"Fun, yes, but you're being pesty!" Julie quieted down, once more drifting back to the last few months at Banyon.

* * * * *

The fatal day was easy to pinpoint. Probe had asked Ben to do a plant tour and presentation for prospective vendors. Full of compliments, the Probe manager, Al Brown, couldn't say enough. Ben agreed, and two weeks later the group descended on the unsuspecting Banyon crew.

Julie and Jim took the visitors on a plant tour, and then Ben gave a formal presentation. While most of the guests sat at the conference table during the presentation, two men stood at the back. That didn't bother Julie as much as the way they asked questions and listened to Ben's answers. They didn't seem interested in getting information, but rather in testing Ben's knowledge. That angered her. Hadn't they already passed Probe's inspection? Was this another test?

After the presentation, Julie took charge of the group, leading them to the cafeteria for an informal wine and cheese reception. Ben was waylaid by the two men at the back of the room.

"Mr. Morgan, we were impressed with what you had to

say, and what you've done here at Banyon. We were wondering if you've ever thought about becoming a consultant? We're with Management Consulting Services at Coopers & Lybrand; you've probably heard of us as a 'Big Eight' accounting firm. We're expanding our manufacturing practices, and we could use someone like you." The taller man had been doing the talking. He looked to be about 45 years old and had a craggy face and blond hair.

As he paused, the other gentleman began. He looked much more like a consultant than the first, and his questions were pointed. "We see a big potential in this market, Mr. Morgan. The United States is getting pummeled from abroad, and this means change. When companies change, they buy expertise to help them over the hurdles, much as you've done here at Banyon. The pay is good, the hours long, but it gives you a chance to see your ideas take hold across the country, in company after company."

They piqued Ben's interest. He was tired of battling corporate. If this offer had been made prior to the last meeting with Walt McVicker's replacement, he would never have considered it. Instead? Well, it was something to think about.

"We're still in the middle of a JIT/TQC implementation. Each day we get better, and I have some bright people coming up behind me. But today? I'd never sleep if I left today. But, who can say about tomorrow or next month?" Ben ended the conversation by opening the door. On their way to the cafeteria, each made one more pitch, and gave Ben his business card for future reference.

Julie, of course, didn't think along these lines at all. She thought Ben was being cross-examined. When he arrived at the cafeteria seeming a little distant and thoughtful, she guessed the worse. She wasn't rude to the two unwelcome guests, but she conveniently forgot to give them any wine before the bar closed. No bar meant departing guests. By 6:00 P.M. all was quiet once again.

* * * * *

Julie's thoughts returned to the seminar in time to hear Ben launch into a thorny topic, the plant performance measurement system. Dealing with this had been the beginning of the end of Ben's career at Banyon. Even though he had eventually won, the unfolding events destroyed whatever loyalty Ben had left.

"Once we took care of the individual incentive system, we were able to make outstanding progress. Employees gave us ideas. What we found is that instead of having 40 engineers in a 400-person plant, we had 400 engineers because of our employee involvement program."

"The benefits are easiest to describe in terms of setups. With the help of individuals on the job we were able to make major improvements in our setup times that laid the groundwork for the flexibility we needed in other areas. One example is the die change procedure on our molding machines. Here, three separate ideas fueled the improvements: (1) we used fast-on/fast-off clamps on the hydraulic and water lines, (2) we eliminated all fasteners holding the die in place, relying on gravity to hold it, and (3) guidepins were used to eliminate all adjustment time. New dies could only go in one way because of the guidepins and the locking mechanisms. These changes allowed us to take setup time on these machines down to 39 seconds."

"What about the setup results in dollars? Many times we heard, 'Your setup dollars are going to go up, as you start setting up more often to accommodate reduced lot sizes.' Well, when you reduce a setup from 2 hours to 39 seconds, you can do the setup 8 times more often, or even 16 times more often, and you're still going to save money. In fact, our setup costs went down 50 percent in a 2 year period."

"Now, I'd like to turn your attention to performance measurement because this is a major problem with JIT systems."

"Typical performance measures in U.S. manufacturing include such things as the material price variance, labor in terms of efficiency and utilization, and burden in terms of spending. In a really exotic system you may see fixed and variable overheads."

"After we implemented JIT, my boss came in to chat with me. Herman is a nice guy; after all he gave me a promotion. He took the financial statement, threw it on my desk, and said, 'You take that just-in-time and throw it out. Your labor efficiency is down 5 percent, your utilization on standards is down 10 percent, and your burden absorption is down 6 percent.' He didn't even give me a chance to respond. By the way, this was at the end of what I considered to be one of our best months."

"That's a good example of employee involvement, right? Now I had a real problem. And I was upset because I faced yet another challenge: getting top management on my side. The stakes were high; I succeeded or I was out of a job. After Herman left, I went out to the plant and looked at the President's line. Mike, one of my key managers, was in the cell working on a problem. I started to talk to him, telling him about the visit and my frustration. I told him that Herman felt that we had lots of JIT-based labor problems."

"That puzzled Mike, so much so that he took me over to one of the machines. 'Ben, I don't understand how that can be so. The chart shows we used to have 10 people assembling, now we have 7. We used to have 5 people in indirect labor doing material handling, inspection, right down the line, and now we're down to 1. How can we be doing worse than before?'"

"Mike's question made a light go on in my head. Now I understood the problem."

"You see, with the cross training we had blurred the relationship between direct and indirect labor. Direct laborers were now picking up parts as soon as they came from the dock and placing them at the point of use; they were doing their own material handling and self-inspection. On issue after issue, I realized we were reducing the number of direct labor hours and redirecting direct labor into indirect tasks. That left us with fewer direct labor hour credits. And guess how we were absorbing overhead? On direct labor hours, a double whammy. Direct labor now was doing indirect work, looking less efficient in the process, and because of the decrease in direct hours, overhead absorption was going to hell in a handbasket. To put it bluntly, we were in deep yogurt."

Ah. The deep yogurt line. If there was one euphemism Julie was going to miss, this was it. What it meant, she was never sure, but it didn't seem to matter. The message was always clear. "Ben, you're going to introduce new slang in the English language on your travels throughout the country." Smiling, Julie drifted away again.

CHAPTER 13

A SECOND CHALLENGE: MEASURING SUCCESS

please, *v.* To lay the foundation for a superstructure of imposition.

Ambrose Bierce
The Devil's Dictionary

* * * * *

"I just don't get it. I know we're more efficient using JIT/TQC, and yet Herman Randolph walked in with financials that would make a grown man cry. We've shipped every order on time. We've reduced waste, setup time, cost, and our lead times are down. What in the devil is wrong? I know accounting systems can be problems, but this is beyond reason." Ben paced. Picked up the report, glanced at it, and tossed it back.

"Ben, stop! What's wrong? You're talking to yourself. Are you answering yourself, too?" Julie was joking, but she was too close to the truth for Ben to laugh.

"Not funny. Now I understand why people leap out windows. Are we getting better at what we do because of JIT/TQC?"

"What? Of course we're getting better. The plant has never run so well. Ben, what's up? I saw Randolph storm out of here. What could he possibly do to us now?"

"He wants us to dismantle JIT because it's causing unexplainable accounting variances. There are days I could kill bean counters. I'm wearing a hole in the rug trying to figure out what to do."

"We ask for their support; they make demands. I thought they'd be pleased with the turnaround. Expect the unexpected, I guess. Can you explain the problem to me? I'm slow when it comes to variances; I only understand advanced mathematics and basic logic. Accounting is something else!" Julie had studied little accounting.

"It's medieval; balance the ledger, and all else be damned. I'll try to explain it. Sometimes just doing that helps me clear my thoughts."

* * * * *

Banyon's accounting system, like that of most U.S. firms, reconciled actual results recorded in the general ledger with cost estimates provided by the standard cost system. In addition to balancing the debits and credits, this comparison generated a series of variances that were basic tools for performance measurement and control.

Material usage was evaluated using both purchase price variance (the quantity purchased multiplied by the difference between standard and actual cost per unit), and the materials usage variance (standard cost multiplied by the difference between actual and standard input for the amount of output). Labor was evaluated on one basic measure: direct efficiency, or earned hours versus actual for the month's output.

The majority of the measures focused on overhead. Using the plant as one cost center, analysis was done on budget versus actual costs, and absorption variances were calculated (for example, how much overhead was applied to product based on direct labor hours used). Being a sophisticated system, the overhead treatment included separate analyses of fixed, variable, and semivariable costs.

Banyon's accounting system treated the plant as one major cost pool with one cost object: product. A simple system of accounts for a complex production setting. Inaccuracy was to be expected, but how could it be so far out of sync with reality? It was often out of sync with common sense; but could it be out of sync with objective, observable success? This was hard to comprehend.

A Broken Control Loop

Before discussing performance measures meaningful in JIT settings, a basic flaw in the traditional standard cost accounting system must be addressed. Some have questioned whether the current accounting system is relevant for evaluating modern manufacturing, or whether it is being improperly used. While arguments can be made for both sides, one thing needs to be understood. The standard cost model, as used by accountants, is an incomplete system.

Control systems use feedback from actual operations to adjust both system and expectations. In contrast, existing accounting systems do not use information about deviations between planned and actual results to adjust or question the accuracy of the underlying standards. Instead, the variances serve two main purposes: to balance the general ledger, and to provide a method for holding managers responsible for the outcome. In standard cost models, the standard is assumed to be right, and reality, wrong. There is no incentive for anyone to prove otherwise, because doing so might generate a variance, and, hence, a reprimand.

In this world, meeting the standard is the hallmark of success. It is a world where mediocrity overwhelms excellence. Don't make waves, and don't cause trouble. Ayn Rand would understand the message.

JIT works toward continuous improvement. Its very essence connotes continuous variance. But the variance is in the accounting system, not in the process. In eliminating the cause for pause, JIT removes variance, the unexpected, from the manufacturing process. It is almost amusing that this short circuits the accounting system.

VISIBLE MEASURES OF SUCCESS

"Julie, you see what's happening, don't you? First, we've reduced the amount of labor in each job. That leads to major problems because it changes the absorption of fixed costs. Then we're mixing direct and indirect costs by setting up production cells. Everyone is doing the right job the first time, taking responsibility for the whole job. If inspection is needed, they inspect on site. The outcome is a blow to labor efficiency because the added time doesn't count as production."

"Wait a minute, Ben. Are you telling me the accounting system likes things the way they were? Late and wrong with lots of waste? Inspecting quality in instead of making good parts? Playing games to keep the numbers in line rather than focusing on the real job: making the best product possible with the least resources? Is that what you're saying with all this talk of variances?"

"To be blunt, yes. That's exactly what's happening. We'll have to be creative again. Get ready for some long hours, Julie. We'll have to work with the rest of the plant to develop performance measures that fit the JIT process. Doing a good job isn't enough to get top management on our side. We'll have to overwhelm them with facts."

New Measures for New Objectives

After examining the President's line for inspiration, Ben and Julie set to work. After thinking through the improvements made, they decided on four basic measurements: lead time, space utilization, quality, and work-in-process inventory levels. Not cost. Cost was caused by inefficiency. Since only activities causing cost could be managed, the rest was just a set of calculations.

JIT erodes the basic assumptions of the standard cost model. As direct labor per product is reduced, the accounting analysis breaks down. Why? Because direct labor is assumed to drive all other costs. Yet, at Banyon it was less than 7 percent of total product cost. Since nonvalue-adding activities were part of standard cost estimates, removing them or shifting them closer to the point of production violated most of the assumptions of the accounting model.

Today, this should be old news. The problems at Banyon were not unique, but they caused ulcers nonetheless. The tail was wagging the dog. No one heeded management experts who suggested that management was done best by walking around. Numbers were used to evaluate performance, giving false security where in reality the process was out of control.

Matching Measures to Performance

As Banyon progressed, they relied on the relationship between structure and strategy to develop measures to match information demands at each level in the organization. The underlying logic is presented in Figure 13-1.[1] Using four levels of analysis, market, business, plant, and shop, different, but linked measurement systems can be developed. At the market level, demands of the marketplace dominate other concerns. If a product can't be sold, there is no need to look further for the source of the problem.

Information at this level revolves around critical success factors. If the product is software, availability, reliability, flexibility, and cost are important. In high-tech industries lead time in new product design spells disaster or success. Conversely, in capital-intensive industries, frequent asset turns are critical. While all organizations need adequate resources to survive, the means to ensure continued viability vary with the industry and its objectives.

At the business level, specific company goals emerge. In high-tech industries market share, cash flow, and sales growth are primary areas for improvement. These goals translate to clear objectives at the plant level, as concerns with cost of quality, lead time, and cost per unit are the bases for success. In JIT/TQC these objectives are framed

---

[1] While many such "pyramid" structures exist in the management literature, this analysis was based on two specific works: the Hewlett Packard Model (see McNair, Mosconi, and Norris, *Beyond the Bottom Line: Measuring World Class Performance* [Homewood, Ill.: Dow Jones-Irwin, 1989]) and recent work by Richard Lynch of Wang Laboratories and Kelvin Cross of Judson, Gray, and Howard, that develops an integrated performance measurement system (for example, K. Cross and R. Lynch, "Accounting for Competitive Performance," *Journal of Cost Management*, Spring 1989, pp. 20-28). The authors especially thank Lynch and Cross for their support and comments.

A Second Challenge: Measuring Success   237

FIGURE 13–1
Hierarchy of Goals and Measures

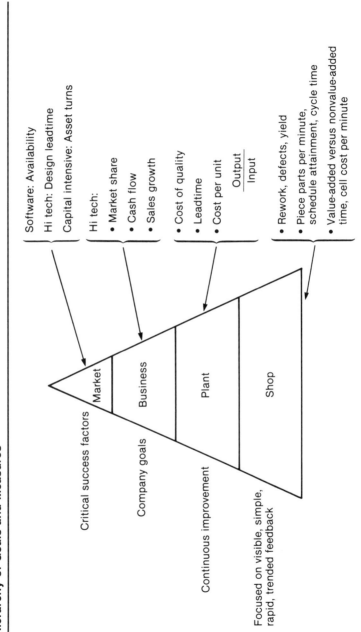

within continuous improvement. Workers search continuously for ways to make product better, cheaper, and faster in order to support company goals.

At the shop level, precise measurements are needed. Cost of quality is broken down into rework, scrap, and yield, which measures the cost of prevention, detection, and internal failure. Principle measures include schedule attainment, cycle time, and parts per minute. Finally, cost per unit measures value-adding versus nonvalue-adding time that, coupled with per hour cell cost, provides the basis for targeted cost reductions.

These objectives apply to the entire organization. If you can account for it, you can control it. For example, lead time to market consists of the time needed for marketing specifications, design, and production. In an integrated system, reductions in lead time can come from two sources: reductions by each function and reductions by working together.

Banyon needed an integrated performance evaluation system that would support plant management while providing information to the corporate parent. Ben had two options. First, he could serve as the buffer between the corporate parent and measurements used to steer the plant. This was his first decision, but unfortunately, this fell apart as JIT/TQC moved farther away from traditional manufacturing.

Second, Ben could change the performance measurements used by Corporate to match the reality of JIT/TQC. Several times in the implementation Ben tried this and failed. Now he had no choice. If he could not convince top management to use a new yardstick to measure the plant's performance, the battle would be lost. It seemed that after every successful skirmish, the enemy brought in reinforcements. Ben felt like David facing Goliath with one small difference. There were no more stones in his pouch.

Doesn't Time Mean Money?

"Julie, where do we start? We've reduced lead times drastically, yet our financial performance stinks! I was taught that time is money, yet we're using less time without making more money. Can you explain it to me?" Ben's look made Julie laugh even if his question didn't.

"I'm sorry, Ben, I didn't mean to laugh. I think the answer to your question has to be somewhere in this article on costing lead time improvements." They turned their attention to the article, looking for clues.

* * * * *

Lead time limits the capacity of a manufacturing system. It reduces the responsiveness of a supplier to a customer. It is false security. Managers love backorders; it assures them that there will be business tomorrow. It also means that customers have to wait for the product, not because of the time actually required to make it, but because of buffers and waste in the manufacturing process.

This is a static system. Product in various states of manufacture is everywhere. Massive storage areas with floor to ceiling racks are crammed with materials. It's hard to see movement amid the clutter.

JIT creates a dynamic system. The goal is to keep material flowing through the factory without a pause. Job orders are eliminated by converting a master production schedule to a daily schedule.

The lead time measure used by Banyon served two purposes: a direct measure of throughput efficiency and production schedule attainment. Throughput efficiency was measured in terms of days of inventory on hand. It was calculated by dividing inventory by daily cost of sales. This calculation provided WIP inventory progress and, over a longer term, progress toward the ultimate theoretical goal. Production schedule attainment was measured by the number of good units produced in the production schedule. Improvement in production schedule attainment indicated readiness to reduce inventory further. A variation was production linearity, or daily production consistency, which also measured JIT effectiveness.

Most managers are shocked when they realize that process time is only 1 to 5 percent of total cycle time. Banyon was no exception. After analyzing the President's line, they found that total cycle time was 46 days, yet less than one hour was value adding. Even factoring in waste for burn-in and similar processes, only two days were essential to the process.

Unnecessary lead time ties up resources that could be used to make more product. Long lead times mean orders and material are waiting in the pipeline. This requires detailed tracking of work-in-process and labor, and places undue emphasis on a forecast. But a forecast is not reality. Marketing can't foretell the future. They are guessing, perhaps using elegant models, but guessing nonetheless. This isn't dangerous unless spending and production are based on a forecast. If they are, every error results in finger-pointing and baseless accusations.

It's a game wherein the object is to blame someone for the waste that results from producing the wrong products and losing orders on the right products. This confusion results directly from the artificially long pipeline between supply and demand. Anything that shortens the pipeline will not only provide value to the customer, but also prevent loss to the supplier.

One final reason why lead time proved to be a good measure is that it reduced uncertainty in the production schedule. That may seem counter-intuitive, but remember that setup times were reduced drastically, and actual production time was down to a day or less. Mix change was no longer an issue. Ben didn't have to worry about building things that weren't needed. Every product was now built to demand. And unless total volume dropped, it was only a minor problem for the plant. Production was flexible and responsive, words seldom used in manufacturing.

With frequent updates on production results, Ben now knew exactly what had been made and what remained to be made. He could respond to problems as they occurred, not a month later when the variances came out.

Space? Where the Buffalo Roam...

"Give me land, lots of land, where the prairie winds blow, don't fence me in." Ben was humming to himself. Julie was sure there was a message in the song.

"Ben, stop!"
"And why?"
"You're making me crazy!"
"Crazier, you mean."
"Funny. Did that song mean something?"
"Maybe. Figure it out."
"It's either buffaloes or vacation time."
"Cold."
"You want to move your desk out to the lawn."
"Not close."
"They're making the plant into a landfill."
"Enough!!"
"Well, then, what is it?"

"We're both spending too much time here, Julie. I get corny, you get cornier. Anyway, getting serious for a moment," Ben paused, looking anything but serious, and moved on. "Julie, what do we call our building and the support costs that go with it when we put together the accounting reports?"

"Is this a test? Capacity costs? The cost of doing business. What do I win?" Julie put out her hand, and Ben dropped a mangled paper clip into it. "Gee, thanks, I'll treasure it!"

"Ah, be thankful for the little things, Julie. The way I figure it, that space is our biggest assumption. We need a lot of things to fill up that space, and if it's empty, we feel like we need more stuff. Ever had an empty closet?"

"Ben, I'm not sure I get it. Can you give me another hint?"

* * * * *

Unused or inefficiently used space is waste. It forgoes profits that could be earned by putting another product line into the plant; it lengthens move and queue to cover the distance.

Recognizing this, Ben used incentives to encourage supervisors to consolidate the space occupied by their lines. If they controlled the space, they were evaluated on the efficiency of its use. Floor space filled with inventory is lost capacity. Factory walls then become constraints on growth.

Creative approaches to increasing capacity, such as using rail cars in the back lot to store inventory, demonstrate an understanding of this problem. Running out of space means that growth will stop unless the resources necessary to increase capacity can be found.

Figure 13–2 shows that Banyon reduced its floor space by implementing JIT/TQC. From a peak of 100,000 square feet, the same production now required just over 40,000 square feet, 40 percent of the original. Ben could take on 60 percent more production in the same facility, increasing the overall profitability and productivity of the basic resource base.

If a space incentive had not been used, it is unlikely that such major improvements would have occurred. The cells would have spread out, increasing move, queue, handling, and scrap. Reducing the distance traveled by the product was a visual way to show what shortening the pipeline meant to the customer.

FIGURE 13–2
Manufacturing Floor Space

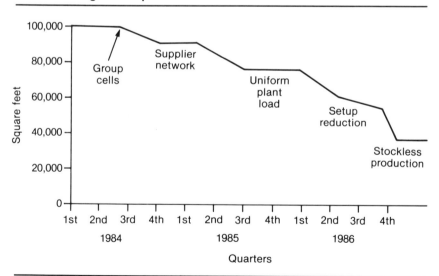

Source: Coopers & Lybrand.

Quality: Key to Ongoing Success

The cost of quality was discussed at great length earlier. The reason for maintaining quality measures was to prove that increasing the quality of the product and the process decreased total cost. In addition, the new measurement system was based on good units produced. Since zero defect production was the key to getting credit for cost relief and for productivity calculations under the gainsharing plan, accurate maintenance of these records was critical.

Defect levels per million parts, as well as extended cost of quality, were the key TQC measures Banyon maintained. They supported the trend of defect levels and served as a visual check of patterns and improvements.

WIP: Liability, Not Asset

"Jim, what do you think of this list of basic measures? There are some subsidiary measures, such as setup time, scrap, and rework, but they fall under one of the major categories. I think we're missing something."

Julie was looking over the list as Jim entered. Walking across the room, he picked up Julie's pad before settling into a chair. It didn't take him long to find the missing measure. "There is something missing, Julie, inventory numbers. If we're talking about improvement, what better area is there? We've cleared mountains of the stuff from the plant floor. I didn't know there were people and machines in some of those corners."

"That's funny. Earlier, Mike Gannon complained he was losing his nests. He was kidding, but it would've been easy to sleep the day away hidden by inventory that never seemed to move. Unless, of course, it was a pile that needed expediting! I don't miss those days. When I come to work now, it's different. We think about tomorrow, about getting better, not about pushing orders out the door."

"Jim, what's a good way to measure inventory? A measure that says it costs money, it's not an asset, it's burying us. That's the message, but how do we convey it?"

"Well, we want the measure to decline, then disappear. One measure is total dollars, or square feet of floor space, or number of components. What's the key to the havoc it causes in the process?"

"My guess is number of parts, but that gets soft. We already measure floor space. I think it has to be dollars, although that makes me nervous given our cost accounting system. Ben and I went over that in detail, and it was frightening. The problem is that every time the level declines we look inefficient because of the way they absorb burden. Heaven save us from bean counters!"

* * * * *

The system Ben and his staff developed used these measures, as can be seen in Table 13-1. Performance was measured and the trends displayed in the plant. Anyone could walk to the chart and see where the line or process started and where it was at the moment. The final target was also marked on the chart, so that everyone would know the ultimate goal. It was an inexpensive way to get good data from production centers to management. This accelerated feedback and made management by walking around a fruitful experience.

TABLE 13-1
Group Cell

Existing Measures	New Measurements
Monthly budget Order accumulated	Work-in-process inventory
None	Throughout time or total cycle time

Actual/standard
  Work order/operation
	Total labor time per unit
	  (direct and indirect)

None	Setup times
Monthly bucket No scrap factors	Scrap and rework

Source: Coopers & Lybrand.

Employees were responsible for updating the charts daily. The reason, according to Ben, was that they got involved in the process. It also provided a way to recognize them when they achieved a target. Rewards and recognition anchored the improvements and motivated further efforts. When a performance target was met, Ben's next question was, "What do you think? What target do you want to set now? Are there any projects you'd like to tackle that will make things even better?"

This might seem like management by stress, but it is a necessary part of continuous improvement. If a worker meets a target and it isn't changed, it becomes an engineered standard rather than a tool for motivation. It is a dangerous tool, nonetheless, one that can be destructive if trust, respect, and human dignity are abandoned. The tool itself is benign. It is its use that determines its final impact on the people system.

Finally, it is important to remember that continuous improvement is gained through process and product redesign, not by pressure on employees to work harder. The latter view underlies traditional manufacturing systems; the former, more humanistic approach, is the cornerstone of JIT/TQC. If the underlying process can be improved, people produce more with less effort.

The idle time on the President's line and the success in electronic counters proved that the same work and more could be done with fewer resources. If 12 workers are taken from rework and put on the line to make good product, everyone's job is easier.

Clear Results

"Ben, did you see the numbers on the President's line? I knew we'd done a good job out there, but I'm still surprised that we got so much more product out using the same resources!"

Julie was looking over the summary reports of the President's line progress from before the changeover to JIT/TQC to the present. The employees on the line had done the charting, and the look on Brenda's face when she submitted the report told the story. They were proud of what they had done; now everyone could see their success.

"I still can't believe it." Ben reread the material. "They've taken lead time from 60 days to 1 day, space from 10,000 square feet to 1,000 square feet, and at the same time made major improvements in quality. Yields have gone from 50 percent to 90 percent on the boards used in the line. If Herman Randolph still can't see that JIT's working, the war is lost." Ben was looking at several reports, including one showing the reductions in inventory [see Figure 13–3].

"No war is ever lost, just delayed in the winning." Julie was optimistic again. The storm over incentives had passed, and life at Banyon had returned to normal. "I bet even Herman will understand the last number. Work-in-process for Presidents has dropped from $200 thousand to less than $50 thousand. We accomplished this with increased volume and new products on the line. Do we give them a bottle of champagne and a bonus?"

Julie had a point. There had to be a way to reward this

FIGURE 13–3
Inventory, May 1984–December 1985 ($ million)

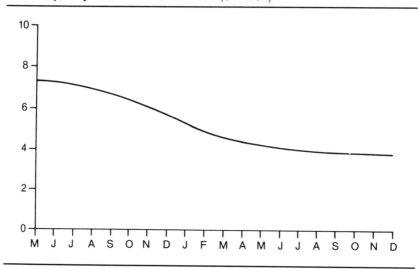

Source: Coopers & Lybrand.

performance. Financially, the gainsharing plan was doing its job, and Ben wasn't going to change it. But he could give awards and give a small reception. Ron Eddy had taught Ben the power of recognition.

"Julie, I think a party is in order. I want you to get plaques, not cheap ones but good ones, and I want them engraved with the name of each person on the line. When we get reports from the other cells, we'll repeat the process. Since Presidents was first, it's logical that they should be recognized first. Let me know when we can have them, and we'll arrange a reception off site. I think these people have earned a bonus from the petty cash fund. It's money well spent."

JIT was working at Banyon despite little support from top management, high-variety production, and other obstacles because the people in the plant tried, because 400 people pulled in the same direction.

* * * * *

Success underscored the tremendous impact made by challenging assumptions used to design workflow and by learning to treat employees as assets rather than as liabilities. Inventory became a liability, workers became assets, an interesting change of positions.

CHAPTER 14

ACCOUNTING COMES OUT OF THE CLOSET

The business world is obsessed with the bottom line. It is the report card used to evaluate management. It is the gauge by which stockholders judge the wisdom of their investments, and it is the basis of bonuses. It is the essence of capitalism, earning a profit from an investment.

The language of the bottom line is accounting. While inadequate in many respects, it is the basic tool of all organizations. It is guilty more for omissions than inclusions. Yet, accounting serves an important economic role in society: it evaluates alternative uses of scarce resources.

Ben's problem was that Banyon did not measure up on the corporate yardstick. Unless he could translate the improvements into accounting terms, into cost savings, and increased profits, he would not succeed in the long run. The challenge was to link the visible signs of success to the dollars and sense of accounting. Ben had to prove that JIT resulted in higher profits, a better bottom line.

* * * * *

"Details, details, details. No wonder accountants are a strange lot, all they do is struggle with details. Let's see, Ben said to start folding things into different pools, to see if different groupings of cost change our reported results."

Julie had been struggling with the project for hours. While she had enjoyed learning about JIT, this was drudgery. She was in front of her PC, becoming friendly with her spreadsheet program; put the numbers in, crunch, and think. "I'm glad I'm not doing this by hand!"

Julie began to see patterns. Ben felt the most accurate data would come from redefining each JIT line as the initial cost pool, rather than using product for the basis as accounting suggested. "Accounting pools labor, materials, and overhead from the ledger to the product. It's simple enough, although that monstrous overhead account would frighten even the stoutest heart."

The figures Julie got from accounting on the costs assigned to product in the President's line are presented in Table 14–1. From the numbers it was easy to see that labor controls should be de-emphasized, that overhead should be reduced, and that profits were to be made by design and choice of materials.

Focusing on work centers seemed to be the right approach. The issue was redefining direct and indirect costs. In traditional accounting this decision would be based on the ability to trace costs to the source. When Julie put all traceable costs together such as depreciation and labor, the numbers were skewed. She got wide swings on some of the unit costs when calculated solely on total units produced per the month.

"The volume effect again. Well, I can't wipe it out. I wonder if it might be better to focus on things supervisors can control. I sure wouldn't want to be held responsible for

TABLE 14–1
"President" Product Costs

Labor	$ 6.40	6 percent
Overhead	17.60	18 percent
Material	75.25	76 percent
Total	$99.25	100 percent

Therefore:
   De-emphasize labor control.
   Emphasize nonvalue-added elimination.
   Emphasize supplier long-term partnership.
   Emphasize material design effectiveness.

Source: Coopers & Lybrand.

someone else's decision to buy one machine over another. I think it's time for input from Ben and John."

CONTROLLABLE COSTS

The issue Julie struggled with is not new. Defining cost to match responsibility in an organization is the objective of an entire branch of accounting. The key is whether the person can control the costs. If not, there's strong evidence that holding him responsible for those costs can create motivational problems.[1] Banyon decided to emphasize control, defining it as cost supervisors could affect without having to ask permission from management.

Under this definition labor, whether indirect or direct, was included in cell costs. Maintenance, supplies, and inspection were identified as controllable and included. Depreciation was not. The supervisor could affect the amount of inspection by improving quality. On the other hand, he had to live with the equipment allocated. In the short run this cost could not be controlled in the same way.

The Logic behind Excluding Depreciation

Line supervisors can request new machines when problems occur with existing capacity, but this is not the normal way that new capital expenditures are made. At Banyon the line supervisor was only tangentially involved in asset acquisition. Of greater concern was the problem of volume change.

---

[1]Recent theoretical work in an area called "agency theory" suggests that in some situations controllability is more directly related to taking responsibility for a pool of costs, because in so doing the individual can exert control upward in the hierarchy. Whether the benefits of increased control upward in the hierarchy can justify the downside risk of demotivation arising from holding an individual accountable for large chunks of cost over which he really *does not* exercise control, is a question for future research. At Banyon, the key person in the system was the line supervisor. It is questionable whether this person could exert enough pressure on management to change spending patterns.

Volume isn't determined by line workers; it comes from an analysis of projected demand, and ultimately, from customer purchasing patterns.

In creating the new system, Ben tried to match the structure of the accounting system to that of the plant. He purposely excluded all costs from reports sent to the production floor over which management had more control than employees. Fixed costs, such as depreciation, could seriously distort the evaluation of cell performance.

* * * * *

"How can we remove the cost of the extra Genrad tester from the President's line cost pool, John? There has to be some way to do that in the accounting system." Ben pored over Julie's reports. She'd run the numbers on the President's line because the real results were plotted already, giving a base for evaluating potential accounting system solutions.

"Ben, have you forgotten all of your accounting? Probably, by choice. There's a method called 'units of production' depreciation that charges the product, or cell in this case, only if the machine is used. The problem we have is that it takes a lot of time to keep track of the transactions. And the President's line is confusing. If a machine is set aside, it doesn't stop losing value. The accounting system has to reflect its value according to the market, and using units of production methods can mean big write-offs downstream or growing pools of obsolete equipment at inflated values if the asset isn't used consistently."

"It sounds complex, John. I want to keep it simple because tracking this detail is nonvalue-adding. If we want to do away with transactions, there's no merit in adding more." Ben returned his attention to Julie's report, looking for an answer.

"I see your point, Ben. For now we won't add it to the pool. But remember, whatever we do for internal reporting, I have to get these uncontrollable costs to the bottom line one way or another. The Internal Revenue Service (IRS) is insistent, as is the Financial Accounting Standards Board

(FASB), that we use full absorption cost in valuing inventory. But I think we can justify separating the costs for ongoing reporting as long as we agree on what costs will go into the direct charging system, and what will be restricted to the financial reporting system."

"Do you agree with our reasoning, John? I mean, every way we turn depreciation causes problems. I know that we can trace those costs to the cell, but I'd like some clean measures that fit with the operating results."

John thought a moment before responding. "I agree, but for different reasons. Even units of production methods rely on some estimate of capacity through the machine. Think about those JIT cells, Ben. The goal is to increase capacity by decreasing setup time and other waste. That means that the unit charge out of the accounting system would always be wrong. While we could fix that, it would require far too much work. I have fewer accountants than before; there's just no time for work like that."

"And it would be waste if you did it."

"Right."

"So, what are your real thoughts?"

"I'd like us to simplify the accounting system. You know, streamline it so it's easy to maintain, relevant, not full of useless detail."

"So, you're in favor of change?"

"That's an understatement. The key is to facilitate decisions. And, I'll need to know who's responsible for them. We need a decision-support system that can trace results to the people who can control them."

"Good. That way I can take responsibility for decisions that I make, like getting rid of that tester in President's. I want that thing off the books; it's really not useful any more. We're looking for a buyer, and it should sell for more than its book value. It's a valuable piece of equipment, but we don't need it."

"Glad you warned me, Ben. I'll alert corporate. That only leaves one major issue, but it's a big one. What are we going to do about the standard cost system? It's only updated once a year. How are we going to use it without blowing your measurements out of the water? Standard costs are the numbers corporate wants; they're the reason you got nailed by Randolph. What should we do? We need to think about it now, but worry about it later. This changeover can only be done one step at a time."

Ben was lucky. John was a supportive controller. When cost of quality reports were requested, he provided them along with a new system of reporting these numbers. Now he was willing to modify some fairly sacred concepts in the accounting system. His attitude transformed a potentially stormy change into a productive analytical exercise.

What's Broken?

Is the accounting system broken? In the last chapter the breakdown in the standard cost system was described. The answer is the evolution of a new form of standard costing that focuses more on getting and keeping accurate estimates. Many companies now use rolling averages of actual costs as the standard for crediting the WIP or RIP (raw-in-process) accounts. Materials are debited to the account when received, for example, the balance is increased. After production is completed, one transaction, a credit, is used to move these costs directly into finished goods. This isn't a new or a revolutionary approach.

The difference appears when the matter of variances arises. For costing to be complete, variances must be used to adjust the standard. But how often? Banyon developed a simple rule. If the difference is less than 10 percent, no update. That doesn't mean the information is discarded, but that the accounting system passed the adjusting entry to the burden or uncontrollable cost pools. Greater than 10 percent? The standard is adjusted accordingly. This handled the gradual change in cost patterns associated with JIT, because at some stage the cumulative difference would exceed the cutoff point. It was a simple, easy solution to an ongoing problem.

The cost per unit per cell, then, was calculated by dividing total controllable costs by the number of good units produced per reporting period. Given the fact that the basic pool of controllable costs was selected based on decisions made at the cell level, the numerator proved to be a good base for evaluating improvement. The denominator, because of the stabilization of volume through uniform plant load procedures, proved to be a good approximation of effectiveness.

The per unit measure, controllable cost per good units, gave clear signals on quality and cost performance together. Because it's a ratio, a change in any factor affecting the numerator or denominator can affect the value, but as long as the original amounts are reported, the data will be in line with what is taking place on the plant floor.

* * * * *

"Julie, this looks like it will work. Look at maintenance on the President's line. Once the process was under control and inventory off the floor, we did more preventive maintenance. The first month controllable costs went up. As time passed, total cost came down as scrap from machine breakdowns and lost time decreased. Quality went up markedly. It makes sense; we put dollars into preventing mistakes. In the long run it decreases controllable costs per unit because maintenance is less expensive than poor quality. There are more good units, and schedules are met. That reduces overtime needed to get product out the door."

"You have the numbers you need for corporate now, Ben. When do you present them?" Julie wasn't anxious. Each time Ben went up against Corporate, he got angry, and he seemed less willing to commit to a future at Banyon. Ever since the meeting with Probe, he had been acting mysteriously.

"Soon, but not yet. I want to have it nailed down, stamped with John's seal of approval, and run past internal audit. When I go, I want to know I'm right."

A CHANGING VIEW OF LABOR

One of the big issues in accounting today is the shrinking role of direct labor, the increasing role of indirect labor, technicians for example, and the impact this has on a system designed around labor. As already mentioned, labor at Banyon was less than 7 percent of total cost. It was not a major component.

Moving to cell configurations highlights the process rather than its individual parts. The system converts materials into product, not people at workstations. Therefore, process efficiency is more important than labor efficiency. As well, the process may be improved by using direct labor to perform indirect tasks, such as moving material to the line, inspecting produced units, and maintaining machinery on a daily basis.

These changes blur the relationship between direct and indirect labor causing the traditional accounting system to break down. If overhead is absorbed on this now ambiguous number, the entire accounting system fails. Having been examined by efficiency experts for years, it is unlikely that huge amounts of waste are buried in the labor cost pool, and JIT's highly visible process flow makes any slack in performance noticeable immediately. Queues build up, the Kanban is filled, and the line goes down. There is no need to add more accounting numbers to the control system; no more control is gained in the process.

* * * * *

"Let's see what the people on the President's line think about these ideas, Julie. They're being evaluated, so it seems right to ask them. Besides, Brenda has kept us out of trouble before. She may see something we don't see."

Ask the worker to help design the accounting system? In an environment built on trust, it is wise.

"Mr. Morgan, Julie, how are you? What brings you to the line?" Brenda spotted Ben and Julie long before they got to her cell. After all, there was no inventory blocking her view.

"We need advice." Ben liked Brenda and trusted her. The feeling was mutual. "We talked last week about the changes we want to make to the accounting system. Have you given it any thought?"

"Among other things, you asked me how to deal with

labor charges. Why keep track of it at all? I can see what my people are doing, and I don't care if payroll designates them as direct or indirect. They're all part of the team."

Brenda continued. "We wonder if we can let labor reporting slip a little, maybe to the end of the process like we do with materials. At the end of the line, one person can generate all the labor charges with one entry. You may think it violates the rules about punching another person's clock, but it doesn't. The real time clock is by the door. Here our time clock is the production schedule and the good units we get out of the cell each day."

"That makes sense, Brenda. And if I know you, you've already set up a system for doing this. Right?"

Brenda briefly, almost imperceptibly, smiled. "Well, I guess you might say so. How does this look?" She handed Ben a single piece of paper she had retrieved from her desk drawer.

What Brenda and her team had created was straightforward. The team was clocked into a production run at the first operation and clocked off at the last. Time spent in the cell was assumed to be needed. If not needed, the cost remained the same. The measure was consistent with continuous improvement.

"Great, this looks great! Julie, what do you think?"

"I think if you're not careful, Brenda will be running the plant." Julie winked at Brenda, deadpanning Ben at the same time.

"I didn't know she wanted the job. Here's my tie, Brenda. Give me your smock. I've always liked blue." Ben was removing his tie.

"No, thank you. If you think I'm going to trade my job for yours, you're crazy, Mr. Morgan. I like it right here. You fight the dragons. You're good at it!"

"Are you sure? If I figure right, with the gainsharing bonuses you're getting, Brenda, I could make more money back here. If you decide to change your mind, I'm ready!"

* * * * *

The new labor reporting system worked well. The accounting system absorbed overhead based on process manpower, not direct labor alone, but total process time. It gave John Rust a system he could sell to the auditors and to Corporate, while eliminating a tremendous number of transactions from the accounting system.

The final benefit from the new labor reporting system was that industrial engineers were now working on process improvements instead of setting process rates; rates didn't add value to output, improvements did. Once again, it directed attention to planning, prevention, and effectiveness, to looking forward instead of backward, to more control, not less. Control moved from individuals to the process. People were no longer the problem; they were the solution.

Figure 14–1 shows improvements on the President's line in total labor efficiency using the new measurements. The results were impressive and moved in the right direction. The numbers meant something to everyone.

Labor efficiency variances were dropped from the reporting system. As part of the controllable cost pool, labor charges were linked to the use of all resources in the cell.

FIGURE 14–1
"President" Labor Efficiency

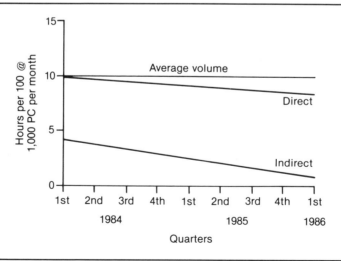

Source: Coopers & Lybrand.

Labor might increase, but in the long run this would mean lower total costs.

The remaining calculation compared the cost of good units from month to month, a simple measure giving real information; not elegant, but effective. Any trade-offs made by the supervisor within the cell would be based on total process efficiency, not on how the change affected the cell's variances. These were moves in the right direction, focusing everyone's attention on making better product, not managing numbers.

REPORTING TO CORPORATE

The day had come. Ben and John Rust were at Corporate to explain the new accounting structures and roll-up procedures they had put in place. They came loaded with an arsenal of slides and charts showing the benefits of changing the performance measurements used to evaluate the plant.

Ben began by describing the JIT/TQC efforts, the visual improvements in throughput time, first pass quality, and space utilization that the new system provided. Describing the system and its benefits provided a logical basis for discussing the shortcomings of the existing plant measurement system. Ben described the diagnostic they used in determining the changes needed to bring the measurement system in conformance with plant performance and process characteristics.

* * * * *

"As you can see from this slide, (Table 14–2), we identified eight major areas where changes were needed to match accounting results to plant performance. After looking at the problem, John suggested that we change our basic cost model from job order to process cost. This was a major shift, resulting in a de-emphasis on labor and material reporting and an emphasis on good units of output."

Ben discussed the major assumptions of the revised accounting system. If the corporate controller was going to ac-

TABLE 14-2
Cost Accounting Diagnostic Areas

Assess changes needed to achieve:
   Job to process (period) costing
   OH allocation—other than direct labor
   Reduced direct labor analysis
   Reduced setup and down-time analysis
   Variable budgeting—OH, volumes
   OH from fixed to variable
   Hourly pay plans—piece to group
   New efficiency measures
      Machine to labor/unit
      Department to product
      Variable OH/unit
      Quality cost/unit
      Enterprise-wide labor hours to hours shipped

Source: Coopers & Lybrand.

cept the new system, he would need to know the assumptions made in designing the system, its integrity, and its auditability.

"The impact of JIT/TQC emerged as we began to analyze overhead accounts. We discovered several major conflicts between the current accounting system and JIT manufacturing objectives. First, by pursuing uniform plant load, fixed overhead costs became variable. Why? Because volume and mix shifts were compatible with the system. JIT is a stressed system; shifts in volume required compensating changes in capacity. Capacity was now directly related to output; the relevant range of production was narrowed."

"The second problem came from the way labor is assigned in a cell. Every individual is an equal member of the team, which meant that the traditional boundary between direct and indirect labor was gone. It isn't a major problem unless the accounting system is driven by direct labor as ours was. Each of you has seen the impact this had on our traditional efficiency and effectiveness measures. In fact, it's the reason we're here today." Ben paused, looking around the room. So far everyone seemed to be paying attention, but that would change if he didn't get to the heart of the issue soon.

"I'd like to turn the discussion over to John because we're now moving into accounting system details. He can do a much better job of answering your questions. We're here to answer them, not to sell you anything." Ben sat down, and John proceeded.

JIT Accounting Meets Corporate

"Thank you, Ben. I'd like to focus on the impact the JIT/TQC methods have on the accounting system. As you can see, JIT changed the basic assumptions of the manufacturing process and required an overhaul of the accounting model. Ben needed new efficiency measures to keep track of plant performance. This was difficult to do as the data coming into the accounting department continued to change." John carefully guided the discussion through the major issues and solutions Banyon had employed in matching accounting to performance.

"The elimination of detailed labor and material tracking accompanying the move to process costing created severe problems. We had to replace this information without overloading the plant with burdensome, nonvalue-added reporting. Common sense suggested that we use the data already generated." John paused, flipping a page of his notes forward before resuming.

"We had two basic transactions within the JIT cell: material receipt and finished goods movement. Using the bill of materials as well as a process flow analysis done by engineering, we were able to reconstruct accounting system transactions without adding complexity to the flow of work in the cell. Material receipts were used to trigger the input transaction to RIP inventory, to relieve the purchase order, to generate payment to the vendor via wire transfer, to delete the open materials commitment record from the MRP system, to update the material cost records, to calculate material spending variances, and finally, to input a record of performance into the vendor history file. An impressive list of transactions, all driven by the receipt of materials *at the cell*, not the loading dock."

"John, can I stop you before you go on? Are you saying that nothing happens when the material is received at the plant door? That looks like a potential internal control problem to me," Hal Wyman, Assistant Controller, had raised the question in everyone's mind: how were they safeguarding the system?

"I had that concern myself, Hal," John responded. "When material arrives, it doesn't sit on the dock or go to storage; it's received on delivery by someone from the cell. You see, they've bypassed nonvalue-adding move and queue transactions. The internal controls are intact as long as we don't allow them to do their own purchasing. Does that answer your question?" Hal nodded, and John moved on.

"When good units leave the cell, the remaining accounting transactions are generated. We 'backflush' labor and material transactions, relieving RIP, and move dollars into finished goods. This eliminates a lot of transactions and gives us everything we need to cost product and maintain inventory. The caveat, of course, is that the total cycle time in the cell must be minimized. We couldn't give up control of in-process work orders if this weren't the case."

Providing Information to Management

Seeing no raised hands, John moved from the general ledger transactions to information being created by the new system. "I'd like to shift your focus from input to output of the accounting system. This is where we add value to the process."

"Cost of quality calculations are done on a product line basis. While we started using the entire plant as the focus, we found the number didn't give us the information we needed to evaluate the progress of each cell. What the quality number provides is a benchmark, a way to compare performance in one area with that in another. Since we've been working with limited resources, these numbers have helped us see where we can get the most bang for the buck with quality upgrades. This has made project selection easier."

John excelled. Ben admired his style, presenting difficult concepts clearly. The paucity of questions indicated that the message was understood, even if not liked.

"Next, I'd like to show you the lead time measures we've developed," John continued. "Another way to think of this is as total throughput time, or how long it takes to produce a product from the point materials are released to the floor until finished goods are delivered to the dock."

"These problems are augmented if setup times are long and piece rate incentives used. Why? Because incentives require long runs of the same product. If an order is delayed due to part shortages, or if the lot size is small, no one wants to run the job. Backlogs and late orders result. JIT removes this problem by shrinking setup time; less time per setup means more setups can be done while maintaining the same level of output. JIT smooths problems in the production process, and that makes the accountant's job a lot easier. It eliminates the need for complex reporting systems to keep track of errors, delayed orders, and waste."

"Excuse me, but I'm having a problem with this," Gordon Shillinglaw, the Corporate Controller, interrupted. "The accounting system doesn't track waste, it tracks orders and costs. I hope we haven't lost sight of the fact that accounting information is used in decision making throughout the organization, and that it serves more than one master. John, you know as well as I do that if the system's integrity is attacked at its base, any other information will be useless. I have a lot of stockholders who look to me to protect their investment. That's your job, too."

"I couldn't agree with you more, Gordon. What I'm struggling with, in fact, is that very concern. Plant level reporting is a challenge because it's a key translation point; corporate, financial, and strategic objectives are translated to daily operating objectives. While I think we've done a fairly good job through the budgeting process translating goals down the pyramid, I'm not as comfortable with the job we've been doing on the way up."

"If managers at all levels aren't given relevant information, the system will break down. All we're trying to do is integrate the plant performance measurement system into the corporate system without losing information or reliability at any level." John handled the second question as well as he had handled the first. It wasn't really a direct answer to Gordon's question, but it was enough to placate him until John reached the audit portion of his presentation.

"Getting back to capacity, it was assumed that adding more machines would solve the problem. But you may not need more capacity; rather, you may need to use what you have better. It can be done by eliminating bottlenecks. This is what we've been able to do in molding by reducing setup time from 1 hour to 39 seconds. If you reduce setup time and improve quality, you increase capacity without new equipment. How we measured this was to divide the time available by the number of units produced to see if that measure of effectiveness changed as setup and quality improved."

Tricking the MRP System

"Another change we've accomplished is the elimination of paper arising from detailed work orders both in accounting and in the MRP system. As we moved to JIT, we decreased lot sizes to match Kanban levels. As lot sizes decreased, work orders increased. It became clear that if we didn't eliminate work orders we would fill the factory with them, each requiring handling, a nonvalue-adding cost."

"In addition to the mass of paper, we couldn't hire enough people to keep the paper flow moving. So, we took the monthly production plan for the President's line, at the time 1,000 units per month, and made it one work order. Total production was divided into even daily lots, adding stability to the process. Everyone knew, day to day, week to week, what was expected. Expediting became unnecessary. We had a lot of expediters. Now they're planners."

John glanced at Ben, looking for some sign that the presentation was going well. The lack of feedback could be good or bad. Ben shrugged his shoulders, a sign that he wasn't sure of the general mood in the room. With no new information, John's only option was to continue.

"We tricked the MRP system because we had to. Every time we decreased the size of work orders, problems increased within the system. Instead of work orders, we began to use the master production schedule as our basic tool. By dividing monthly output by 20, we developed a daily production rate. By using a flat bill of materials, we avoided stockroom transactions."

"Parts are taken out of stores as needed; transactions are generated on completion of specific work orders or daily runs. The MRP system only sees one monthly order, but everyone else works from daily orders. Finally, we make sure the materials group is informed of part movements, not through the MRP system, but rather by sending them 'partial completion' notices each day. They know planned production loads, and what's in process. Doing the reconciliation is simple."

"What this means for the accounting system is the marriage of two accounts: raw and in-process inventories. All material was at the cell. Now, when materials are received they go directly to the cell and directly to RIP. When we complete a unit, the RIP account is backflushed to transfer cost per unit to finished goods, using the logic embedded in the MRP system."

"Material handling has been greatly reduced, and transactions in the entire system minimized. This frees time in accounting to work on planning and analysis. In a given month we now have 20 to 22 inventory transactions compared to thousands prior to the change."

John turned the presentation back over to Ben with a quiet sigh of relief.

Moving through Labor

Ben described the changes the plant was making to its basic labor pools and cell costs. Line after line showed improvements in asset utilization, total effectiveness, and responsiveness. The proof seemed overwhelming.

"We've done cell design and line balancing on the fly with operators taking the lead role in finding and implementing process improvements. They're involved with the process directly; they can see where changes will make a difference. By charting in the cell, they can see if the change is making a difference in productivity. This information is not useful by person, because the goal is to make the system work better. That may mean shifting more work to one person. This shift doesn't mean one person is more efficient, the other less. It simply means the process is more involved. If you use any kind of idle time charge in this setting, it's like reading yesterday's news. You can see if everyone is busy, you don't need a measure for that."

"The gainsharing system made this even more important. The calculations are done on net sales less controllable costs. To know how to improve this measure, you need root cause data, not packaged summaries. What is important is the process, not the cost. If the process is right, costs will improve."

"This is our problem with many of the accounting reports. The accounting information sent out in the past made people happy or sad, but not smart. It doesn't identify root cause. By using JIT and TQC concepts, you can pinpoint the reasons for cost symptoms and take corrective action quickly."

Inventory Accounting

The next slide described the inventory accounting system Ben and John wanted to put in place. This was critical. If the managers in the room accepted the logic of the new system, the plan was home free. Otherwise? Ben had better get a new job.

As can be seen in Figure 14–2, the system was elegant in its simplicity. Two main transactions occur, with adjustments based on cycle counts and scrap tickets for control purposes. The difference was visual. It was then that questions began to fly. Seeing the details of the inventory system freed the tongues of managers not wanting to interrupt until they had a clear understanding of the proposal.

"Are you saying you want to move to the second system?

FIGURE 14–2
Inventory Accounting

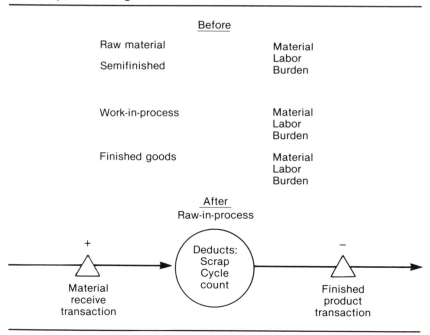

Source: Coopers & Lybrand.

To just two transactions, two inventory accounts, and no direct labor reporting? It sounds like you're throwing away the entire accounting system, Ben. John, does this hold together? Are we going to provide what the auditors need?" Gordon was ready for details and wanted answers to nagging questions.

John was back in the limelight. Ben handed the slide projector control to John, hoping he was ready for the barrage.

"I've checked the system backwards and forwards, Gordon. We absorb overhead as always, although what's in the pool is different. Our operating reports separate controllable costs from burden, making it easier to hold people accountable for their costs. Using actuals and periodic updating keeps our inventory costs in line with the ledger. And in the end it all balances. The difference is that now I can generate cost of quality reports, analyses of potential savings, and a long series of things that I never had the time to do before. And I can even do that with the reduced staff resulting from the last headcount reduction. It works; it's not elegant, but it works."

"And the auditors?" The questions were coming from Gordon Shillinglaw who was doing his best to find chinks in the armor.

"The auditors like it. The RIP is greatly reduced and cycle counting so accurate that their work is cut in half. They can come any day and verify the accounts without having to shut down the plant to do it. And since all dollars eventually get to the right place in the books, they're happy. I see no problem from them, and they're delighted."

"This is how they described it to me, Gordon. Their concern is the impact these changes will make on their ability to express an opinion on our financial statements. JIT affects operations directly, which affects accounting and controls. But the system's integrity isn't affected; it's easier to audit because of high levels of process control and the repetitive nature of the basic transactions. They want to be informed as we make changes and define new internal controls. And we know that they have to approve the new methods, or we'll be in trouble come time for the audit. But so far, so good."

John continued. "I anticipated your questions, Gordon. I had them, too. To address your concerns directly, I put together this slide (Table 14–3). It shows the primary changes, their impact on the internal control system, and how we deal with the exposure. As you can see, the three major problems we face are the elimination of receiving transactions, the elimination of stock issue transactions and storeroom controls, and their impact on the inventory valuation process." John was prepared for the question, but that didn't mean the answer would pass muster.

"When we eliminate transactions, the auditor loses a physical trail of process flow. This affects the valuation of inventory and raises concerns of units in house. Two solutions ease these worries: first, we modified the accounting

TABLE 14-3
Audit Considerations (Assess)

Elimination of receiving transaction:
  Concerns: inventory valuation; period cutoff
  Solution: modify accounting system
Elimination of stock issue transactions and storeroom controls:
  Concern: control of inventory
  Solution: physical counts
Inventory valuation:
  Concern: how to value inventory
  Solution: value transactions at standard cost

Source: Coopers & Lybrand.

system to ensure that inventory valuation and period cutoff demands can be met by employing a rolling average of actual costs as our standard costing measure; second, we employed frequent physical counts to validate inventory levels. This is possible because we've reduced the level of inventory so significantly. We're sensitive to the auditors' concerns. We simply don't want to sacrifice internal information to provide them with details. For now, the auditors are comfortable with our solution. Are you?" John paused, hopeful and anxious.

"I'll give it careful thought, John. For now I'm satisfied that you're paying attention to the needs of Corporate and the auditors. But I'm going to reserve my opinion on the solutions until I have time to examine them more carefully." Gordon signalled that the meeting was ready to end. It was none too soon as far as Ben and John were concerned.

Final Points

Ben took the floor again. He wanted to drive home the message about the benefits of JIT/TQC once and for all.

"What we're doing is making improvement a dynamic force in the plant. The focus is on improvement, not on marking time. We need to be able to take the plant's pulse periodically to make sure the patient is still breathing and that stress isn't shutting down the system. But we don't need the data to make sure the process is running; without piles of inventory we can see it."

"The system works because it's simple. When we need to evaluate performance or check on production, all we have to do is count the number of good units. Since we only have a day or two of work-in-process, it doesn't take long. And the Kanban trays make counting even simpler. Each tray holds four units. Also, folding labor into the general pool saves a lot of time. More important, it's diverted attention from personal performance to improving cell output."

"What we've done, in effect, is to collapse the costs on the floor into two components: materials and conversion. It's a lot like a process accounting system now, only simpler because the equivalent units issue is removed. In process accounting, simple measures are used to track overall performance. We've turned the plant into a process flow, and now we're looking for your approval to make the accounting system match the manufacturing process."

Before the meeting was over, Ben and John had preliminary approval for the system. While Gordon was hesitant to give a formal seal of approval, the assistant controller took a strong stand for it. In the end, common sense won out. Ben left the meeting with a new set of performance measurements for the plant and the renewed respect of Corporate. By the end of the meeting the conversation was not on whether to let Ben continue, but on how to leverage the improvement process into other plants in the corporation. Finally, the battle had been won. Ben had turned a nightmare into a JIT success story.

EPILOGUE

"The improvements we made were finally incorporated in the accounting system, and they provided a reliable, productive way to evaluate our progress against our goals. This was the last major battle of the campaign. Once it was won, Corporate was on our side, the JIT/TQC process stabilized, and I was able to sit back and relax."

Ben was wrapping up his presentation. Julie looked around the room, trying to gauge the crowd's reaction. She saw enthusiasm on some faces, skepticism on others. This brought back memories of Banyon's early efforts, the conferences she and Ben walked away from filled with skepticism, and the thrill when it all started to make sense.

"We started out with such a naive view of JIT, Jim. Do you remember? We were sure we could get rid of inventory and make a lot of money in the process just by moving a few machines. We were looking only at the benefits, and we kept missing the point. It's the process that's important, not the results."

Whispering, Julie and Jim reminisced. The implementation had changed the way product was manufactured, and it had transformed the lives of everyone in the plant. Equality, participation, and communication had created a unique environment of openness and trust. Ben was leaving; that meant uncertainty in the future. They hoped that the culture and the people would be strong enough to deal with the changes that were sure to come.

* * * * *

"Julie, how do we get Ben off of a 'marriage of JIT and TQC'? We're not there yet, although I won't rule it out someday. Every time he brings it up, I cringe."

"He's having fun with us. Did you see his new license plate? It's 'JIT/TQC.' He's become the consultant and advertises success as he goes."

"That's hard to figure. I mean, Ben can help a lot of people, but he's not my idea of a consultant. He's as honest as the day is long. But I can't see him selling unnecessary work. Maybe that alone will make him a success."

"Jim, we would have failed several times without consultants. Ben knew when he needed help, and he used it wisely. I think that a lot of people are in the same boat."

Both returned their attention to Ben. He was fielding questions, trying to get the message across. But he knew his audience wouldn't understand until they, too, were at a crossroads and faced a crisis. The solutions for each company would be different, but the message would always be the same:

> You have to trust people. That's the hardest part to learn. We all feel a need to control our world, to make sure it goes our way. But true control and power comes from sharing responsibility. I don't lose control when I share my thoughts and goals with others. I gain, because others help me make sure that what I'm doing is right and work with me to find the solution.
>
> Without people like Carolyn, Brenda, Jim, and Julie, we would have failed. JIT is more than moving machines, it means changing the way you think about yourself and your relationships with others. JIT is people working together. No boss, no subordinates. Just a team.

Ben left Banyon shortly after putting the measurement systems in place. Perhaps he felt he was no longer needed and that his job was done. Ben was the agent of change, the entrepreneur. The system didn't need that any more. It needed quiet, calm leadership, and consistency. The changes made had to settle in and become part of the basic structure of the plant.

After Ben left, the JIT/TQC effort slowed down, more because of the leadership transition than anything else. The basic systems Ben had put in place were robust. They were based on people, on motivation, not control. The greatest assurance that things will be done right is congruent goals, a motivated work force, and a clear understanding of priorities. Even absence of leadership wouldn't shake the system.

Interestingly, Ben's weakest supporter tried to fill his shoes. Herman Randolph struggled for a year to remake Banyon to fit his own view of leadership and control. In the end, it didn't work. Outside the plant he took credit for the improvements that Ben and the workers had put in place. Within the plant he used the carrot and stick to gain loyalty and control. Ultimately, he failed. Only someone within the plant could understand what it took to make it work.

After floundering for a year, Herman was promoted to corporate. He took John Roscoe's place. Roscoe had failed to see the wisdom of JIT and the benefit of the change in the incentive system. His negative attitude toward the change militated against him, and he left. Roscoe's superiors credited the enormous improvement at Banyon to Randolph's management, and in their eyes, he was Roscoe's natural successor.

Randolph's successor at Banyon was Julie. She had grown up with the system, listened, knew the plant, and could help people sort through problems. She had become a natural facilitator. That was shown time and again throughout the JIT/TQC implementation. With Julie at the helm, the system picked up steam once more. It became the showcase of the corporation, a success in spite of the opposition.

Jim? He continued at Banyon, eventually leaving to take over another plant. He never forgot the lessons he'd learned from Ben, and it served him well.

> "Success" is never merely final or terminal. Something else succeeds it. . . . The world does not stop when the successful person pulls out his plum; nor does he stop, and the kind of success he obtains, and his attitude towards it, is a factor in what comes afterward.
>
> John Dewey
> *Human Nature and Conduct*

CHAPTER 15

POSTSCRIPTS

enough, *pro.* All there is in the world if you like it.
Ambrose Bierce

There are a lot of details and changes that make a JIT implementation complete. The principle intent here has been on the process of change. Because of this, a series of issues critical to ongoing success has been neglected. This chapter will fill in the missing pieces.

WHAT TO DO WHEN VOLUMES FALL OFF

The JIT/TQC effort at Banyon was a success due in no small part to a promise Ben made to keep employment at existing levels. There would be no layoffs; if there were, suggestions from the work force would stop. Participation only works in a climate of trust and security.

This sounds good, but what happens when volumes fall so significantly that the plant loses money because of temporary sales shortfalls?

Ben had this problem at Banyon. And as with every other situation, the answers came from the people.

* * * * *

"I had a 'no layoff' policy once I implemented JIT. The employees improved quality, decreased costs, and decreased lead times. To have rewarded them with a layoff when volumes stabilized or fell would have dried up cooperation, support, and ideas."

"The way we handled this was simple. We knew that 23

people had to go. We projected that volumes would be down for about three months because of problems with a major customer. So, I had Julie call a plantwide meeting. I explained what was happening. Then I asked for volunteers for a temporary layoff. We offered to pay their insurance, to guarantee their seniority, and to ensure they could collect unemployment. For many it sounded like a paid three-month vacation."

"Twenty-eight people signed up. Grandparents wanted to travel and spend time with their children and grandchildren. Mothers enjoyed time off with their families. The plant also employed many gentlemen farmers. They could always use the extra time."

"We only needed 23 people, but there was no good way to choose, so we didn't. We let all 28 take leave. The mix? It was terrible. Half the volunteers came from electronic assembly. But this was the solution we reached together. We took it, and we managed. Three months later, volumes were up and everyone was back on the job."

"I guess we were lucky. We didn't face a major cutback while I was there. When we began to free extra space and meet deadlines regularly, we brought in work from other plants. And Corporate sent most new products to us. In the end, the plant was back at capacity with a larger work force than ever. JIT meant more than doing a better job; it meant security for everyone in the plant."

* * * * *

Volumes fall off, and unforeseen problems occur. They can't be avoided. What cushioned the impact at Banyon was that the solution was a joint effort of management and labor; it was made in light of joint goals and priorities. Volunteers are happier at home than workers forced off jobs. The solution kept the culture of trust in place.

DESIGN FOR MANUFACTURABILITY

At several points the impact of design on the process was mentioned; it wasn't enough. Design is the critical dimension in the success or failure of JIT/TQC and the company itself.

Recent studies have shown that more than 75 percent of a product's cost is set in design. The machines used, the process flow, the materials, all of this is set by the design engineer. Once a product is designed, changes are costly. Each engineering change causes waste because it means dismantling existing processes and products. It can result in unprofitable product lines, a fact hidden by traditional accounting.

The Japanese expend the bulk of their efforts in design and planning. They design not only for ease of production, but also for customers' expectations. A product designed with a six-year life when only one is required is wasteful. What a designer likes and what a firm produces are unimportant. Only the customer's expectations matter in making design decisions.

* * * * *

"We had new products that demonstrated Design For Manufacturability (DFM). We found that writing test programs to check quality on the line took as long as designing the product itself. This was unacceptable if we were going to respond quickly to market shifts."

"Why did it take so long? Think about the product. It had thousands of electronic components, each with its own value. We knew the value of each piece alone, but as part of a circuit, the transistors, diodes, and other parts took on new values. Circuit performance didn't match stand-alone value. That meant the test programmer had to start from scratch."

"Think about it. A thousand connections on a circuit board, and no clue to tolerance or performance level without testing for failure. It's an expensive way to learn. More than that, the complexity of handling the data meant that the programmer could never really understand all the detail. It required brute calculating power."

"In the corporate excess capital resources fund was a Data General computer available for $25,000 that sold for more than $300,000. I couldn't afford list price, but the corporate price was fine. The computer was tied to the test device, and tolerances were set from known good and rejected units in a fraction of the historical programming time. The problem was solved. Years of engineering time were saved by this approach."

* * * * *

There were other areas where design changes made a big difference. In the assembly of the President's counter some basic problems were discovered. One day as Ben walked by the line, he was called over by the line supervisor.

"Mr. Morgan, I want to show you something. Here, sit down at this work station. Can you do the final assembly step? I'll help if you need me."

Brenda walked away. Ben was dumbfounded. But he knew Brenda had a reason for asking him to try to do the work. He set to work, or at least he tried. No matter what he did, he couldn't get the counter together; there were too many things to do at once. A person with only 10 fingers was in trouble. After ruining five units—they were made such that when the case snapped shut, it could not be reopened—he went in search of Brenda.

"How do you put these things together? You need 12 fingers. I think we should get the design engineer out here to fix the problem. Surely something can be done to make it easier."

* * * * *

A few simple changes in design reduced rework and scrap in final assembly by 200 percent. They were simple solutions to problems that should have never occurred. JIT/TQC highlighted design; improvement became a team effort.

CLOSING THE LOOP: SUPPLIERS AND JIT

When most people think of JIT, they think immediately of logistics, of getting suppliers to deliver small batches daily. It puts the cart before the horse. If the internal process of the plant is not under control, it is pointless to force vendors to make daily deliveries. Quality is a different problem. Bad material can stop the JIT line; it needs to be controlled from the start. Quality, not timing of raw materials delivery, is critical. But what about closing the loop?

American JIT manufacturing will not look like Japan's. Vast distances between suppliers and customers make daily deliveries difficult and expensive. In this case classifying inventory into "A," critical cost/delivery items, and "C," non-critical items, can help.

"A" items may very well require daily delivery. They are probably expensive. Keeping a large inventory increases cost. So vendor arrangements are needed. But nuts, screws, and bolts? You don't want to stop a line for a nickel bolt, so keep ample quantities on hand.

The Essence of a Supplier Network

Banyon got into JIT because Probe set up a supplier network. But Banyon was not ready to push JIT into the supplier chain until they were experts. Probe trained Banyon, but Banyon was in no position to train its suppliers. They tried, once, to get JIT deliveries. The vendors who were willing to respond asked for a plant tour so they could start making the necessary changes to their operations. Ben had nothing to show them.

Once JIT/TQC is up and running, vendor networks make a lot of sense. What are they? Their primary characteristics are:

- Single sourcing.
- Long-term contracts (18 to 36 months).
- Short-lead times.
- Monthly rolling forecasts (one year out).
- Frequent deliveries.
- 100 percent good quality.

It is critical to have the right material at the right time in the right quantity and without inspection at delivery. It is a partnership between supplier and customer, an informal vertical integration that blurs the boundaries between organizations.

An example of the analysis Banyon made is presented in

TABLE 15–1
Materials Management (Purchasing Pareto Analysis)

Part Type	Number of Parts	Dollar Value
"A" or "B"	853	96%
"C"	5,240	4%
Total	6,093	100%

Table 15–1. They employed the $^{80}/_{20}$ rule in determining which items to control—853, or 14 percent, of the total parts accounted for more than 96 percent of the cost. Here, vendor management is critical. For "C" items, keep enough on hand to keep from running out. The EOQ model works quite well, as does the MRP system.

Keeping the vendor network in line requires the development of measures that can be used to assess performance. Table 15–2 outlines the elements used by Banyon to assess preferred vendors. After completing the exercise, Banyon went to single sourcing based on contract for its major materials. This runs counter to tenets of purchasing practice by tying the two companies together. But the demands JIT places on the supply chain require partnership. The alternative is loss of control and effectiveness.

JIT is an integrated management system. It promotes the interdependence of one process with another and the pro-

TABLE 15–2
Supplier Performance

Item	Rating	Score
Price	−Price increase +Cost reduction	
Quality	−Require inspection −Defects received +Statistical process control	
Delivery	−Shipped late −Shipped more than one week early +Agreement to ship	

cess with the people. It minimizes variance in the process itself, allowing for simple controls. It relies on responsive, people-oriented systems and management styles that support continuous improvement. JIT is management, not machines.

> . . . Four underlying themes shape the behavior of the truly superior manufacturing company. . . . The first is, management makes the difference. The kind of impact management has on manufacturing performance . . . is on the order . . . of 50 to 100 percent differences observed. . . . Second is the importance of adopting a holistic perspective. . . . Third, the whole organization must relentlessly pursue customer value and competitive advantage. Finally, continual learning and improving is central to the entire process.[1]

---

[1] Robert H. Hayes, Stephen C. Wheelwright, and Kine B. Clark, *Dynamic Manufacturing: Creating the Learning Organization* (New York: Free Press, 1988), pp. 341–42.

INDEX

A

Accounting for Competitive Performance, 236
Ackoff, Russell, 25–26, 30, 32, 36, 193
Creating the Corporate Future, 25
Age of the Smart Machine, 147, see also Zuboff, S.
Agency theory, 250
Anderson & Anderson, 21
Andrews, Jim, 68, 72–74, 77, 87, 90–91, 104–105, 124, 131–132, 135, 149, 154, 160, 168, 183–184, 187, 206, 227, 243, 270–272
Association for Manufacturing Excellence, 2
AT&T, 99, 105
Audit considerations, 268
Avco, 178–180

B

Banyon, first steps, 41
Basho, 126
Benefits, 23
Beyond the Bottom Line: Measuring World Class Performance, 236
Bierce, Ambrose, 25, 232, 273
The Devil's Dictionary, 232
Bonus, *see* Incentives
Bottlenecks, 35, 36, 100, 146
eliminating, 263
Boyer, John; *see also* Regent Electric
Brady, Jack, 217–218
Brown, Al, 227
Buckets, 35, 98, 100
Buffering, 18
Buffers, 40, 50, 99–100, 143, 220, 238–39
eliminate, 96

C

Cause and effect diagram, 115
Cause for pause, 14, 15, 19, 20, 39, 44, 84, 185, 234
eliminate, 95–96
Cell concept, 37
charting, 265
common components, 37
costs, 250
first, 124
flexibility, 37
group, 244
implementation, 100
JIT, 28, 96, 131, 146, 150
idle capacity, 147
performance/evaluation, 251
standardized assembly path, 37
structure, 101

Change, impact of, 30
The Changemasters, see also Kanter, Rosabeth Moss
Charts, 20, 62, 66, 73, 131–32, 140, 210, 244–45, 258, 265
　incentives, 180
　procedures, 72
　product flow, 94
　progress, 93
　SPC, 62–63, 76, 182
　techniques, 78
　updating, 245
Checkpoints and measures, 71–72
Cherry-picking, 27
Church, Alexander Hamilton, 37
Chou, Dr., 11
Clark, K., 155
　Dynamic Manufacturing: Creating the Learning Organization, 155
Communication, 106–7
Competition, 85
　understanding, 85
Conformity with requirements, 45
Consensus building, 202
The Constraints of Corporate Tradition, 150, *see also* Kontrow, M.
Consultants, using, 109–11
Continuous improvement, 24
Continuous Improvement: A Close Look at Japanese Manufacturing, 126
Contracts, long-term, 41
Control
　formal, 128
　informal, 128
　multiple dimensions of, 128–29
Control in Business Organizations, 128
Controller. *see* Rust, John
Coopers & Lybrand, 16, 27, 53, 71, 83, 104, 136, 138, 141, 145, 158, 177, 180, 219, 228, 242, 244, 246, 249, 257, 259, 266, 268

Management Consulting Services, 228
Corporate human resources, 217
Cost accounting, 259
Costs
　controllable, 250–54
　of goods, 82
　reduction, 98
　system, 252–53
Costing the mistakes, 81–82
Creating the Corporate Future; see also Ackoff, Russell
Crosby, Phil, 45
Cross, Kelvin, 236
Cross training, 170
Customer service, improved, 35
Cycle of improvement, 19
Cycle of success, 26–27, 42, 44
　initiating, 112–129

D

Dantel, 57–59, 61, 63
Data, root cause, 265
Data General, 275
Defective product, 18
Defects, 116–18
　cause of, 116
　prevention, 11
Design
　engineers, 90
　review, 90
Design for manufacturability (DFM), 147, 274–76
Developing a plan, 25–26
The Devil's Dictionary, 232
Dewey, John, 272
Dynamic Manufacturing, 279

E

Economic order quantity (EOQ), 38, 39, 142, 278
Eddy, Ron, 108, 110, 112, 114, 116, 118–19, 133, 167, 247
Education and awareness, 29–31

Effectiveness measure, 263
Employee involvement, 62, 93
  seminars, 106
Entrepreneur, 41, 158, 183, 271
Excel, 67
Expediting, 3

F

Failure
  external, 82–83, 89
  financial impact of, 82
  internal, 81, 83, 89
  product, 91
  testing for, 275
Federal Accounting Standards Board (FASB), 251–52
Fennel, Ron, 42
Fitness for use, 45, 54
Floor space
  manufacturing, 242
  reduced, 242
Flowchart, 34, 36, 54; *see also* Charts; Cycle of success; and Implementation
  starting, 43
Focus diagram, 117
Focused factory, 37
Ford, Henry, 37, 169
Future Shock, 155

G

GRI, 7, 44, 46, 98, 119, 174
Gainsharing, 102, 178, 187–88, 194–207, 210, 213–15, 219, 225–26, 243, 247
  adopting, 225
  bonus, 216, 256
  criteria for, 197–98
  deficit, 204
  definition, 199
  details of, 206
  moving into, 226
  payout, 216
  pool, 205
  Scanlon Multicost plan, 219; *see also* Scanlon Multicost plan
  suggestions, 205
  system, 223, 225, 265
Gannon, Mike, 17, 40, 42, 55, 61, 64, 66, 68, 131–35, 147, 149–52, 157, 160, 167–68, 171–72, 175, 183, 197, 205, 230, 243
Getting started, 23–24
Grapevine, 128
Graphs, 20
Group discussion, 29
Group interaction, 30
Groupthink, 114

H

Hall, Robert W., 74
  Attaining Manufacturing Excellence, 74
Harley Davidson, 105
Hayes, R., 155
  Dynamic Manufacturing: Creating the Learning Organization, 155
Hewlett-Packard, 40, 79, 90, 98, 105, 236
Hierarchy of Goals and Measures, 237
Housekeeping, preventive maintenance, 31–33
Human Nature and Conduct; 272 see also Dewey, John
Human Resources Association of Greater Milwaukee, 175

I

Idle time charge, 265
Implementation, 174, 238
  ABCs of, 133
  brain trust, 42

Implementation (*continued*)
  failed, 106
  flowchart, 42, 44
  guide, 106
  key element, 167
  plan, 55, 67, 133
  process, 36, 101, 156, 158, 167
  puzzle, 61
  task force, 65
  team, 45, 63, 101, 106, 135
    choosing the, 107
Improshare, 179
Improvement
  creating a climate, 51–52
  evaluating, 254
Incentives, 29, 74, 107, 162–63, 174–93, 241, 246
  bonus, 63, 182, 198–204, 247–248
  changing, 213
  chart, 180–182
  committee, 194, 198, 202, 214–215
  consultant, 195; *See also* Washbone, Linda
  historical standard, 186
  implementation, 177, 188, 194–195
    damage, 211
  individual, 95, 102, 162, 171, 174–194, 197
    shortcomings of, 176–178
  issues, 169, 184
  piece rate, 262
  plans, 175, 178–180, 185–193, 211, 218, 221
    existing, 199
    group, 183
    modern, 189
    Scanlon; *see also* Scanlon Multicost plan
    seminar, 175
  pool, 220
  problem, 183
  process, 193
  profit sharing, 195
  programs, 35, 171

  space, 242
  team, 182
Incentive system, 64, 110, 164, 166, 173–75, 177, 187, 212–13, 225, 272
  changes to, 177
  comparison of, 180
  components of, 191
  design of, 175
  effectiveness of, 176
  equality, 201
  individual, 225, 229
  redesigning, 176
  starting, 197
  traditional, 176
Individual(s), 196
  goals, 196
  involvement, 30
  worker, 48, 99
  value of, 48
Inspect time, 12
Inspection, 12, 18, 56
Interdependence is reality, 17–18
Internal Revenue Service (IRS), 251
Inventory
  buffers, 17
  changeover time, 16
  controls, 98
  costs, 102
  excess, 142
  finished goods, 16
  idle, 50
  levels, 134
  management technique, 96
  mistakes, 139–40
  raw, 16
  raw-in-process, 144
  reductions, 64, 102, 246
  valuing, 267–268
  work in process (WIP), 16, 17, 99, 139, 145, 159, 170, 235, 239, 241
Inventory-based idle time, 13
Ishikawa, Dr., 114–16
  cause and effect diagram, 115

J

Japanese, 37, 39, 51, 85, 115, 125–26, 275, 277
  manufacturing, 126
Job order, 258
Job shop, 3, 35
Johansen, P., 126
Johnson Controls, Inc., 32
Journal of Cost Management, 236
Judson, Gray, and Howard, 236
Juran, J., 47
  Juran on Leadership for Quality, 61
  method, 61
  Upper Management and Quality, 47
Just-in-time (JIT)
  accounting, 260
  adopting, 225
  awareness, 31, 68
  back office, 14
  balance, 105
  benefits of, 64, 269
  candidates, 105
  capacity, 145
  cells, 28, 96, 105, 121, 151
    capacity, 147
    configuration, 142
    group results, 146
    progress, 131
  changing to, 113, 245
  characteristics of, 169
  communication, 197
  continuous variance, 234
  conversion, 134
  cornerstone of, 245
  dangers of, 161–166
  definition, 190
  discipline, 15
  doing, 75
  downside, 165
  effectiveness of, 239
  efforts, 212, 223
  elements of, 114
  expanding, 159–61
  features of, 112, 165
  hard facts, 95–111
  human side, 103, 150–68
  impact of, 259–60
  implementing, 61, 75, 91–94, 97, 103–6, 113, 121, 123, 133–34, 144–45, 154–56, 165, 196, 210, 214, 228–29, 242, 272–73
    summary, 166–68
  incorporating, 144
  islands of, 28
  Japanese, 125
  learning about, 248
  management, 153
  manufacturing objectives, 259
  operations, 267
  performance measures, 234
  physical characteristics of, 97
  process, 235
  putting it to work, 120–25
  selecting a candidate, 55
  seminars, 169
  and suppliers, 276–79
  target, 98
  teaching, 113–14
  technical side, 103, 127
  technical view of, 97–103
  themes, 27, 97
  tying to the past, 13
  understanding, 133–34
  using, 232, 265
  what it is and isn't, 10–11, 94
Just-in-time-based labor problems, 230

K

Kanban, 39, 40, 98–101, 114, 123, 141, 255, 263, 269
  definition, 99
  in action, 141–142
Kanter, Rosabeth Moss, 153, 155
  The Changemasters, 153
Keep product moving, 11–12
Kontrow, M., 150
  The Constraints of Corporate Tradition, 150

L

Labor, 16
  direct, 16, 235, 250, 254, 256–57, 259
  efficiency, 257
  exempt, 16
  indirect, 16, 250, 254, 256, 259
Lead times, 35, 134, 232, 235, 238–40, 262
  costing, 239
  decreased, 273
  improved, 144
  limits, 239
  measure, 239
  reduce, 93, 123
Line balancing, 31, 36
Linked flow of materials, 40
Lock-step path, 36
Locking in the solution, 41
Lower control limit (LCL), 73
Lynch, Richard, 236

M

Major cost, 29
Management by stress, 245
Manufacturability, design for, 274–76
Manufacturing
  cell, 37
  holistic, 96
  lead time, 16
  optimum, 75
  perfection, 31
  synchronized, 97
Mares, W., 196
Marketing
  industrial, 86
  research, 86
Material usage, 233
Materials management, 278
Materials resource planning (MRP), 5, 41, 140, 146, 260, 263–64, 278
McDonald's, 49
McGuire, K. J., 126
McNair, C. J., 128
McVicker, Walt, 212–13, 217–18, 228
Measuring, Planning, and Controlling Quality Cost, 85
Measuring success, 232–47
Merchant, K., 128
Mercury Marine, 178–79
Method/Process Improvement, 101
Morse, W. J., 85
Motivational factors, 56
Move time, 12

N

NAB 1, 185
Nonvalue-adding, 143, 185, 249, 251, 260–61, 263
  activities, 14, 18–19, 60, 185, 235
  operations, 169
  pause, 39
  tasks, 147
  time, 136–37, 146, 238
Nozaki, Mr., 125–26

O

Opportunities, 16
Organize for success, 28–29
Overheads
  fixed, 229
  variable, 229

P

Pareto analysis, 116, 278
  diagram, 116, 118
Participation concept, 30
Pearce, Drew, 163, 165, 175, 177–79, 182–83, 185, 188–92, 197, 210–11, 213–14, 216–17
People intensive, 127
People-oriented, 19, 128
  systems, 279
Performance
  assessment, 278

Index **287**

evaluation, 41, 128
measurements, 121, 229, 258
supplier, 278
Personal dynamics, 56
Philips, Greg, 135
Pilot site, 96, 98
  choosing, 103
Planning process, 28
Plant load, uniform, 98
Plaques, 247
Polaroid, 72
Poston, H. M., 85
Prevention
  cost of, 79
  definition, 79
Preventive maintenance, 132
Pride of ownership, 32
Primary process, 62
Probe, 5–7, 9–11, 17, 20, 23, 34, 40, 44, 46–47, 52, 55, 76, 78, 84–87, 91, 97, 103, 105, 119, 135–36, 148, 158–59, 167, 171–74, 227, 254, 277
  Probe Awards of Excellence, 3, 6, 47
Process
  accounting system, 269
  analyzed, 116
  assembly, 105
  budgeting, 262
  changes, 273
  charting, 73
  communication, 203
  constraint, 100
  control (PC), 72, 91, 126, 172; *see also* Statistical process control (SPC)
    levels of, 267
  costing, 50, 258, 260
  creating simple, 49–50
  design, 91, 274
  flow, 49, 50, 103, 139, 152, 156, 171
    analysis, 260, 269, 275
    design, 18, 97
    diagrams, 106, 139
    management of, 14
    redesigning, 37–38
    visible, 51
  focused on, 96
  improvement, 75, 93, 151, 165, 205, 257, 265
  individual, 100
  inventory, 139
  manage, 172
  manufacturing, 99, 102, 239, 269
  negotiating, 114
  organizational change, 195
  problems, 106, 116
  production, 84, 97, 141
  quality, 95
  rates, 257
  refining, 170
  simple, 49
  standardized, 147
  supply, 100
  time, 12, 106, 257
  variance analysis, 186
  waste, 164
Process Technologies, Inc., 86–87
Product
  design, 86
  failure, 91
  families, 37
  flow, 132
Production
  linear, 35
  schedules, 256
Profit and loss (P&L), 169
Profit sharing plan, 178
Pull system, 15, 39–40, 100
  definition, 100
  linked, 39
  overlapped, 39, 40
  setting up, 39–40
Push system, 15
Putting a plan together, 26–28

Q

Quality, 11, 21, 44, 225, 235, 254, 276–277
  acceptance level of, 44

Quality (*continued*)
  achieved, 92
  in the age of efficiency, 47–48
  analyze, 115
  building, 92
  challenge, 91
  charting, 91
    techniques, 78
  concept of, 47
  of conformance, 85
  conscious, 77
  control (QC), 61, 80, 125, 143, 187, *see also* total quality control (TQC)
    check, 50, 72
    classes, 68
    concept of, 48
    embedding, 80
    implementation, 206
    indifference to, 80
    levels of, 71
    problems, 206
    program of, 56
    system, 73
    test results, 59
    total, 74
  cost of, 16, 76–77, 82, 83, 88–89, 91, 238, 243, 261
    analysis, 88
    defining, 78–84
  definition of, 45, 61
  demands, 63
  design, 85, 90
    constraints, 90
    issue, 90
  detection, 84, 92
  dollars and cents, 76–94
  effort, 54–57, 63, 124
  elements of, 80
  focus on, 52
  history of, 46–48
  improvement, 33–34, 54–55, 61, 64, 66, 72, 74–75, 89–90, 108, 143, 153, 246, 263
    defining and finding, 45–46
    implement, 70
    plan, 89
  program, 67, 106
    start-up, 133
  increase, 123, 243
  inspecting, 45, 80
  issues, 82–83, 85
  learning about, 44–45
  level of, 155
  maintaining, 243
  management, 45
    basics of, 45
    process, 84–87
  map, 92
  performance, 34, 44
  planning, 47, 61
  problems, 57–58, 63, 84, 90, 139, 170
  procedures, 92
  process, 95
  program, 93, 154
  progress in, 100
  reports, 253, 267
  responsible for, 123
  seminar, 84, 87
  strategy, 54, 84, 86
  team for, 54–55
  technology of, 47
  tracking, 72
  upgrades, 261
  zones of, 74
Quality assurance (QA), 33, 42, 46, 57, 66–68, 80, 88
Queue, 99, 241–242, 255, 261
  minimize, 123
  time, 12

R

Rand, Ayn, 234
Randolph, Herman, 188–90, 207–9, 211–12, 217, 229–30, 232, 246, 253, 272
Raw-in-process (RIP), 253, 261, 264, 266–267
  inventory, 260, 264
Raw materials, 57, 102
Regent Electric, 4, 17, 20, 22–23, 91

Boyer, John, 4, 12, 19–22, 26, 36, 41, 91, 93
Responsibility, 32
Rogers, Dan, 200, 203
Root cause, 265
Roscoe, John, 208–12, 214, 217–18, 272
Roth, H. P., 85
Rust, John, 77–79, 185–87, 197, 217, 251–54, 258, 260–63, 265–69

S

Sacrifices, 23
Safety nets, 40
Scanlon Multicost plan, 179–81, 189, 191, 198, 219, 226; see also Incentives
  exploring, 180–81
  gainsharing plan, 219
Schedules
  maintenance, 75–76
  production, 256
Schonberger, Richard J., 34
  World Class Manufacturing, 34
Schoner, Richard, 95, 175
Scrap, 18, 81, 89, 145, 156, 158, 162, 170, 238, 242–44, 254, 265–266
  examining, 92
  reduced, 276
  reports, 81
  standards for, 81
Setups, 63–64, 158
  external activities, 38–39, 156
  internal activities, 38–39, 157
  problems, 63
  reduction, 38–39, 64
  time, 12, 243, 252
Shillinglaw, Gordon, 262–63, 266–69
Simons, J., 196
Slack resources, 75
Space utilization, 258
Specifications
  customer, 90

marketing, 90
Stanadyne Diesel Systems, 98, 105
Stand-alone value, 275
Standardization, 38
Statistical process control (SPC), 6, 34, 46, 52, 56, 66–67, 71–74, 84, 87, 172
  charting, 62–63, 76, 182
  definition of, 73
  implementation, 71
  planned approach, 53
Strategy, 55
Supplier networks, 277–79
  setting up, 40–41
Synchronizing the flow, 31

T

Frederick Taylor, 13, 47, 48
Team-based technique, 113
Teams; see also Implementation
  concept of, 44
  spirit, 113
  structures, 113
Time buckets, 12
Toffler, Alvin, 155
  Future Shock, 155
Tokai, 125–126
Total preventive maintenance (TPM), 32–33
Total productive maintenance, 125
Total quality control (TQC), 46–57, 62, 67, 69, 74–75, 77–80, 84, 86–87, 89–92, 106, 163, 166–67, 174–75, 179, 181–82, 184, 190, 195–96, 198, 205, 208–10, 213–14, 228, 238, 271, 273–74, 276–77
  adopting, 225
  anchoring, 196
  balance, 105
  basics of, 49, 53
  benefits of, 64, 268
  changeover to, 245
  concepts of, 54
  cornerstone of, 245

Total Quality Control (*continued*)
  efforts, 212, 223, 258, 272
  impact of, 259–60
  implementing, 55, 61, 75, 92–94, 133, 196, 210, 214, 242, 272
  measures, 243
  results, 91
  using, 232, 265
Total time, 12
Tracking inventory, 14
Transportation, 18

U

U-shaped cell configuration, 37
Uniform plant load, 35–37, 100, 102, 144, 254, 259
Unions, 181
Upper control limit (UCL), 73
Upper management and quality; *see also* Juran, J.
Us versus them, 30, 165, 196
Utilization asset, 264

V

Value-adding, 20, 137, 145, 169, 185, 187, 238, 240
  activity, 32, 75, 169
  time, 89, 134, 136–38, 144
Vendors, preferred programs, 41
Vertical integration, 40
Volume
  change, 250
  increased, 246

W

Wang, 105, 236
Warner Electric, 178
Warranty costs, 91
Washbone, Linda, 191–92, 194–95,
  197, 199–202, 208, 210–12
Waste, 13, 14, 17, 20, 83, 115, 137, 144–45, 235, 239–41, 252, 255, 275
  building, 102
  concept of, 11, 14–15
  dollars of, 144
  eliminate, 49, 50–51, 98
  expediting orders, 50
  institutionalized, 69
  process, 164
  reduced, 232
  tracking, 262
  visible, 50
Western Electric, 38
Wheelwright, S., 155
  Dynamic Manufacturing: Creating the Learning Organization, 155
Williamson, Dick, 28, 39, 42, 57, 61–62, 66, 68, 71–72, 94, 101, 124, 131–32, 157, 183, 185–87, 205–06
Within Context: The Implementation of JIT Manufacturing and Its Impact on Management Accounting, 128
Woods, Joe, 149, 159
Woodward, Joan, 128
Work in process (WIP), 64, 139, 141, 240, 243, 246, 253, 266, 269; *see also* Inventory
Worker involvement, 78
Working Together: Employee Participation in Action, 196; *see also* Simons, J. and Mares, W.
World Class Manufacturing; *see also* Schonberger, Richard J.

Z

Zero defect, 33, 115
Zero inventory, 96
Zuboff, S., 147